THROUGH PAINTED DESERTS

OTHER BOOKS BY
DONALD MILLER

Blue Like Jazz

Searching for God Knows What

To Own a Dragon

THROUGH PAINTED DESERTS

Light, God, and Beauty on the Open Road

DONALD MILLER

THOMAS NELSON
Since 1798

NASHVILLE   DALLAS   MEXICO CITY   RIO DE JANEIRO   BEIJING

Published in Nashville, Tennessee, by Thomas Nelson. Thomas Nelson is a registered trademark of Thomas Nelson, Inc.

Thomas Nelson, Inc. titles may be purchased in bulk for educational, business, fund-raising, or sales promotional use. For information, please e-mail SpecialMarkets@ThomasNelson.com.

Library of Congress Cataloging-in-Publication Data

Miller, Donald, 1971–
    Through painted deserts : light, God, and beauty on the open road / Donald Miller.
        p. cm.
    Rev. ed. of: Prayer and the art of Volkswagen maintenance, 2000.
    Includes bibliographical references.
    ISBN 978-0-7852-0982-9 (pbk.)
    1. Christian life—Miscellanea. 2. Miller, Donald, 1971—-Travel—West (U.S.) 3. West (U.S.)—Description and travel. I. Miller, Donald, 1971– Prayer and the art of Volkswagen maintenance. II. Title.
BV4501.3.M543 2005
277.3'0829'092—dc22   2005008472

Printed in the United States of America
08 09 10 11 12 **QG** 14 13 12 11 10

Mom,

Here is the first book, rewritten a bit. I didn't know, when I was living it, that it was about leaving home. I think you always knew. Thanks for letting me go. This will always be yours.

CONTENTS

AUTHOR'S NOTE

IT IS FALL HERE NOW, MY FAVORITE OF THE FOUR seasons. We get all four here, and they come at us under the doors, in through the windows. One morning you wake and need blankets; you take the fan out of the window to see clouds that mist out by midmorning, only to reveal a naked blue coolness like God yawning.

September is perfect Oregon. The blocks line up like postcards and the rosebuds bloom into themselves like children at bedtime. And in Portland we are proud of our roses; year after year, we are proud of them. When they are done, we sit in the parks and read stories into the air, whispering the gardens to sleep.

I come here, to Palio Coffee, for the big windows. If I sit outside, the sun gets on my computer screen, so I come inside, to this same table, and sit alongside the giant panes of glass. And it is like a movie out there, like a big screen of green, and today there is a man in shepherd's clothes, a hippie, all dirty, with a downed bike in the circle lawn across the street. He is eating bread from the bakery and drinking from a metal camp cup. He is tapping the cup against his leg, sitting like a monk, all striped in fabric. I wonder if he is happy, his blanket strapped to the rack on his bike, his no home, his no job. I wonder if he has left it all because he hated it or because it hated him. It is true some do not do well with conventional life. They think outside things and can't make sense of following a line. They see no walls, only doors from open space to open space, and from open space, supposedly, to the mind of God, or at least this is what we hope for them, and what they hope for themselves.

I remember the sweet sensation of leaving, years ago, some ten now, leaving Texas for who knows where. I could not have known about this beautiful place, the Oregon I have come to love, this city of great people, this smell of coffee and these evergreens reaching up into a mist of sky, these sunsets spilling over the west hills to slide a red glow down the streets of my town.

And I could not have known then that if I had been born here, I would have left here, gone someplace south to deal with horses, to get on some open land where you can see tomorrow's storm brewing over a high desert. I could not have known then that everybody, every person, has to leave, has to change like seasons; they have to or they die. The seasons remind me that I must keep changing, and I want to change because it is God's way. All my life I have been changing. I changed from a baby to a child, from soft toys to play daggers. I changed into a teenager to drive a car, into a worker to spend some money. I will change into a husband to love a woman, into a father to love a child, change houses so we are near water, and again so we are near mountains, and again so we are near friends, keep changing with my wife, getting our love so it dies and gets born again and again, like a garden, fed by four seasons, a cycle of change. Everybody has to change, or they expire. Everybody has to leave, everybody has to leave their home and come back so they can love it again for all new reasons.

I want to keep my soul fertile for the changes, so things keep getting born in me, so things keep dying when it is time for things to die. I want to keep walking away from the person I was a moment ago, because a mind was made to figure things out, not to read the same page recurrently.

Only the good stories have the characters different at the

end than they were at the beginning. And the closest thing I can liken life to is a book, the way it stretches out on paper, page after page, as if to trick the mind into thinking it isn't all happening at once.

Time has pressed you and me into a book, too, this tiny chapter we share together, this vapor of a scene, pulling our seconds into minutes and minutes into hours. Everything we were is no more, and what we will become, will become what was. This is from where story stems, the stuff of its construction lying at our feet like cut strips of philosophy. I sometimes look into the endless heavens, the cosmos of which we can't find the edge, and ask God what it means. Did You really do all of this to dazzle us? Do You really keep it shifting, rolling round the pinions to stave off boredom? God forbid Your glory would be our distraction. And God forbid we would ignore Your glory.

HERE IS SOMETHING I FOUND TO BE TRUE: YOU DON'T start processing death until you turn thirty. I live in visions, for instance, and they are cast out some fifty years, and just now, just last year I realized my visions were cast too far, they were out beyond my life span. It frightened me to think of it, that I passed up an early marriage or children to write these silly books, that I bought the lie that the academic life had to be separate from relational experience, as though God only wanted us to learn cognitive ideas, as if the heart of a man were only created to resonate with movies. No, life cannot be understood flat on a page. It has to be lived; a person has to get out of his head, has to fall in love, has to memorize poems, has to jump off bridges into rivers, has to stand in an empty desert and whisper sonnets under his breath:

> I'll tell you how the sun rose
> A ribbon at a time . . .

It's a living book, this life; it folds out in a million settings, cast with a billion beautiful characters, and it is almost over for you. It doesn't matter how old you are; it is coming to a close quickly, and soon the credits will roll and all your friends will fold out of your funeral and drive back to their homes in cold and still and silence. And they will make a fire and pour some wine and think about how you once were . . . and feel a kind of sickness at the idea you never again will be.

So soon you will be in that part of the book where you are holding the bulk of the pages in your left hand, and only a thin wisp of the story in your right. You will know by the page count, not by the narrative, that the Author is wrapping things up. You begin to mourn its ending, and want to pace yourself slowly toward its closure, knowing the last lines will speak of something beautiful, of the end of something long and earned, and you hope the thing closes out like last breaths, like whispers about how much and who the characters have come to love, and how authentic the sentiments feel when they have earned a hundred pages of qualification.

And so my prayer is that your story will have involved some leaving and some coming home, some summer and some winter, some roses blooming out like children in a play. My hope is your story will be about changing, about getting something beautiful born inside of you, about learning to love a woman or a man, about learning to love a child, about moving yourself around water, around mountains, around friends, about learning to love others more than we love ourselves, about learning oneness as a way of understanding God. We get one story, you and I, and one story alone. God has established the elements, the setting and the climax and the resolution. It would be a crime not to venture out, wouldn't it?

It might be time for you to go. It might be time to change, to shine out.

I want to repeat one word for you:
Leave.

Roll the word around on your tongue for a bit. It is a beautiful word, isn't it? So strong and forceful, the way you have always wanted to be. And you will not be alone. You have never been alone. Don't worry. Everything will still be here when you get back. It is you who will have changed.

1 LEAVING

HOUSTON, TEXAS, AT NIGHT, AS SEEN FROM INTERSTATE 45, is something beautiful. The interstate approaches and collides with the city's center in a tight, second-level loop that hugs skyscrapers three-quarters around downtown before spinning off north toward Dallas and south toward the Gulf coast. It is, as you know, an enormous city, its skyline brilliant with architecture and light. A landlocked lighthouse on the flat surface of south Texas.

Tonight she shines. The towers are lit and the road is ours alone. A bank sign marks the time at 2:30 a.m., alternately flashing the temperature at seventy-three degrees. Houston has an empty feel to it at such an hour. Her size demands traffic and noise. But this is a southern city and people sleep at proper hours, leaving the landscape to changing street signals with nobody to obey their commands. Night travel is best. Mild, thick air pours through the windows like river water, flowing in circles around our heads. Paul and I are quiet, our thoughts muffled by the tin-can rattle of his 1971 Volkswagen camping van. We are traveling north toward Oklahoma and then, perhaps, the Grand Canyon. After that, we have no plans except to arrive in Oregon before we run out of money. We share a sense of excitement and freedom. Not a rebel freedom, rather, a deadline-free sort of peace. There is nowhere we have to be tomorrow. There is no particular road we have committed to take, and I suppose, if one of us could talk the other out of it, the canyon itself could be bypassed for some other point of interest. Tonight we are travelers in the truest sense of the word, a slim notion of a final destination and no schedule to speak of. We are simply moving for motion's sake.

Our plans were shared with friends, but few understood. "Going off to find yourself" was the standard interpretation. I don't think that is really our point. We are shaped by our experiences. Our perception of joy, fear, pain, and beauty are sharpened or dulled by the way we rub against time. My senses have become dull and this trip is an effort to sharpen them.

"Does it snow much in Oregon?" I say to Paul in a voice loud enough to be heard over the wind and the engine.

"Snows a couple feet every winter out in central Oregon. Not a whole lot along the Pacific, though," he says, reaching to adjust the driver's side mirror.

"Do you think there will still be snow on the ground when we get there?"

"I doubt it. Most of the snow melts off in March. We will get there a couple months too late. There might be some snow in the mountains. We will see."

My mind has been swimming in mountain landscapes. Paul lived in Oregon most of his life and he's told stories of the geography. From him, I know the look and feel of Jefferson Park, of the Three Sisters and Crater Lake, all of them stitched together by a Pacific Crest Trail running up the Sierra Nevadas and then the Cascades, from Mexico to Canada. They've got trout the size of sea bass, bars thick with pretty girls, a cliff-bordered ocean, waterfalls, canyons, and just about anything Ernest Hemingway put in a novel. In Oregon, men live in the woods and let their beards grow. I know it happens the way Paul says it happens because he doesn't shift his eyes when he talks and his stories are never long.

Paul and a friend left Oregon several months ago and had been traveling around America in this van. Paul's friend found a girl in New Orleans and decided to stay, to play jazz on the street and try to make a new life in the South. Paul left New

2

Orleans and made it, on his own, as far as Houston, which is where he ran out of money. He got a job at an oil refinery, walking along the top of tanker cars, checking valves to make sure they were closed securely, climbing the ladders of vertical pipe at the end of the evening to look out over the landscape of smokestacks and yellow light, to breathe the sulfur and salt and humidity as a way of noting its human beauty, but all this was done in a longing for his home, the way a man will hold the woman he has while thinking of the woman he loves. Somehow Paul met my friend Fred, and though he was only in Houston for a few months, we accepted him into our small group of friends. He was mostly quiet, but if you prodded him enough you could get him to talk about life in the Pacific Northwest, about the wilderness winding along river basins, along canyons, about the wildlife timidly footing through forests, still like statues when you came across them, flashing away like lightning when you raised your rifle. He'd talk like this a little and then get to missing it and just as soon shut up, passing the talking to someone else—someone from Houston who only had stories about bars and girls and football scores. His stories got inside me like Neverland. I knew anybody from a place like that could never stay in a place like this.

Houston is no city for a guy like Paul; he doesn't fit. Time moves quickly here; people are in a panic to catch up. Paul exists within time but is hardly aware of how it passes. I check my wrist every ten minutes out of habit, and I don't think he's ever owned a watch. He is a minimalist. Everything he needs is in this van. His gear includes a tool box, a camping stove, a backpack, and about ten Louis L'Amour books. I think he has a pair of jeans, some shorts, and tennis shoes stuffed behind the seat, but nothing more except the clothes he is wearing. He is living proof you can find contentment outside the accumulation of things. The closest I've come to this sort of thinking was pondering the writings of Hank Thoreau. But I went to Walden Pond a year ago, just to see and feel the place, just to walk alone around the water, and they've made a suburb out of it. It hurts to hear the traffic rolling in through the trees. People commute from the land of Thoreau's solitude to Boston, to work at banks, to work at law firms. And I wonder if Walden exists anymore. I am not talking about the real Walden, the one in Boston; I am talking about the earth God meant to speak before we finished His sentence.

PAUL AND I HAVEN'T KNOWN EACH OTHER VERY LONG. Fred brought him up to a beach house that some of the guys and I rent every year in the winter when the phosphorus in the water dies. You can walk along the empty beach in the middle of the night and the waves glow bright green. There are no lights out on Crystal Beach, just scattered houses along the dunes, and out in the pitch black of the Gulf your eye will find an oil rig, and then suddenly from the east, a stream of green, a naturally lit wave will light out west for a hundred yards before folding into its own floating glow. It's the liquid equivalent of the northern lights. You can walk along the wet sand and turn to see your footsteps glow and fade out, the ones in the distance glowing least, the ones at your feet shining out in active chemistry. My friend Kyle discovered the phenomenon a few years ago and so we go out there every year and make fires on the beach and drink beer and every once in a while one of us will get up and walk out toward the waves to ponder the natural wonder.

He was doing pull-ups on a beam under the house when I arrived. *Who's the surfer?* I thought to myself. Paul is Oregon at heart but looks like California. He has wild blond hair and a smile that endears him to women. He's framed tightly with muscle, carrying his midsize stature in efficient, able-bodied strides. A swimmer's arms, not bulky with excess, but efficient, thick, and sun weathered.

There were old friends to catch up with, so we didn't talk the first day. Night came and I slept in a hammock on the porch. I was awakened shortly after sunrise by someone dragging a kayak over the dunes and onto the beach. I watched as Paul lifted the kayak to his shoulder and stumbled fifty yards to the shore. He dropped the boat into the water, pulled the two-sided paddle from the inside, and lowered himself into the opening. He launched out, through the short breaks, and slid along the still side of the Gulf for a few minutes, getting a feel for the kayak; then he turned away and paddled into the ocean till I lost him in the horizon. A half hour or so passed and he didn't return. Concerned, I rolled out of my hammock and stood against the railing. Still no sign of him. I kept mistaking waves for him, before finally finding his paddling motion, the oar coming out of the water like a pump, shoving back in on one side, then the other.

That evening, around the fire, Paul told us about his morning ride. He said he had found a school of dolphins and ridden above them as they crisscrossed beneath the kayak, playing with him, surfacing less than ten feet from the boat, and then diving into the deep. "It was as if they wanted to race," he said. "They were gliding beside me the way a dog runs beside a moving car."

These sorts of exploits earned our admiration, and once assured he was not interested in our girlfriends, we included him on road trips. Paul was welcome company, and his van came in handy. We made weekend runs to New Braunfels and central Texas, only stopping to pee off bridges, always holding it in through the pain and torture until finally we would hit a river or an overpass and we would fold out and stand at attention along the railing, holding our heads up toward the sky and breathing sighs of relief.

Soon we began talking about an extended trip, one that would have us living in the van for months, meeting new people and discovering regions of the country we had never seen. We plotted hypothetical routes up the East Coast or north to the Great Lakes. We bought a map and traced back roads connecting Civil War battle sites. We considered the Bible Belt and the Florida Keys. We pictured ourselves in New York and actually made a call to inquire about Yankee tickets. Paul and I began to consider the trip seriously. We spent days on the Internet and at the library flipping through glossy pages of mountains and rivers and cities at night. When our dreams gave way to plans, our other friends faded back into thoughts of responsibility and comfort. They became apprehensive; it would mean leaving their jobs or taking a semester off from school. Soon, Paul and I were the only ones willing to go.

THERE WERE, IN OUR GOOD-BYES, SENTIMENTS OF permanence. Some good-byes were more substantial than others. Kristin's last embrace felt difficult. Our relationship had come to an end because of this trip. I could not ask her to accept a halfhearted promise of returning soon, so a few days before we left, I called it off.

We parted with dignity. In our last hours she had asked, again, my reasons for leaving. I told her of the need to travel, to gain memories, and to be, for a while, completely free. She could not understand but accepted my explanation with understanding and an assurance there was something better for her just as there was for me.

Our time together ended too soon. We were to be at a friend's house where our close-knit group had gathered to say good-bye. Paul's van was already there when Kris and I arrived. We could hear people talking inside, so we walked in without knocking. The room was filled with familiar faces. Paul was on the couch with Bob, Jim, and Kyle. He was vaguely answering a question about our itinerary. Tia, Heather, and Kurt were standing in the kitchen. Jeremy, who was sitting on the stairs, playing his guitar, was the first to notice us.

"You know, I never took you as the hippie type," Jeremy said.

"Never took myself as the hippie type," I said. He took his hand off his guitar and reached out for mine. Gripping my hand tightly and matching my eye, he said, "I'm going to miss you."

"I will miss you too," I replied.

Within seconds we were surrounded, and Kristin slid off into the kitchen to avoid the reality of the moment. There were sincere good-byes; tones of loss were in our voices. It felt good to be in the spotlight, I have to admit. We were vagabonds, drifters, rebels setting out to see America. There were stories and laughter and promises to write. Fred gave us silver crosses on leather straps, and Dan gave us wool blankets he took from his Coast Guard barrack. I sensed an innocent envy from the guys. We wished they could join us, and they wished likewise, but school and work owned their youth. Trips like ours are greener grass left unknown for fear of believing trite sayings, sayings that are sometimes true. But theirs is an existence under the weight and awareness of time, a place we are slowly escaping, a world growing fainter by the hour and the mile. Our letters will arrive like messages in bottles cast from the luminary of distant shores.

EACH MILE DRIVEN LESSENS THE WEIGHT IN MY CHEST. Our friends are back in their homes, long asleep. And we are fading from the familiar into the unknown. The glass towers have given way to suburbs and darkly lit shopping malls. We are in that part of Houston where the sons of the sons of cowboys live in master-planned communities and play golf on weekends. They married their high-school sweethearts and exchanged horses for Volvos, half of them Southern Baptists who aspire to be politicians.

The van moves slowly. I am able to focus on a reflector mounted to the concrete barrier separating the north from the southbound lanes. As we approach, I turn my head to watch its white brightness dim as we pass.

"At the rate we're going, we may not reach the Northwest till next winter," I observe.

Paul leans his weight into the gas pedal. "At this rate we may not even get out of Houston till winter."

Paul is more comfortable with the slow progress than I am. We are cruising at a sluggish fifty miles per hour, and when ascending an overpass, the van chugs and loses a few notches on the speedometer. From the passenger's seat, I can see into the console, where the miles are clocking at a snail's pace.

Paul has nicknamed his van "the road commode," and it's a fitting name. The box-shaped van barely passes state standards. Throwbacks from the sixties, these vans are mobile intimations of the Woodstock era. Volvo-encased couples pass us on the street, look into each other's eyes, and remember when. I understand why this is the hippie "vehicle of choice." The van can comfortably sleep four (five if you lay a board across the two front seats). Paul has reconstructed the sink cabinet with wood scraps. It sits directly behind the driver's seat. Beyond the sink, parallel with the back window, there is a bed folded in a bench. Another bed can be created by turning a crank that lifts a tentlike contraption on the roof. There are two boxes of books on the floor between the sink and the bench, and another box of groceries and utensils in the open space beneath the sink. Several blankets are folded and sitting on the bench, and both of our backpacks lean against the side seats where a person can easily get through to the back. The interior is a black, waxlike plastic and rubber. They built this van when plastic was a new material so it's more rigid than the stuff they make now. A working stereo hangs out of a hole in the dash, and there are a couple knobs that work vent directors within the console. The gearshift is long and comes out of the floor. Volkswagen vans have rear engines, so we are sitting at the absolute front of the van. A glimpse over the dash allows me to see the headlights and the front bumper with the road sliding beneath.

STRETCHED BEFORE US IS AN ENDLESS SYSTEM OF interstates, highways, and back roads, a trail system of sorts, connecting city to city and state to state, Home Depot to Starbucks. Every intersection passed is an artery leading to workplaces, schools, and homes. Small towns dot the interstate for more than fifty miles north of Houston. Each city its own world; high school football games, church picnics, and Boy Scout meetings keep lives moving in a comfortable rhythm. Tonight they are but clusters of streetlights strung from neighborhood to neighborhood. Each neighborhood with its homes, each home with its family, and each quiet soul sleeping one thin wall from another. Charles Dickens tells us every heart is a profound mystery to the heart beating nearest it, and I am starting to understand him. Watching the dark towns pass gives them a new significance. During the day the roads are clustered with cars at stoplights, but tonight the thick, dark lines simply separate one neighborhood from another, one socioeconomic group from the one it once was. And it is odd for me to consider the thousands of sleeping people, quiet in their homes, their clocks ticking on the walls, the dogs breathing at the feet of their masters' beds, and to realize there are six billion people living in six billion settings. These homes house families we don't know. So many sleeping people, all of them spirit, bound by flesh, held up by bone and trapped in time.

Rarely do I question the mystery of it all. We are atoms connected to create big, awkward, intelligent animals, animals complex in construction, equipped with minds, hearts, and the like. Spinning secretly around us is an intricate system of interconnected physical laws, completely dependent upon one another for effectiveness. And we are in the middle of it; actors on Shakespeare's stage, madmen in Nietzsche's streets, accidents in Sagan's universe, children in God's creation.

And I suppose part of my wanting to leave Houston is to attempt an understanding of this mystery. My life, this gift I have been given, has been wasted, thus far, attempting to answer meaningless questions. Recently I have come to believe there are more important questions than *how* questions: *How do I get money, how do I get laid, how do I become happy, how do I have fun?* On one of our trips to central Texas, I stood at the top of a desert hill and looked up into the endlessness of the heavens, deep into the inky blackness of the cosmos, those billion stars seeming to fall through the void from nowhere to nowhere. I stood there for twenty minutes, and as it had a few times that year, my mind fell across the question *why?*

The question terrified me at first. I had only recently begun questioning my faith in God, a kind of commercial, American version of spirituality. I had questions because of the silliness of its presuppositions. The rising question of *why* had been manifesting for some time, and had previously only been answered by Western Christianity's propositions of behavior modification. *What is beauty?* I would ask. *Here are the five keys to a successful marriage,* I would be given as an answer. It was as if nobody was listening to the question being groaned by all of creation, groaned through the pinings of our sexual tensions, our broken biochemistry, the blending of light and smog to make our glorious sunsets. I began to believe the Christian faith was a religious system invented within the human story rather than a series of true ideas that explained the story. Christianity was a pawn for politicians, a moral system to control our broken natures. The religion did seem to stem from something beautiful, for sure, but it had been dumbed down and Westernized. If it *was* a religious system that explained the human story, its adherents had lost the grandness of its explanation in exchange for its validation of their *how* lifestyles, to such a degree that the *why* questions seemed to be drowning in the drool of Pavlov's dogs. And it wasn't just the church that was drowning; it was all of humanity or, at least, all of the West. Our skyscrapers and sports teams, our malls and our master-planned neighborhoods, our idiot politics, our sultry media promising ecstasy with every use of a specific dishwashing detergent. What does all of this mean? Are we animals nesting? Are we rats in one giant cage, none of us able to think outside our instincts? And does my faith live within these instincts, always getting me to my happiness, or is it larger, explaining the *why* of life, the *how* a shallow afterthought?

It wasn't just my faith that was being shaken. I began to wonder what personal ideas I believed that weren't true. I believed I was not athletic enough; too stupid, I believed I had to go to college; I believed the Astros were a more important team than the Mets; I believed jeans that cost fifty dollars were better than jeans that cost thirty; I believed living in a certain part of town made you more important than living in another. I looked up at the cosmos and it had no scientific proof that any of this was true. The cosmos wasn't telling me I was stupid; it wasn't telling me one pair of jeans was better than another. The cosmos was just spinning around up there, as if to create beauty for beauty's sake, paying no attention to the frivolity of mankind. And I liked the cosmos. I liked the cosmos very much. It seemed that it understood something, perhaps, humanity did not understand.

And so in exchanging the *how* questions for the *why* questions I began to probe the validity of presuppositions. There wasn't a science stepping up to insist authority. All of these ideas seemed subjective, and once they seemed subjective, they began to feel subjective. Far from depressing, this led to something quite beautiful. Girls who I once ignored as not pretty enough became, to me, quite lovely, their gentle way and deep humility and tenderness and femininity, their true images no longer being compared to the lies of commercial propaganda. If I couldn't grasp an idea, I didn't fault myself as dense; the cosmos didn't seem to be suggesting there was any more value to a dumb person than an intellectual. And jeans got a lot cheaper too.

I confess I wanted to believe life was bigger, larger than my presuppositions. Out there under the cosmos, out in the desert of Texas, beneath those billion stars and the umbrella of pitch-black eons of nothingness, on top of that hill, I started wondering if life was something different than I thought it was, if there was some kind of raging beauty a person could find, that he could get caught up in the *why* of life. And I needed to believe beauty meant something, and I needed God to step off His self-help soapbox and be willing to say something eternally significant and intelligent and meaningful, more meaningful than the parroted lines from detergent commercials. I needed God to be larger than our free-market economy, larger than our two-for-one coupons, larger than our religious ideas.

"You feeling tired yet, Paul?" He is looking groggy at the wheel.

"I've been tired for a while," he says.

"Why don't you pull over the next time you have the chance? I've got to use the restroom and we can switch."

Twenty miles pass and we see a rest area sign. Paul slows the van and coasts down the entrance past some trees and into the parking lot. A dozen or more tractor trailers are parked in long spaces. We pass them and pull into a spot near the restrooms. Paul turns off the engine, and we are immediately enveloped in the whistle and hum of a million crickets. Texas silence. I arch and stretch my back. Stepping out of the van, we are slow and road-travel weary as we move toward the restroom.

"I don't think I remember how to use my legs," Paul says, walking in an exaggerated wobbly motion.

"I'm pretty sure you just put one foot in front of the other, but it definitely doesn't feel right," I joke.

The temperature has dropped and a layer of moisture soaks the ground. Brainless june bugs make loud, fast dives at a light on the wall of the rest area. One broken-winged bug struggles on the sidewalk. I squash him under my boot and say softly, as if to myself, "All your questions are now answered."

Paul swings the heavy bathroom door open, and we are mugged by a foul stench.

"People really should eat better," he says.

We both hold our breath but can feel in the warmth of the room, in the moisture on the floor, the foul scent that surrounds us and seems to brush against our pant legs.

I beat Paul back to the outside world and gasp for air like a diver finding the surface of the ocean. Making my way across the lawn, I stretch out on a picnic table to flatten my back. The stars in this part of the country are distant and faded. They are grouped together in patches and encompassed in a hazy, humid-gray darkness. There are a few dark patches more milky than others that I recognize as high clouds, and they move slowly, engulfing twinkling stars, one at a time.

The road from Houston to Dallas cuts through the heart of the big thicket. We are encaged in a fence of tall pines. A blanket of pine needles and scattered cones lies across the lawn. Behind us, an island of trees is surrounded on four sides by the highway, the rest area, and its entrance and exit. Before us, across the parking lot, a dense forest, dark with shadows, extends perhaps as far as Nacogdoches. Save the choir of crickets, the air is silent and still, the truckers are asleep in their trucks, and the rest area is quiet and peaceful.

"Should we sleep here?" Paul asks.

We've not driven more than four hours, and we did that slowly. We've not made enough progress to stop, regardless of the time. I tell Paul I can probably make it through Dallas, and perhaps as far as Oklahoma. "Why don't you fold out the bed and sleep while I drive?" I suggest.

"Sounds good," Paul says, stretching his back and walking aimlessly around the picnic table. His jeans are faded and torn on one knee. They look like they've been through a cement mixer. I notice that one of the rips on the inside of his pant leg is patched with a red patterned cloth. "Is that a bandanna? You patched your jeans with a bandanna?"

He gives me a defensive look. "These are my favorite jeans."

"Did you do that yourself?" I ask.

"Yeah, so what?"

"Nothing, just wondering, that's all." Paul comes back to the table and sits down. There is a short period of silence, then I speak up. "Paul."

"Yeah."

"I was wondering. It's gonna get a little cold on the road, and I was hoping you could sew me a quilt or something, just maybe a scarf. Do you knit?"

Paul ignores me. I'm looking out into the sky, trying to find some stars. "It's going to get pretty cold out there, and I myself can't sew a stitch."

"Seems like you've got enough hot air," he says to me, walking over to the table, where he pushes me off so he can sit down. I fold down the bench of the table and into the wet grass. The ground is cold, but it is a refreshing change from the fixed-position seats of the van. Paul pulls a pipe out of his pocket and packs the tobacco with his thumb. He pulls out a lighter he told me his father gave him, some army issue contraption that was passed down from his grandfather. As he lights the pipe, the first plumes burn off white as cotton, and the smell of flowers and almonds drifts out across the lawn, back toward the van.

The highway has the ear of an ocean, trucks in distant hum roll close until their roaring engines push through our stretch of the highway, then fade off toward Dallas. A pair of head-lights sweep like searchlights through the trees as a semi grinds slowly into the rest area and his brakes squeal and hiss as he maneuvers his truck into a space on the far side of the rest area.

He turns off his lights and the place darkens again.

"I suppose we should get moving," I say, still lying in the grass.

"I'm about to fall asleep," Paul tells me. "Can you drive?"

"I should be fine," I say, standing up and wiping the blades of grass off my back.

Paul opens the side door and folds out the bed. He lays himself on top of the mattress and closes the door behind him with his foot. I hear his boots drop in the space between the front seats as I climb through the driver's side door. I sit for a second and think about where we are going. To Dallas, then to Oklahoma, then to Arizona, then who knows. Whatever is between Arizona and Oregon.

The clutch pedal offers little resistance. I pin it against the floor with the weight of my foot alone. With the shifter in neutral, I try to start the van. It turns several times before I let off the ignition. No start. I pump the gas and try it again. Still no start. I once had an old Datsun that gave me the same trouble. The carburetor would flood every other time I went to start it. Remembering a trick I used on the Datsun, I hold the van's gas pedal to the floor for a few seconds to drain the carburetor and then pump it once. Turning the key, I hear the engine fire immediately. With the shifter in neutral, I move it over and back. The clutch grinds as it finds reverse and the engine whistles and ticks as I back out of the parking space. I enter the on-ramp, slowly, and even as I step the pedal to the floor, there is no surge of power. The van feels gutless and old. It is creating a hisslike whistle and there is a steady, quick tempo to the valves as they click. We enter the highway at a turtle's pace, like a semi pulling a full load. There is a large-winged, yellow-blooded insect stuck in the driver's side wiper.

One wing shakes in the wind and the other is mostly steady as it is fastened to the wiper itself. I hadn't noticed it from the other seat.

The interstate is laid across slight, long hills. A lone truck's red taillights glow in the distance, disappearing and reappearing as we rise and descend. My headlights cast a ghostlike glow on the blurry road as white striped lines approach from the distance, slow at the outstretch of my headlights, then quickening as they near until they fire like lasers at my left wheel. Stately pines, keeping a careful, untrusting distance, slide by on the left and right. I half roll up my window as the air is coming in cool.

There is a solace in night travel that is absent in daylight. Daylight is broad and exposing; gas stations, factories, and forests are all brought to life under the sun. Night covers them. It is as though a cloth has been draped over the cares of the day, pouring them into our memories for meditation and reflection. It occurs to me, as it sometimes does, that this day is over and will never be lived again, that we are only the sum of days, and when those are spent, we will not come back to this place, to this time, to these people and these colors, and I wonder whether to be sad about this or to be happy, to trust that these hours are meant for some kind of enjoyment, as a kind of blessing. And it feels, tonight, as if there is much to think about, there is much we have been given and much we have left behind. The smell of freedom is as brisk as the air through the windows. And there is a feeling that time itself has been curtained by darkness.

2 HILL COUNTRY

THE SUN IS SHINING THROUGH THE WINDOWS IN THE back of the van, and I slide deep into my sleeping bag. Warm in my cocoon, I position the pillow above to block the light. Car doors slam in the distance, and I hear the sound of children laughing. Sleepily, I wonder where I am. Fresh, but fading in my mind, is a dream that had me on a horse being chased by men with guns. All of it was so real . . . the safety of the here and now comes back slowly.

"Don." A muffled voice speaks softly.

I lie silent . . .

"Don . . . hey, bud, it's nine o'clock in the morning."

I am not sure whether I am imagining the voice or the one speaking.

"Don, you awake?"

Like a turtle from its shell, I take my head out of the bag and open my eyes to the brightness of late morning. I close them again at the flood of washed-out colors and light.

"Yeah, I'm up." I cover my eyes with the pillow. Paul is sitting with his head turned, pressed against the ceiling. He is pulling a boot over his foot.

"What time is it?" My voice is smothered by the pillow, my stench breath absorbed by the cotton.

"It's nine o'clock. How long did you drive last night?" Paul asks.

"We're close to Dallas," I respond. "I didn't make it to Dallas, but we're close, I think."

I slide back into my bag and mumble empty words at the bright morning sun. Last night I had caught myself closing my eyes for seconds at a time, so I pulled over.

"I'm gonna get us moving again," Paul says. "Do you want to sleep some more?"

"I'm up," I respond, rolling over and burying my face in the pillow.

Paul maneuvers out of the bed and between the two front seats. "I'll be right back; I'm gonna use the restroom." The van door opens and closes and the space around me has a sudden quietness to it. Pulling my head out of the bag, I see Paul walking down the sidewalk toward the restrooms. Outside the back window, I notice the headlights of an RV. They are high, broad apart, and tainted brown with road dust. It is parked so close that, were it not for the glass, I could reach out and touch it with my foot. The small rest area looks less significant than it did last night. What I thought was a thicket of trees is only a weak scattering of saplings mixed with shrubs. It is more of a roadside pullout than a rest area. There are restrooms and picnic tables. A trash can is mounted at its top to two rusty poles with a large, lazily placed trash bag hanging off its rim. I change my position to lie on my side, stretching my back. Still in the sleeping bag to my neck, light illumines floating, rolling, falling particles of angel-bright dust meandering ever so lazily down morning beams, filtered through a dirty window. Cars pass in quick, colorful blurs. Yawning, the van air comes in stale.

Outside the window, somewhere behind me, there are children laughing. I catch their small frames in the corner of my eye. Turning over, I find two red-haired kids staring at me through the window. Surprised by my sudden turn, they step back and release a sudden spurt of laughter, covering their mouths and pulling close to each other in one motion. There are a boy and a girl. They look like brother and sister. My reflection in the window is unshaved and disheveled—my thick hair standing in the front like a wave frozen in the ocean. As I allow my eyes to fall back to the children, they release another giggle. The girl, in an act of bravery, steps forward and knocks on the window. The boy pulls her back by the sleeve of her sweater. I play the part of the hippie and hold up two fingers to make a peace sign. Another spurt of laughter erupts and they become red-faced, not looking for long, but taking short, split-second glances, followed by a gasp and a laugh and pulling close to each other. I can't help but smile. Suddenly two women walk by and the children attach themselves, disappearing behind the RV.

WE ARE ONE DAY OUT AND HOME SEEMS AN OCEAN away. My watch ticks inside my boot. I don't need it. I'm not late for anything. There is no disgruntled friend waiting for me at a coffee shop or office. The people I used to be surrounded by are getting along without me. I am in a van, south of Dallas, heading I don't know where, and I have to tell you, it feels pretty good. I wonder, though, if the good feeling will last. I do this with good things; I think joy into its coffin; I analyze too much. I don't want to think about life anymore; I just want to live life.

Sometimes I admire people who don't ask *why* questions, who only want to know the *how* of life: How do I get paid, how do I get a wife, how do I make myself happy, whatever. The *why* path isn't so rewarding, if you think about it: Why are we here, why do we feel what we feel, desire what we desire, need what we need, hate what we hate? I saw this Calvin and Hobbes cartoon once that had Calvin's teacher asking the class to turn in their homework. Calvin raised his hand and asked why we exist. The teacher told Calvin not to change the subject but to turn in his homework, and what difference does it make anyway? Calvin leaned back in his chair and mumbled to himself that the answer to the question determined whether or not turning in his homework was important in the first place. I think that is what I am talking about here, about needing the answer to the former question before the latter becomes important, about *why* questions determining whether *how* questions are important. And that is what I mean by admiring people who don't think about the *why* questions, because they can just get a job, a big house, a trophy wife, and do whatever they want and never ask if it is connected to anything, whether their *how* is validated by their *why*.

Paul opens the door just as I am thinking this through. "You up, Don?"

"Yeah, I'm up."

Climbing into the seat and pulling it forward with a shift of his weight, he turns the key and the engine offers several slow revolutions before bellowing out a loud, unsteady start. It runs only for a second and stalls. I reach for my boots, throw them to the space between the seats, and then follow, climbing out of the bed to the passenger's seat. Meanwhile, Paul is pumping the gas and fiddling with the key. I'm struggling with my feet and my boots and the small space I have to work with.

Just as I begin to tell Paul about the trick with draining the carburetor, the van gives a sudden start. Paul lays into the pedal and the engine screams uncomfortably and cold at 4000 RPMs. He holds it there for a moment, then releases the pedal and pumps it again. The cold, sleeping metal rubs against itself and wakes in a grumpy, old dog growl. Normally you wouldn't rev an engine that has been sitting all night, but with an old wreck like this, there is no other way to wake it. You've got to put some gas in the carburetor and light the plugs.

"How are we on gas?" I ask.

Paul looks at the console. "We've got a quarter of a tank. We should stop soon."

"Coffee would be nice too."

Paul nods in agreement and backs the van up slowly, no more than a few inches, and then pulls forward, tugging the steering wheel with both arms, hand over hand, easing us only a small space from the bumper on the car in front of us.

LIGHT REFLECTS IN SHARP POINTS OFF WINDSHIELDS in motion. Stripes of gray asphalt, two lanes in each direction, are banked and separated by grass and trees. Weeping willows hang depressed limbs low, sweeping the ground and rolling slowly around themselves in a light breeze as behind them, shapeless clouds bring the bright sky close and cast an eye-squinting reflection off a sign that marks Dallas at forty-seven miles.

From the south, there is no industry to indicate a great city is near. Soon we will crest a hill and beneath us will rest a modern skyline complete with a towering cluster of buildings, factories, and freeways in a grand display of the New South. Dallas is the Seattle of Texas. It is what Chicago used to be. But no single man built the coming town. Dallas blew in on the wings of a Gulf coast hurricane and rained glass and steel onto a field of bluebonnets. It's an odd town, though. A big, Republican, evangelical city where you can't drink, girls wear black dresses for dates on Wednesday, and the goal is to join the local country club like your daddy and his daddy before him. When you build a city near no mountains and no ocean, you get materialism and traditional religion. People have too much time and lack inspiration.

We crest a hill and there she stands, just as I recalled, puffed up and proud of herself, all bustling with activity and shining in the late morning sun. Cars line the distant freeways thick and slow, bumper to bumper, moving together as if they were connected like an endless train. The highway rolls straight toward city center, through suburbs, past parks and soccer fields and strip mall after strip mall after strip mall. If there is one thing they have in Texas, it is land. There is no need to build things tall and close together; everybody gets an acre; you get an acre to live on, an acre to work on, an acre to park your car in, and an acre in case you need an extra acre. Driving to work or the store may take you an hour because nothing is close together; no space is conserved because, save the cosmos itself, there is nothing quite as big as the Lone Star State.

There is but one Texas, and for Texans there is need for nothing more. A country within a country, these people believe they have found the promised land. Businessmen wear thousand-dollar suits with ten-thousand-dollar Stetsons. They drive king-cab trucks to their office jobs while their wives drive SUVs filled with kids in transit to and from school, band practice and football practice and cheerleader practice, and so on. And they have these little white stickers on the backs of their cars that read, "Michael . . . Plano Football" or "Michelle, Redmond Cheerleader" advertising their child's achievement like a political statement, teaching their kids that what really matters, what Daddy really loves, is what you do. Give me something I can brag about to complete strangers stuck in traffic. Brilliant. I will have to send my mother a sticker that says "Vagabond" or "Late Sleeper." I turn on the radio to find a station with a deejay ranting about how we need to stop the Mexicans from crossing the border, his cohost humming "The Battle Hymn of the Republic" in the background. It reminds me of those history lessons in which we learned the great honor the men at the Alamo displayed as they stopped the nation of Mexico from taking back its land. I turn the knob even farther to find somebody playing a Robert Earl Keen record. And I remember, if there is one thing that all this empty pride produces, the crop that all this land harvests, it is good music. I don't think there is any better music than the music that comes out of Texas. Robert Keen, the guy on the radio, used to room with Lyle Lovett back at Texas A&M, and he and Lovett used to sit on the porch of their house in their underwear, right when the Lutheran church across the street let out, and they would sing as the women would walk to their cars, looking down at the asphalt, and the men would sneer over at the ugly concert, all the while blocking their children's eyes. I let the station stay, and Paul comforts himself in his seat, reaches over, and turns the volume up. Robert Earl Keen Jr.'s voice comes soft and thoughtful over his guitar in "Road to No Return":

> But each new morning sunrise
> Is just as good as gold
> And all the hope inside you
> Will keep you from the cold
> Bare your soul and let your spirit burn
> Out along the road to no return

As the city passes, we fade from metropolitan landscape to farmland, bound slow but sure for Oklahoma. I am glad to be done with the city. I like the slow pace of agriculture, where you ask the crops to come, and they come when they come, not when you ask them, so slow you can't see them for months. They unfold under an inch of soil like children in wombs, keeping their own time. No wishful thinking can do a thing to speed them up.

The air is cooler today than yesterday. These clouds came to us from the north, and soon they will pass and leave a deep-blue sky that will blanket the state with, quite possibly, the last cold front of the season. The temperature tints the air with cleanness. And all of it reminds me that I am alive, that I am having some kind of experience, some kind of thing is happening to me the way it is happening to the crops, how for months they come into themselves under the soil, made from the elements in the soil, how from out of dirt gets built a little bud of corn, a little human in a womb, without explanation, without an obvious reason or purpose, just stuff getting born, just stuff dying and going back to dirt, just rolling around the cosmos like foul weather. It strikes me that I am like this and Paul is like this, and my family and my friends, we are all just getting born, just growing up, just dying off.

I wonder what it must feel like, for those without a faith system, to wake up one morning and suddenly ask *why* questions, the way I asked them on that hill in west Texas. I would think it would be difficult to explain pain and suffering, to explain beauty and meaning and purpose with only subjectivity as framework. When I think of this, I think of that Douglas Coupland book with all the nursery rhyme characters who are lost, looking for something good that was supposed to happen but never happens because the plastic surgery didn't work or the drugs started to own them or the depression that is always, always waiting just outside the door found a crack it could slip through to whisper hard and unwanted truths into the ears of the characters whose stories were supposed to come true, were supposed to end with a *happily ever after*. And I wonder, quite honestly, if I will end up like this, if I will discover that my Christian faith, my American faith, was a fraud, and that there was nothing behind it, that it wasn't even pointing me toward something real and authentic, and I, too, will join the ranks of the dispossessed, staring up into the cosmos asking why, only to have the cosmos shrug its broad black shoulders as if to return the question.

I would imagine having the capacity to ask *why* questions but not having any answers would just make life feel something like rehab.

It's interesting how you sometimes have to leave home before you can ask difficult questions, how the questions never come up in the room you grew up in, in the town in which you were born. It's funny how you can't ask difficult questions in a familiar place, how you have to stand back a few feet and see things in a new way before you realize nothing that is happening to you is normal.

The trouble with you and me is we are used to what is happening to us. We grew into our lives like a kernel beneath the earth, never able to process the enigma of our composition.

Think about this for a moment: if you weren't a baby and you came to earth as a human with a fully developed brain and had the full weight of the molecular experience occur to you at once, you would hardly have the capacity to respond in any cognitive way to your experience. But because we were born as babies and had to be taught to speak and to pee in a toilet, we think all of this is normal. Well, it isn't normal. Nothing is normal. It is all rather odd, isn't it, our eyes in our heads, our hands with five fingers, the capacity to understand beauty, to feel love, to feel pain.

If I do lose faith, that is if I do let go of my metaphysical explanations for the human experience, it will not be at the hands of science. I went to a Stephen Hawking lecture not long ago and wondered about why he thought we get born and why we die and what it means, but I left with nothing, save a brief mention of aliens as a possible solution to the question of origin. And I don't mean anything against Stephen Hawking, because I know he has an amazing brain and I know he has explained a lot of the physics of our universe, but I went wondering about something scientific that might counter mysterious metaphysical explanations, and I left with aliens.

Hawking can only move a finger. The rest of his body is limp. He has a computer they built at USC and he uses his finger to feed words into sentences, and under his wheelchair is a speaker and when he presses a button, the sentence he made on his screen is spoken through the speaker. We crowded into a room just before he rolled on stage, turned the wheelchair toward the audience, and sat in stillness and silence like a slight sack of rice set low in a chair overflowing with wires. The room fell to a hush as the answering-machine voice of his computer offered a welcome and a greeting and then a long pause, and then one sentence and a pause, and another and a pause, and then another, each sentence revealing some bit of new knowledge about black holes and string theory and time travel and, well, aliens. And I confess I was taken aback. I had previously considered two theories about the universe, the first a rather archaic idea I had picked up in church as a kid regarding God speaking the cosmos into being, and the other a series of accidents that stemmed from nothing and meant nothing and were adding up to nothing. While I subscribed to the breath of God idea, the idea of accidental propulsion was beginning to weigh heavy on my mind, both as an explanation for our existence and as a motive for philosophical suicide, a faulty rotted *why* holding up the meaningless *how*. And to put a point on it, here was the greatest physicist of our age, a man who could recite more than seventy-five pages of theory to his assistant from memory. A man who discovered and explained much of the physical behavior of matter at the openings of black holes, a man on par with Einstein himself, explaining that one possibility for the creation of our universe might be a cosmic seed planted billions of years ago, set in motion by an advanced species of aliens.

It turns out the droplet of our knowledge is a bit lost in the ocean of our unknowing. So much so we are still stabbing at fairy tales. And what I really mean by this is that science itself is not capable of presenting a why. That is, in order to subscribe to a *why* (an objective rather than subjective why) you have to subscribe to some sort of theory about God or aliens. And yet the mind needs a *why*, just as the body needs food.

"What in the world are you thinking, bud?" Paul asks.

"What's that?" I respond.

"You're just staring at the dash like you're in a trance." Paul has a smile on his face. He has been watching me for a while.

"I guess I was just zoning a little." I sit back and hang my arm out of the window, making a cup with my palm to feel the air against my hand, thinking again about the mystery of the elements, of invisible wind, not seen but there, en masse, collecting to push against the skin of my hand.

"Are you homesick already?" Paul asks.

I give a slight, defensive chuckle. "Not quite yet. It's gonna take a little longer than this."

"Then what are you thinking about? You look sad or something."

"I wasn't thinking about anything, Paul."

"You sure?"

"I'm sure," I tell him.

THE VAN IS MOVING SLOWLY, EVEN SLOWER THAN normal. We are ascending a hill that is significantly larger than anything we have yet seen. Texas curls up at the border, as though the land mass wouldn't fit inside the map, so it rises at the edges. The road is straight and narrow, and there is a good quarter mile of concrete between us and the summit. The shoulder of the interstate passes slowly. I can make out the gray and green definition of small stones and broken glass.

"You want me to get out and push?" I ask.

Paul begins to rock backward and forward in his seat. I can feel his weight sway the van. I place both hands on the dash and begin to push, clenching my teeth and wrinkling my forehead as if to be working hard. Paul looks down at the speedometer.

"It's no use. We're down to 42!"

I sit back and bend my legs to set my boots against the dash. Again, I push and grit and wrinkle my forehead. In an exasperated voice, still pushing against the dash, I ask if we are moving any faster.

"Bud, this isn't good." Paul is looking frustrated. "We are down to 35."

I take my boots off of the dash and lean over to look at the console. "What do you think it is?"

"This piece-of-crap van is what it is. They didn't say anything about this in the brochure," he says.

"Worthless salesman," I add.

"We're not getting any power," Paul explains. "I should have adjusted the valves before we left."

As we crest the hill, two trucks and an RV pass us quickly and loudly on the left side. From atop the hill I can see the road dipping low into a ravine and then rising through trees in a four-lane bend toward another hill of greater size.

"We've got to get some speed on the downhill," I comment, just above a whisper, as if talking more to the van than to Paul.

Paul has the pedal to the floor and the van is gaining speed. He announces our progress in increments of 5. Fifty feels like 90 compared to the 30 we've been moving. The van rattles and whines and enjoys the slope of the road like an old man who has been hit with a burst of energy. Showing off, it lifts its shaky needle to 55 and then 60, before steadying at 62. We roar through the bottom of the hill, begin to climb, and the van slows. This time there is no rocking or pushing and what was funny only seconds ago has lost its humor. We crest and descend five or more hills at turtle, then rabbit, then turtle speed. Each ascent frustrates us to the point of silence. Paul voicelessly expresses his concern. His hands are tightly gripped on the steering wheel, and his slightly wrinkled brow frowns toward the noonday horizon, as if to wish he was there and not here.

An hour into our trouble we meet with Oklahoma. The welcome sign is of no consequence as we are preoccupied with the trouble and the van. What would have exacted a "Yeehaw" or a stirring and not quite accurate chorus from the state's own musical has been deluged by our circumstance.

Having brought up the valves a half hour before, I ask Paul if he thinks we should pull over and adjust them.

"Well, we'd have to wait for the engine to cool. That could take several hours, and the more I think about it, I'm not sure it's the valves. It could be the carburetor. It feels like it's not getting enough gas. I can hardly feel it when I step on the pedal." As he says this, he deepens his foot into the gas but there is no thrust. We crest another hill, descend, and begin climbing the next. These hills are long hills; they are several minutes to the bottom and twenty minutes to the top. At common speeds a road looks small and thin, but at van pace it is broad-shouldered, wide-laned, and dashed with long, distantly spaced lines. We have slowed to an embarrassing speed of 23.

As we crest a hill and turn a bend, we find a small store and pull into a dusty roadside parking lot. A few weathered pickup trucks are parked outside. Paul kills the engine and we sit for a minute, listening to the metal tick itself cool. Paul silently gets out of the van, and I follow him. As we are walking into the store, two young boys come out with small paper bags filled with candy, each holding a cold bottle of Coke. They notice the van and strike up a conversation.

"Where are you guys from?"

Paul, slightly surprised at their friendly interest, answers in a soft, withdrawn voice. "We drove up from Houston."

The boy who asked the question leans into the other and they both speak at the same time.

"Jessie's been to Houston . . ."

"I've been there," one of the boys offers. "My uncle lives there, and we went down at Christmas. That's a big city."

The other joins in before Jessie finishes his sentence. "I've been to Dallas, to Six Flags too. You sleep in that van?" The boys walk to the side of the van, looking at it in wonder. The nameless boy speaks before we can answer his first question. "Ben Bonham had a van like this but he sold it and got a car."

Jessie, disagreeing with the other, starts at him with a child-like arrogance. "Nu-uh, Ben still has it. He has two cars. A van and a car."

"He did too sell it. He only has one. I bet you a fireball he ain't got it."

"I know he still has it. I seen him the day before yesterday."

The boys trail off, across the parking lot and back through some woods, all the while talking about Ben and his car and how he does and doesn't have a van like ours. Paul looks at me and shrugs his shoulders and we walk into the store. As we enter, my eyes adjust slowly to the dim light and for a second everything is covered in gray. Deeper into the store, past the counter and the woman behind it, things begin to sharpen. Part quick-mart and part grocery store, the shelves are half-empty and in disarray. A layer of set-in dust covers the floor, and the place smells more like a feed store than a grocery store. We pace the short aisles, past the chips and candy, around the end cap of Styrofoam coolers and then back, down the cat food and aspirin aisle, toward the woman at the counter.

"Can I help you find something?" the woman asks.

"Yes," I respond. "We're looking for carburetor cleaner."

"Car stuff is behind you," she says, pointing over my shoulder.

We turn to see a small sampling of motor oil and pine-tree air fresheners. There is one can of Fix-A-Flat, but no carburetor cleaner. A plaid-shirted, red-faced man, who has been standing at the counter, talking to the woman all this time, walks toward the door and stands in the bright light, looking out at the parked cars. "You boys having problems with that van out there?"

Paul answers as he walks down the aisle, toward the man. "Yes, we think it's the carburetor."

"What's it doing to you?" the red-faced man asks.

"We get no power when we're going uphill. It slows down to about 25 or so."

The lady behind the counter speaks up, addressing the plaid-shirted man. "I don't think Michael Johnson's place is open today, is it?"

"He's out of town. Won't be back till Tuesday," the man answers, not looking at her, only staring out at the van and picking at his teeth with a toothpick. He is thin and weathered from a lifetime in the field. Layers of sun on his gray-brown face probably add ten years to his aspect.

"Ben Bonham could help you boys. I think ol' Ben is home."

The lady joins in, as if to remember, and agrees with the man. "Ben sure could help. He knows about those vans. He used to have one."

"Yeah, Ben could help you boys. Ben's as good at fixing those things as Michael Johnson is. He's just up the road a bit if you wanna go out there."

"Does he have a shop?" I ask toward the man, but glancing at the woman to include her in the question. The man and the woman begin together but she quiets to his response. "He works out of his home, just over the highway a bit." The weathered man takes the toothpick from his mouth and points, in a general motion, across the road and toward a side street, starting to tell us how to get there. He puts the toothpick back in his mouth and goes to the counter where the woman hands him a pencil and a piece of paper. Writing and talking at the same time, he begins his directions.

"Go out across the street and head up Dagg Road. That's Dagg right there," he says, as he points with the pencil to a dirt road just out the door and across the paved street. "Head on out Dagg till you get to Midland, and Midland isn't marked but Dagg dead-ends there so you'll know it when you come to it . . ."

The man goes on like this for a while, carefully writing down each street. As he finishes, Paul thanks him for his kindness. The plaid-shirted man accepts our handshakes and farewells in a removed, masculine way. We climb back into the van and edge slowly across the parking lot, rough and rattling, kicking up dry dust.

A DOT ON THE HIGHWAY, THIS TOWN IS ALL MOBILE homes and pickups. Each trailer differs only in fencing and color. Families with money have built carports and fencelike trimming to cover the tires or their trailer hitch. Paul navigates us through streets long given to potholes and sections of shell and dirt. We arrive at what looks to be Ben's place. The trailer sits at the edge of town and backs up to a piece of land that is raised in the front and dips down to a man-made pond and a squab of wiry berry bushes and woods. A large tool shed sits between the trailer and the pond. On its doors are hung ancient, rusted tools.

We turn up the drive and notice a Volkswagen van, abandoned and surrounded by a tall mesh of weeds. Paul cracks a smile and I make a comment about how someone owes someone else a piece of candy. Around the front of the trailer is an enclosed porch, complete with floor-to-ceiling screens and a thin glass door. Aside from Ben's van, there are no cars and we begin to wonder if anyone is home.

It is an uncomfortable position to burden a stranger with your troubles. Doctors, lawyers, and mechanics are constantly queried for free advice and labor. The expressions on our faces note our disdain for our state and there is an uneasy, brief moment of stillness as one waits for the other to approach the door. Paul goes and I follow at his shoulder, through the glass door, into the porch. He knocks and there is an immediate stir. As we step back, the door opens and then draws closed, leaving only a crack of darkness. A rotund female figure is outlined in shadows through the dim opening.

"Yes?" her voice is small and secretive.

Paul, standing in front, takes the conversation. "Does Ben Bonham live here, ma'am?"

"He is my husband."

"The people in town told us he might be able to help with our van. We were just passing through and the mechanic in town is away."

The door opens a little more and a friendly, round, elderly face claims her voice. "Ben is out right now, but he should be in soon. Where are you boys from?"

Shifting to Paul's side, I involve myself in the conversation.

"We've come up from Houston and are heading to the Grand Canyon."

Our conversation goes on for a while about the Grand Canyon and her twice having been there, once with Ben when the kids were young and another time only three years back. The dialogue never stales as brief moments of silence are quickly absorbed by another story or bit of trivia about the canyon and her two trips there. Several minutes later as Mrs. Kate Bonham still stands in the doorway, a long, sixties Cadillac pulls behind our van. Kate's gentle smile tells us it is Ben. She slips back into the trailer.

We meet Ben at the back of our van and I explain to him our dilemma. All filled with kindness and pride, Ben sets his coat and lunch pail on the hood of his car and opens the engine compartment to the van. His hands are aged eighty years or more. They are stained with grease and time.

"I got one like this myself, boys. Put it out to pasture a few years back, but liked her while she ran. I blew a piston trying to turn my tractor over when I rolled it. What seems to be the problem with yours?"

Paul and I are silent, imagining a seventy-five-year-old man rolling a tractor and then attempting to right it again with a Volkswagen.

"I say, what's the problem with yours?"

Paul shakes off his daydream and answers quickly, making up for the inattentiveness. "It doesn't have any power. We do about 25 when we're going uphill. I thought maybe it was the valves . . ." Paul is interrupted by Ben before he can finish his sentence.

"Valves wouldn't do that to ya. It's a gas problem. Sounds like the carburetor." Ben rolls up his long, stained sleeves and leans under the hood, over the engine. He is a short, pudgy man whose height gives him an advantage leaning into the low compartment. His overalls are long and extend past the heels of his steel-toed boots. "I never did like these dual carburetors. Did you know that you can get a kit to change it to a single carb? I did that to mine and had it for the better, that's for sure."

"I didn't know that," Paul responds, hands in pockets, peering behind Ben's shoulder and watching his hands shake wires, pulling them taut.

"Does it chug when you give it gas?"

Paul, hesitating as he considers the question, speaks softly and reserved, inches from Ben's ear, "It does. That's the problem."

Ben playfully barks a command at me, "Start it up, boy."

I round the van to the driver's side, wait for the signal, and turn the key. Without pushing the pedal, the engine revs fierce and loud. Ben releases the lever and it dies. "Start it again, son!" His voice comes muffled and distant from within the engine compartment. I turn to see Paul twisting his fist and fingers in a sign to start the van. Again, Ben controls the RPMs from the rear and the engine whines loud and inconsistent. He releases the gas and it dies.

"You're missin' some linkage here." Ben shows Paul the lever on the right carburetor. Two holes in the lift are empty. "You boys are working off of one carburetor. See this here . . . ," Ben moves aside, still holding the lever with his right hand, ". . . this connects to this other and gets a tug from the gas pedal to give gas to the carb. It's a wonder you got to twenty-five miles per hour with just one carb." Paul, looking relieved to know that the problem is a simple one, crunches down and pulls at the lever. Ben disappears behind the van and reappears in the distance, walking toward the tool shed. He returns with a small piece of baling wire. "Let me in there for a second, son." Paul moves aside and Ben's efficient fingers go to work twisting the wire to link the two levers. Upon Ben's signal, I start the van, pump the gas, and the van gives a loud, dual-carburetor wail.

"She sounds all right to me. I think that might do it."

Ben's proclamation is met with gratitude and an offer to pay. He will have nothing to do with that and changes the conversation to neglected introductions. After telling him where we are from and where we are going, we listen again to stories of two trips to the Grand Canyon, several years ago with the kids and a few years back with just the wife and the dog, which "isn't around because it got run over just last month." It was a good dog named Bear and was hit by a truck. Had three legs to begin with.

"You boys should like that canyon. Amazing thing she is. Deep as hell herself with a river at the bottom to boot! We never went to the bottom, but seen it in the picture cards and the Colorado runs right through her like a cut. Folks go boating through her too. We saw it in a video. You boys going down?"

"We hope to," I answer. "We're just sorta playing it by ear. Hey, listen, give me your address and I'll send you a postcard when we get there."

"I will," Ben answers, smiling and huffing toward the trailer for a piece of paper and a pencil. He returns with an opened scrap envelope from a piece of junk mail and a dull pencil. Paul and I are silent as we watch him write his name and address next to the same name and address printed on the envelope. Ben's eyes are lit like a boy's at Christmas. He hands me the envelope and reminds me again what it is for. "A picture card will do. Kate and I really like it there."

"Ben, are you sure we can't pay you?" Paul asks. "You've done so much."

"Get outta here, boys. I gotta get washed up. I smell like a mule and Kate doesn't like that." Still wearing a giant smile, he shoos us with his hands as if we are chickens being scurried through a gate. Paul locks eyes with him as he turns to go. I close the door on the passenger side and give a soft three-fingered wave and grin. Paul backs out of the drive, rolling off into the worn grass to pass Ben's car. The old man watches through the glass, inside the porch, and waves as he sees I am still looking at him.

We weave back through the dusty streets and onto the road that will take us to the interstate. "Ben has the life, doesn't he?" Paul comments, breaking a minute or so of silence. I nod my head in agreement, rolling down the window to get some fresh air.

"Works all day, comes home to the woman he loves. You couldn't ask for a better life," Paul says.

3 THIN ICE

WE MOVE WITH NEW AND APPRECIATED QUICKNESS toward a sinking sun that sets to flame the backs of close and distant hills, causing clouds to flare in violent strips and tall trees to lay their shadows across the road like nightclothes across a bed. Oklahoma has no better show than evening.

Our conversation has lulled from praises of Ben Bonham to comments about the sunset to silence. Out the passenger-side window the blur of green opens and closes with each passing red-dirt road. My mind focuses on life beyond the trees and the hills and this road cutting through them. It is there I imagine a small home surrounded by forest and a man sitting by a fire, reading the pages of a book he has read before and will read again. He is tired and nodding, and though his eyes still brush the words, he has long stopped reading. The fading light through the windows and the warmth of the fire soothe him into a sleep from which he will not wake till morning, finding himself still dressed with a book across his lap. Miles from the cabin, in another home, still in the here and now (albeit in my imagination) I see a family at evening supper, perhaps saying grace. And at that table there is a woman who is glad to have her husband home as he has been to such and such a place to do business. Ever nearer, and perhaps in a home just off this interstate, down a dusty driveway weaving through maple and pine that spread March over these rolling hills, there is a young girl at her desk, constructing a letter to the boy who has taken her heart. And just outside my window, a hundred thousand voices fire through phone lines that parallel this road, each voice carried swiftly to a listener who trusts his response to the broad-shouldered poles and sweeping lines marking the miles from home to home and business to business.

And the sun is being swallowed by the hills, leaving ample room on left and right for blood-red glow and backlit clouds. To the east, darkness and shadows. Our headlights press softly against the oncoming road.

The radio lacks a CD player and is probably the one that came with the van. There's a tape player, though, and in the glove box I find a few tapes. Secretly I scold myself for not bringing music of my own. Amid scraps of insurance papers and part-shop receipts, my fingers find a tape.

"Lynyrd Skynyrd?" I question aloud.

"You can't beat Skynyrd," Paul defends.

"I could if I had a bat."

Other tapes include U2's *Joshua Tree* and a fellow named George Winston. "Who's George Winston?" I ask.

"He's a piano player."

"Is it classical?"

"Not really, it's just kinda mellow. Like Mogwai, without the wires or the beat."

"Mogwai without music, you mean."

Paul smirks. "Trust me. It's good."

Music is the sound track of life. The absence of it is unforgivable on a road trip. This is a James Taylor moment and we are stuck with a piano player who wants to sound like Mogwai and a Southern funk band that, somewhere along the line, fell into thinking Alabama is a sweet place to call home. Catchy meaninglessness. A more thought-provoking, smooth desperateness is in order. Lyle Lovett would hit the spot right now. John Gorka or Clem Snide would make fine background music for a journey such as this. But I am without, and silence being the next best thing to noise, I resolve to myself to listen to that which is so commonly called nothing. Tonight's silence is road and tires, engine and wind. Each so well-composed and rich and made for each other. All that thumping beneath the van and the whistling from the wind against the mirrors. Each resonance rivals for the lead, taking it one from the other and in no specific order. There is a faint squeak that, when focused upon, becomes great and overbearing. It is best left beneath the noise of the road and the tires and the wind and the engine. Everything is like a symphony, if you think about it. Birds are perfect, and crickets come out of the wet woods like a choir. *And this is another accident,* I think to myself, *that we have ears to hear, and that nature itself worked perfectly to calm the soul, and wind from a tornado has that perfect pitch of fear, that train rumble of death, and music, music, if it is an accident, may be one of the greatest miracles of them all, as beautiful as romance or color or the power of water.* All this silence is thick and buzzing and it takes some effort to break it. "Maybe later," I comment, placing the tapes back in the glove box. "Maybe quiet for now."

Paul is the kind of traveling companion who will go along with anything. He doesn't strike me as the kind of guy who has a lot of needs, the kind of guy who needs to stop and see some monument or pull over every few hours for a refill of coffee. There aren't many guys you could drop off in the middle of the forest who could make it without losing their minds, but Paul strikes me as that kind of guy. I guess what I mean is, he isn't one of the millions of us who are always looking for an escape, for distraction. He doesn't need to be talked to, but he isn't a recluse, and he doesn't need to hear music all the time, but he likes music, and he doesn't have to have something in his mouth to keep his mind off his mind, but he will be the first to praise a good meal. I guess you could say he is healthy or something. Guys like that are a bit of a mystery to me, if you want to know the truth. I feel like I am always looking for some kind of escape, you know, some way to not think about thinking, or to not face the blunt force of reality.

"So what are you going to do with your life, Paul?" I ask him, wondering out loud, I guess, what the mystery next to me is about.

The mystery leans his shoulders forward, placing both hands on the wheel. "This and that," he says.

"Sounds like a good plan," I say in a tone to request a more specific answer.

"Well, you know, get a degree, a dog, a job, a wife, a kid," he says.

Paul dated a girl back in Houston named Lynette. They seemed to hit it off. I know he didn't promise her anything when he left, but I never really got a feel for how serious they were.

"Is Lynette in your plan?"

He pauses before offering an answer.

"I'm not too sure about that. She's a sweet girl, but I don't know. There's a girl I dated back in Oregon. We went out for a couple of years. She might be the one, but I'm not sure about her either."

"What's her name?"

"Michael Ann. I met her in junior high and we dated off and on through high school. She's a good girl, you know, real, I don't know, outgoing or whatever. We've had some good times together. We used to hike down to the head of Jack Creek and fish till sunup. She's a girl you can take fishing, you know what I mean?"

That last statement tells me as much about Paul as it does about Michael Ann. I've heard it said there are two types of men in this world—one is looking for a woman to make his life complete and the other is looking for a woman to join his complete life. I don't think one is any better than the other, but Paul is definitely the latter. Paul continues with his stories of fishing, rock climbing, and hiking. Michael Ann has small roles. She fell in a stream in story two and beat him to the top of Smith Rock in story three. It becomes obvious, to me, that Michael Ann is not the one for Paul. It is one thing to have a woman join your complete life and another to have her tag along. As he winds to the end of story four, I keep him talking with a question.

"Describe the perfect woman."

Paul sighs and sits silent for a second. "In fifty words or less, right?"

"As many words as you want."

"That's a tough question. I think I'll know her when I meet her."

"But you must have a general idea. What does she look like? How does she act?"

"Okay, now we're on to something. She's got a great smile, right." He sort of gestures in the air as he says this, emphasizing the importance of her lips. "She doesn't have to look like a model, all skinny and slinky, you know, but I've got to be attracted to her. That's a given. She's going to be an athlete and like the outdoors. I plan to do a lot of camping, so she should probably look good when she hasn't showered for a month."

"A month?" I question.

"A month. You know the girl, Don, that type who never wears makeup and can jump in a creek and all that."

"Good thing we left Texas," I say.

"You can say that again. Those girls look like china dolls. You try to hug them and you are afraid you are going to break them or something." He pauses for a minute, raises his eyebrows, probably picturing some little girl turning to glass and cracking in his arms. "I also want to travel," he begins again, "so she'd have to be willing to live on the road. I'd like to hike Europe sometime, living in youth hostels, never knowing what we are going to eat the next day, that sort of thing. And when we hunt, she has to help carry the deer back to the truck." He finishes and sort of looks at me to see what I think of this girl he has described.

"Do you think that she will ever give up professional wrestling to settle down with the likes of you?" I ask.

He eases back into his chair, pauses, looks down at the console and then out onto the dark road. "Professional wrestling, huh?" he says.

His tone turns mellow. "I guess I'm looking for what any guy is looking for. I want a companion, you know. Just someone to share life with. I want her to be my biggest fan and I want to be her biggest fan too. I want us to raise kids in a home where they know their parents are in love with each other and with them. I guess that's all I want."

Realizing he had taken the question seriously, I offer a penitent comment, just above a whisper, loud enough to know he can hear me. "That sounds like a pretty good want."

"It ain't bad," he says. "It isn't too much, you know. I don't want the perfect girl, really. You figure every girl is beautiful, you know. It's our arrogance that makes us think one is better than the other."

"What do you mean?" I ask.

"I don't know. I was just thinking about girls the other day and wondering, you know, why some girls just get ignored and others get worshipped, and I really got this feeling in my chest like all of that wasn't true. Can't be true. Doesn't make sense. Like maybe if you can't love a girl who isn't all perfect, then you can't really love a girl who is. Not for real. Not unconditionally."

"That's pretty profound, Paul," I say, after a bit of silence.

"How about you, Don? What are you looking for in a woman? What gets the fire burning for you?"

"Oh, you know, this and that."

"I answered. You've got to answer," my friend says, directly.

The van chugs a good quarter mile before I speak up. "Well, she's going to have to love to sleep."

"Sleep!" The driver's eyes light up.

"Yeah, I like to sleep. That's my favorite thing to do. Do you have a problem with that?"

"No, I mean if that's your thing." He tries to speak without laughing but his voice comes distorted through a grin. "Sleep is a good thing, Don. I sleep almost every night."

"You bet you do. Sleep is entirely underrated. All these Tony Robbins wannabes talk about how the early bird catches the worm. I'd like to see them go one week without sleep and try to function."

"Preach it, brother!"

"All I'm saying is, I don't want a girl who's going to wake up in the morning and expect me to be mowing the lawn by ten o'clock."

Paul's laugh is a silent laugh—teeth-showing grin and a light gasp. "I can just see you, Don. The sun is in midsky and there you are mowing the lawn in your pajamas!"

Making sure I don't lose face with my new friend, I switch moods on him. "I'm kidding. No woman will let you sleep till ten. That's a fantasy, right?" I ask.

"Yeah," he says. "That's a fantasy."

"You know what I want in a woman, Paul?"

"What's that?"

"A friend. A true friend, someone who knows me and loves me anyway. You know, like when I'm through putting my best foot forward, she's still there, still the same. I meet these people and it's all conditional, like you were saying. They are in it for themselves. They are friends with you because you fit the image they want to portray. It's a selfish thing. Do you know what I mean? I'd like to get a girl who doesn't think like that. Don't get me wrong. She's got to be proud of her husband, I know that. I don't mind trying to make it easy on her in that way. But all in all, there's got to be some sort of soul mate thing going on. That's gonna take work, I think. There are some people in this world who love their spouse because they provide them with the life they want, and there are others who love their spouse just because they've chosen to, or because love has chosen them, or whatever. Something way back endeared one to the other and they made a decision to lock into it."

Paul gives an understanding nod. "You hit on a fear of mine," he says. "It's like I don't want a girl to get too wrapped up in me because she'll just get let down. Living with a woman is going to be tough. They tend to be really domesticated, you know. They fold things and clean things and know what they are going to have for dinner several hours before it's time to eat. Sometimes I wonder whether I'm cut out to live that way. I don't know whether a woman is going to put up with me. Is that what you're talking about?"

"Maybe. I'm not sure where you were going with that folding clothes thing. I'm just saying I want her to love me at my worst. I don't know if that's a low self-esteem thing or something else."

Paul tilts his head and motions out a slow *no*. "I don't think so. I mean, nobody's perfect. We can't be perfect."

I get quiet for a minute, just thinking about the *why* of what Paul and I are talking about. It's like I was saying, we always think of the *how* in life but not the *why*. We want to know how to get a mate, how to get sex, how to whatever, but why? Why are we designed to be in relationships? Why are women so much more beautiful than men, and why is there more than sex in life, why is there love, why is there oneness between men and women, closeness, that soul mate thing that happens? Darwin doesn't explain that crap.

"You never answered my question, Don." Paul breaks the silence.

"What's that?"

"A woman. What are you looking for in a woman?"

"Your guess is as good as mine." My mind returns slowly to our previous train of thought. "I like to read, so maybe she will too. I don't know exactly. My guess is, I can't imagine her. I mean this system, you know, this crazy system, these chemicals that jolt through our brains and make us love another human, they are a complete mystery, and we can't say what kind of girl we are going to be attracted to, the chemicals

44

decide that, and nobody has figured out the science yet. Who knows what it is? Maybe it is brown hair that makes my chemicals start, or squinty eyes or small breasts or big breasts or her voice or her smell; we just don't know. It makes no sense, you know, and yet we all live by it, and we ask these questions, and we just live within these presuppositions without ever asking where the presuppositions came from. We're just puppets, you know, because of the chemicals."

"Puppets," Paul repeats in a hush. He nods his head a bit and looks into the rearview mirror and adjusts it. "Puppets," he repeats.

"Puppets," I say as Paul comforts himself in his chair and nods his head a bit more.

"I have to tell you, though," he says. "It doesn't bother me."

"What doesn't bother you?" I ask.

"Being a puppet. Girls. Being a puppet man who is attracted to puppet girls. Doesn't bother me a bit."

I think about it for a second. "It doesn't bother me either, I suppose," I say, smiling.

"Nice puppet girl with a big puppet smile and a dress and that puppet girl smell."

"Those big puppet eyelashes," I add.

"Puppet lots of things," he says with a smirk.

Paul cracks a smile and rolls up his window. His action makes me realize that the air is thin with a dry coolness. Reaching around the seat, I grab my jacket and push my arms slowly through the sleeves. No glow now on the horizon. We have ventured one more day on our journey. Time moved quickly today. It passed like a whisper. The hills have completely buried the sun. We pass roadside houses, windows aglow with the flame of television and ten o'clock news. Paul sits quiet in reflection. With the road atlas across my lap, I follow the thin line of Interstate 35 with my flashlight. She runs straight into Oklahoma City. My thinking is that we will cut there and head west, crossing into

New Mexico, Arizona, and then north toward the canyon.

"What are you getting on the map, Don?"

"Looks like Interstate 40 from Oklahoma City. That should take us right to the canyon. Would you rather take back roads?" I ask.

"No, let's head straight there. I'm looking forward to seeing Arizona and we should be able to make it by late tomorrow. Do you want to drive through the night?"

"Wouldn't bother me," I respond.

It occurs to me we haven't stopped in a while. Save a quick visit with Ben Bonham, we've covered more than five hundred miles, and at the van's slow pace, that is quite a bit of ground. It feels again like we are leaving, like we are leaving who we were, moving into the people we will become, hopefully people with some kind of answer about the *why*, some kind of thing to believe that makes sense of beauty, makes sense of sex and romance, makes sense of gravity and oxygen. It wouldn't bother me to have something to tie the whole thing together, something that would explain the red glow against Paul's face, the red glow that seems to be coming off the console . . .

Leaning over, I see that the engine light is lit. Paul notices I am leaning over to look at the console and ignores me.

"Did you notice the engine light is lit, bud?" I say, after a moment of silence.

Paul looks down at the light. He looks out the side window. He doesn't want to answer the question.

"Paul, did you notice the engine light?"

"Yeah," he says. "It's been bugging me."

"How long has it been on?" I ask.

"Twenty miles," he says.

"Twenty miles?" I say.

"Twenty miles," he says.

"Twenty miles?" I question.

"Twenty miles. Ten times two." He lets on that he is agitated by my questioning.

"That light has been on for twenty miles?"

"Yeah, twenty miles. It'll be twenty-one by the time you stop asking me about it."

"Twenty-one miles," I respond.

"Right in there somewhere. Yeah."

"Did it ever occur to you we should pull over and check the engine?" I ask.

"It did," he says.

"It did?"

The driver breathes deeply. "Do we have to do this again?"

"Help me out here. Why aren't we checking the engine?"

"I've had it with this van, Don. It wouldn't bother me to see the thing go up in flames."

"Are you serious?"

"Yeah. This van has given me more headaches than, well, anything. I figured we'd just drive it into the ground."

"Paul, what are we going to do when the van breaks down in the middle of nowhere?"

"Don't worry. I have a plan," he says, after a slight pause.

"Fill me in, would you?" I ask.

"You won't like it."

"Try me," I say.

"Well, see those train tracks? They've been running alongside the road for a while. I figured we'd just jump a train heading west."

"You want to jump a train!"

"I said I had a plan. I didn't say it was a good one."

"You're being serious about this, aren't you?"

"I've always wanted to jump a train, Don. Imagine it. Riding the rails. Setting out across the Painted Desert, legs dangling off the edge of a boxcar."

It is my tactic in a moment like this to remain silent. The agitator sits and meditates on his crazy idea. Anyone can convince himself an idea is logical, but when that idea is spoken, when it's out in the air like Paul's is, and it rests in the ear of

47

a being more rational, the instigator is forced to reason. I don't argue his point; that would suggest there is merit to it. Not a lot of merit, but enough to justify a response. My silence speaks louder than words. It forces him to sit alone in a room with his own thoughts and know I am not willing to join him. Or at least this is what I hope. Plus, I don't know what to say. I don't guess his plan is all that bad. I'm not especially fond of the van either. I know we are going to have to pull over and fix it every hundred miles, and if we jumped a train, I could always tell girls about it in the future. And I'm not going to tell Paul, but I grew up near a train track and have always been fascinated by stories of people who jump trains. Still, it frustrates me that he didn't include me in his thinking.

"When were you going to tell me about this?"

"Soon. I promise. I didn't know how you'd feel about it."

"Isn't jumping trains a little dangerous? What if we run into some hobos?"

"Wouldn't happen. Hobos don't ride trains anymore," he says.

"They don't? Well, that's good, I guess."

The lunacy of my friend's plan is beginning to dilute. I imagine the Painted Desert passing before my eyes, the rocking of the slow-moving train and all that red and orange and purple falling off the horizon, a world of desert pushing color off the earth.

"Why don't hobos ride trains anymore?" I ask.

"It's too dangerous," my friend says.

"Why is it too dangerous?" I ask.

"They don't do it anymore because the gangs have taken over."

"Gangs?" My voice gives a hint of surprise.

"Gangs."

This is hard to picture. Bank robbers ride trains. Hobos ride trains. Cowboys ride trains. Gang members ride around in low-rider cars and shoot indiscriminately at other gang members. They don't ride trains.

"Paul, gang members don't ride trains," I tell him.

"They do. I read about it somewhere. They jump trains out of LA and all. Sounds crazy but it's true."

I don't feel like arguing with Paul. If he wants to run his van into the ground, that's his business. And so for whatever reason, I sit silently, listening for the engine to give. But she doesn't. Miles pass and she doesn't. I look over to see Paul. He's deep in thought and aglow in red light. I can tell by the look on his face that he wants the van to die. It's like a vengeance thing. This old heap has been kicking him around for months and now he's killing it. Slowly but surely, driving it into the ground. The engine light casts a demon-red glare in his eye. It's like he's possessed.

Reaching into the glove box, I slide a stick of gum out of its wrapper. "Would you care for a stick of gum, Paul?" I ask, breaking his stare into the oncoming road.

"No thanks," he says, looking over as if to remember I was sitting next to him.

"Minty fresh," I say, holding up the package.

"No thanks," he says, turning his gaze back to the road.

The possessed man drives, looking down at the engine light and then over at the tracks. He's thinking of the van's suffering and remembering all the times he pulled over to save it. Not this time. No, sir. This time it's the junkyard.

"You look pretty angry," I say to him, breaking the silence.

"I'm not angry," he says. "I'm frustrated because this warning light is shining in my eyes. I can't focus on the road."

Taking the moist gum out of my mouth, I lean over and press it tightly against the round glowing plastic of the engine light.

Paul nods and smiles for a second. "These things really are easy to fix," he says, motioning toward the gum.

"You're not kidding," I agree.

Fifty more miles pass and the cold begins to get to me. I clasp my hands together and rub them for warmth. I ask Paul if his fine automobile comes equipped with a heater. Without answering, he reaches over and pulls a lever from blue to red, turns a switch, and the van delivers a modest, cold breeze, more from the floor than the round, adjustable vents in the dash. In an attempt at efficiency, the Germans engineered these vans to be air cooled. Two wind vents stand out in the rear of the van. They catch wind and funnel it through the engine compartment. That same air (at least in the mind of the engineer) makes its way through shafts to the van's cab, having been warmed by the engine. So goes the Volkswagen heater. I would imagine if one is traveling through the desert in midday, that technology might make sense. Not tonight. The heater is being defeated by the elements.

"Doesn't work that well, does it?" Paul concedes. "Grab my fleece, would ya? It's on the bed." Stepping through the seats, I enter the cave of blankets and scattered clothes. Paul's fleece rests in a wedge between the bed and the side panel. The warmth of the blankets and the softness of the pillow are too much to reject. Tossing Paul's fleece at the back of his head, I lay my mind on a pillow and watch the road pass outside the cold window.

4 DISCOVERING GEORGE WINSTON

WHILE I WAS SLEEPING, PAUL DROVE THROUGH Oklahoma and into the Panhandle. The yellow light from a truck stop street lamp fills the van. Trucks grind gears and turn like elephants into the parking lot. The lights and the noise bring me out of sleep. I toss my nose into the window and follow with my elbow, all tangled in a net of blankets and clothes.

"Where are we?" I ask, slowly opening my eyes to the parking lot.

The van rocks as Paul drops his weight on the bed, rolls himself over, and kicks one foot against the heel of his other, a struggling attempt to remove his boot. "Back in the Lone Star State, my friend. Can't you smell the manure?"

"We're still in Texas?"

"Where the stars at night are big and bright," he says.

"I thought we were in Oklahoma."

"We were. We are in the Panhandle now. Back in Texas."

"This is a big state, man," I say, still pressed against the glass.

"You're not kidding. We've been driving for days and can't get away from it."

Another truck grinds, hisses, and spills light over our pile of clothes and blankets. Its light swings shadows through the van, moving their focus over and beyond us, out toward the truck stop pumps, store, and restaurant.

"Did the van give out?" I ask, wondering aloud why we stopped.

"She's purring like a kitten."

"Why did you wake me? I was dreaming about a great girl."

"You were cheating on me!" Paul says, leaning his head into his pillow. "I thought we had something, man."

"You're ugly as hell," I say to him. "Boys will never like you."

Paul covers himself in blankets and rests his head against the side panel. "It's because my breasts are so small, isn't it?" Paul says, lifting two points off his shirt.

"That's a start."

"So who was this girl?" Paul asks, still pulling points off his shirt.

"What girl?"

"The girl you were dreaming about. She have a name?"

"You'll laugh," I tell him.

"I won't. I promise."

Sitting up and throwing my blankets off, I begin, "She was a cowgirl." Paul covers his face with a pillow.

"You said you wouldn't laugh," I say.

"A cowgirl," he says into the pillow.

"Her name was Cheyenne. Call her by her name."

Paul slips the pillow down his face and looks me full in the eye. "That's a beautiful name, Don. You think your dream was influenced by the smell of the pasture across the highway?" His heckle is delivered with a straight face but changes to a grin as he anticipates my response.

"It is a beautiful name for a beautiful girl. You'll never get one like that."

Paul keeps laughing. I look out the window and talk under my breath . . . sarcastically, as though in a daze . . .

"She needed me. We were running from the bad guys who killed her father on a ranch outside Little Rock."

Paul slides himself down on the mattress and tucks the pillow under his head. "A ranch outside Little Rock," he repeats. "You ever actually ridden a horse, Don?"

"Scared of them," I say matter-of-factly.

"I see," he says.

I grab my pillow and swing it directly at my friend's face, still looking out the window. "I rode like the wind, I tell you," I say in my best Charlton Heston voice. He lies motionless. Lying back down, I continue my story: "There were three of them. Chasing us on horses. All of them had guns. We had ducked behind a rock and I was telling her how much I could bench-press so she would feel safe. I was telling her she would be okay. They were coming with guns and she was worried."

"She must have been comforted when you told her you could bench almost sixty pounds."

Despite my friend's harassment, I want my dream again, and am disturbed by its ending. I resolve I will not finish rescuing Cheyenne tonight, so I leave Paul in the van to walk across the parking lot toward the truck stop. Gray pebbles and patches of oil, dripped from long-removed trucks, pattern the lot. A wind, sliding off some distant Canadian glacier, presses against the parking lot with frigid hands. It builds strength in treeless pastures and pelts the dimly lit station and store. Texas hasn't seen a colder night since Ann Richards was elected governor. Tom and Huck never had it so bad as we do tonight.

I rattle some change in my pocket, counting with my fingers. About seventy-five cents or so. One cup of coffee.

Money is an issue on this trip. I have $300, sock-wound in my backpack, and most of it will convert to gas. My half of the fuel bill will reach $200 in 3,000 miles. That leaves little to spare. More money will come when my truck sells back home. After retiring the car loan, I will have another $1,000. The strategy is to not deplete the $300 until the truck is sold. It's a gamble. Coffee is worth it, though. I am sure I will be driving through the night. Besides, if I don't drink something warm, my insides will freeze.

"Where's your coffee?"

The store clerk motions with her eyes toward the wall that

is closest to me. Two glass pots sit on brown burners. One is labeled decaf and I reach for the other. "How much is a cup?"

"Fifty cents," she shouts across the aisles. I pour the black liquid (it looks like it's been sitting for hours) into a Styrofoam cup and search for the lids. Rounding the aisle toward the counter, I meet face-to-face with the clerk, a young brown-haired girl in a Bon Jovi T-shirt. She is keeping company with a man standing no less than three inches taller than me, greasy, and leaning in on the counter. He's dirty with black on his fingers that wrap around the brown cup he brought with him. *Truck drivers own their own cups,* I think to myself. The look on her face and the shy grin on his tell me he's hitting on her. Brunette, fit, half-pretty, she's used to it. Truck drivers probably come in at all hours for a shave and a shower and haven't seen a woman in a thousand miles.

"This man isn't giving you a bad time, is he?" I say, sort of under my breath as I count the change in my hand. I only meant it as a joke, but the girl looks back at me a little shy. Rural people don't get urban humor; they really don't. You just stay out of folks' business out here, unless you know them. She looks at my size and at his and back at me as if I were crazy and then silently punches in the code for a cup of coffee. "I didn't bring my own cup. You'll have to charge me for the cup," I say to her, motioning toward the truck driver's cup. "Where did you get your cup?" I ask the man. He stands silent, just looks away and then back at the girl. All my jokes are falling limp.

"Cups are free," she says slowly, watching for the reaction of the driver. He perceives her look as an inquiry into what he thinks of me, and he responds with a threat.

He leans in at the side of my face. "You got a problem with me, hippie boy?"

There is a thick silence now. A portable heater sits behind the counter at the girl's feet. It rattles as it turns, glowing with strands of heated steel. "No problem. I got no problem," I say, setting two quarters and some tax on the counter.

54

"You what?" His breath reeks. He is so close, I imagine him biting my ear. "Why don't you get in that van of yours and head back to Austin?" he continues.

"I'm not from Austin," I say, watching the girl slowly pick up the change.

"I don't care where you're from, boy, so long as you go back."

I look over at him with a half smile. "Look, Buck"—his name is embroidered on his shirt—"I was just making a joke. It was supposed to be funny. I didn't mean to interrupt you. I am sure you were wooing this girl here, and I didn't mean to interrupt." The man pulls his head back, glances confused at the girl, looks back at me, quiets his tone, and reveals his ignorance. "How did you know my name?" The girl smiles as she notices the tag across his heart.

"We hippies know everything, Buck." I step back a foot or so to make some space. I take a sip of coffee and look over at the girl, kind of including her in the conversation. I speak softly. "Let's see . . . I learned to tell people's names from a guru named Monty, an Indian fellow who knows about what people are called from their smell. You were either a Buck or a Francis. I went with Buck to give you the benefit of the doubt." I nod my head as though I am revealing interesting facts.

"Don't you make funny with me. I don't know you. How did you know my name?" he questions again.

"I know a lot about you, Buck," I tell him, looking him straight in the eye.

I ask the girl if she has enough of my money for the coffee and she says yes. I start walking toward the door. Buck gathers his meager senses and realizes how I knew his name. His hand slaps the name on his shirt and he starts after me. Out the door and into the cold wind, every nerve longs to check shadows over my shoulder. I hear the door close, but walk quickly and wouldn't hear it reopen if it did (due to distance and sound of wind). I am looking for Paul in the van, wondering if he can see Buck walking behind me. I don't want to turn around and see a fist and I am hoping Paul will show his face and warn me with a look of shock. I can hear Buck's footsteps now, coming from behind, running, but I don't turn. I hear them again, then again, and realize I am just imagining these sounds. I walk toward the van and don't turn around. My mind pictures him coming up quick and throwing his fist against the back of my head. I feel my heart speed up and adrenaline pumps through my arms. Still, I keep pace and don't turn. The van sits miles across the parking lot. It seems like it was half as close when I walked in. It feels like the thing is getting farther away, for heaven's sake.

I turn at the far side of the van. The corner of my eye finds no presence, and through the driver's and passenger's windows (standing outside the van looking through), I see Buck watching through the glass door. I give Buck two fingers in a peace sign and a nod. He stands motionless, his dark eyes staring me down.

The van starts at first command and I let it idle as I watch the man leave the door and resume his position against the counter. He is mumbling his pick-up lines through an embarrassed grin and coffee-lacquered teeth. Minutes pass as I allow the van to idle and once again I notice the wind, pushing up against the van, gently rocking the thing, rocking Paul in his bed, setting a temperature against the glass so cold you can almost see it.

With Huck Finn asleep in the back, and with one last look about the place and a sip from the coffee that is warm enough to stage a dance of steam, I release the boat into the river of distant taillights and eighteen-wheeled shadows. All shadows set against the dark, dark sky with stars that wander at will.

I reach with my free hand for the tape in the glove box, then turn the knob on the radio. It bleeds light across its face and I slip the tape through the opening. George Winston begins his private concert. The music seems to match the night, more or less soothing, like the whole thing, the evening and the music, was made to rest in the background, to color the walls behind thoughts and van rattle.

At a distance to the left, across the oncoming lane and across a field, sit lights on barn roofs or a grain tower or processing plant. The cluster of lights rests out on the horizon like a constellation, too small to be a town; maybe it's another truck stop with a farm or grain tower next to it. *If there is one thing we have in this country, it's land,* I think to myself. *Nothing but blank and empty land.* You get to feeling everything is concrete when you live in Houston, but it isn't. Houston is just a speck of rock in the middle of endless fields of nothingness. Cities rise up on the oceans, but in the middle you've got dirt, crops, ranches, and government yards that stretch on for hundreds of miles. One red light blinks atop a building in the constellation and the other lights are white and yellow, resting on the ground like smoldering ashes. Slow to my notice come other constellations, way out on the horizon to the right, up on some slow slope of hill. George Winston serenades me through a weak speaker on the driver's side and a strong speaker in the door panel of the opposite seat. And so go miles and miles. The tape flips sides automatically so it keeps music going in an endless loop. No lights now on the road ahead, save the soft yellow faded lamplight of the Volkswagen against the asphalt.

"It ain't that bad being a puppet," I say under my breath, checking over my shoulder to make sure Paul is still sleeping.

"It ain't bad seeing beauty, or having some chemical in my head trick me into thinking something is nice, some night is a good night, a cold night, or whatever. Some girl is beautiful. That ain't bad. Nice to meet you, my name is Don. What's your name? Nice to meet you, Cheyenne.

"You know, Cheyenne, you get out on an open road like this in the middle of the night and you want some kind of explanation for everything. It wouldn't bother me if aliens left us here, so long as they were good aliens who wanted to love their pets. I wouldn't want my brain sucked out to be used as a battery, like they do in the movies. But if they were loving aliens, that would be okay. Do you believe in aliens, Cheyenne, or do you believe in God? I believe in God. I think He is looking down, or up, from somewhere outside all that black out there.

"What do you think, Paul? You think we came from aliens?" I look over my shoulder again to see Paul, still lying motionless.

5 THE GAZE OF RA

ANCIENT GREEK TRADITION HAS PROMETHEUS STEAL-
ing fire from heaven, fire used to light the path toward civiliza-
tion. You can see the sun this way, if you wish, as Prometheus
riding his horse into space and time, a lantern in his hand, held
out toward the planets, a bit of it split into the belly of a furnace, forging steel, the steel splintering off to spark and die
away on a blacksmith shop floor, little smidgens of fading
heaven, little cosmic mysteries, plucked from the sparkling hair
of God. In Egypt the sun was the eye of a god: the sun god Ra,
in the evening, closed his eyes and opened them again in the
morning, thus the light by which we work and see and have our
being is the gaze of a god. I like the Hindu tradition that has
Shiva and his lover, Parvati, engaged in foreplay, Parvati coming from behind Shiva and covering his eyes, stopping the light
from shining down off the Himalayas. Imagine young Indian
children being beckoned to sleep by the erotic ritual of divin-
ity. The gods are randy, night after night, the teenagers must
have giggled. It is enough to make a Hindu blush.

In the Hebrew tradition, which splintered off into the
Christian tradition, which is how I was raised, light is a
metaphor. God makes a cosmos out of the nothingness, a
molecular composition, of which He is not and never has
been, as any*thing* is limiting, and God has no limits. In this
way, He *isn't*, and yet *is*. The poetic imagery is rather beautiful, stating that all we see and feel and touch, the hardness of
dense atoms, the softness of a breeze (atoms perhaps loose as

if in play) is the breath of God. And into this being, into this existence, God first creates light. This light is not to be confused with the sun and moon and stars, as they are not created until later. He simply creates light, a nonsubstance that is *like* a particle and *like* a wave, but perhaps neither, just some kind of traveling energy. A kind of magnetic wave. Light, then, becomes a fitting metaphor for a nonbeing who is. God, if like light, travels at the speed of light, and because space and time are mingled with speed, the speed of light is the magic, exact number that allows a kind of escape from time. Scientists have played with atomic clocks, matched exactly, setting one in a plane to fly around the world, and another motionless, waiting for the return of its partner. When they reunite, the one that traveled rests milliseconds behind the one fixed. The faster you move, physicists have found, the less you experience time. And if you move at the speed of light, you will never age; you are outside of time; you are an eternal creature. But before you strap on your running shoes, you should know scientists warn us that with speed, matter increases in density, so an attempt at the speed of light will have you imploded by the time you hit Wichita, your atoms as dense as bowling balls. And to make matters worse, your density increases on a curve; the faster you go, the greater the density, and though you can get close to the speed of light, matter and that magic speed can never meet; the faster you go, the steeper the trajectory on the graph. You and I, made from molecules, cannot travel at the speed of light and cannot escape time, at least not with a body. Consider the complexity of light in light of the Hebrew metaphor: we don't see light; we see what it touches. It is more or less invisible, made from nothing, just purposed and focused energy, infinite in its power (it will never tire if fired into a vacuum, going on forever). How fitting, then, for God to create an existence, then a metaphor, as if to say, here is something entirely unlike you, outside of time, infinite in its power and thrust: here is something you can experience but cannot understand. Throughout the remainder of the Bible, then, God calls Himself light. The perfection of the Hebrew metaphor is eerie, especially considering Eratosthenes wouldn't play with sticks and shadows for several thousand years, discovering Ra was, in fact, never closing his eyes.

WITH THE VAN BEHIND ME A HUNDRED YARDS, I STOP to take in the horizon. The air comes into my lungs cold while rich blue neon outlines the distant mountains, each ridge black and jagged. *This is going to be a good one*, I think to myself. My breath makes no mist, though the temperature is certainly cold. Perhaps it's too dry for that. Looking back, the white van sits gray on the side of the empty highway. No cars for miles. No trucks and no noise. I can only hear a faint flow of wind slide down from the hills, rolling like water from high pressure toward some swirling low. The interstate slices through a field of sand before climbing into a distant pass behind me, and this desert floor, still dark with night shadows, lies flat for miles before giving rise to those sleeping peaks in the east. And the sand has the ghostly stare of a blank canvas, as if to hope something beautiful will be painted on its surface, as if to want for flesh.

I press into the desert, aiming for a spot to watch the sun break. Every ten steps I check the east and it changes as I walk. Black gives to blue and it is a blue like no blue on any painting or picture. This is living blue, changing from one hue to another, shifting slowly the way color only does at morning.

Spilled on the brown, then, are dry and shadowy lakes of deep, rich darkness; the absence of light. My tracks are laid out, marking my path, and as I look back, I see the van is now a small form beside a black threadlike strip. To the east, the first tint of red arrives in weak shades through overpowering blue. There are clouds now, and as the light comes in slow, the great vapors establish form; tall clouds with thirty-thousand-foot lifts. And though tremendous in size, they are guarded by the length and depth of a black-blue sky, held back by mountains.

Morning lifts with her finger first, stretching her long bones into the clouds. Engaged, I set myself down on the cold morning sand, my hands beside me and half buried in the frozen dirt. I pull them out, dust my hands against each other, and slide them into my jacket pockets. The black hills ghost to gray, revealing crags and cliffs lifting up toward their summits.

Suddenly I hear my name called. Standing and wiping my hands against my pants, I see Paul at the front of the van, looking in my direction as if to wonder whether I am a man or a rock. I wave my arms and he starts across the road and disappears into a ditch. After a few minutes, the noise of Paul quietly precedes him, the soft steps of his feet against the sand. He is coming slowly, keeping an eye on the horizon. His arms are folded tightly and his shoulders are lifted to warm his neck. Unfolding his arms he wipes his eyes, lets go a yawn, and turns his head toward sunrise. He lessens his stride as he nears, takes a place ten feet from my side, and, together, we watch Prometheus gain on the mountains.

6 TROUBLE

THE VAN IS A RATTLETRAP. IT ECHOES THROUGH THE desert with odd ticking and muffler thump. The asphalt is long and straight, not too hot, but retains, always, the knowledge of summer: a general sense of respect and even fear of high temperatures. Each passing range opens to the same view as the valley that prefaced, each mile looking precisely like the last. The terrain is nearly Martian, I say to Paul, who agrees with a nod. We had stood for a half hour in the desert, letting the sun have its time. And I wondered at the metaphor as it spilled beauty against the brown. As the sun went higher, the color faded and the earth gave way to nothingness, as though the color were a trick, as if the sun were teaching us there is no such thing as beauty, only what it chooses to shine a certain light upon that stimulates a certain chemical in our brains, as though the two were old lovers, teasing each other, reliving some forgotten memory.

But if they were teasing each other, they have certainly stopped. What we have here in all this dead dirt is the stuff of life without life's spark. All of us are made from this stuff, this dirt. Everything in life is just this magical soil, fairy dust, if you will. Plant a seed in the soil and that seed will find the magic around it to make some sprig of wood that, with time from the fairy dust around it, will make a tree, and with the aid of water and more dirt and a hundred years, a tree the height of a skyscraper and the width of a house. All of it from dirt. Grass grows the same way, carrots, potatoes, onions, apples on trees, barley for beer. Rocks are dirt fired in the furnace of the earth's belly, steel is processed rocks, diamonds are rocks forged in the compression of earth's weight, and people, you and I, are dirt lit with, depending on what you believe, the magic seed of the aliens, or the accidental nothingness of Darwin's dreams, or the warm breath of God, the spark of life, giving an embryo a heartbeat, the magical glint that brings the dirt alive, sets in its DNA a coded direction and a mysterious motion that becomes greater than a tree in complexity, able to question its own being, able to guess at its creation, able to love and to hate, to live inspired, then to die, to return to dirt, to the vast abyss of nothing that is a desert in midday, a sea of brown, only beautiful when the sun tricks the eye, only beautiful in the playful metaphor of light.

In all our technology, we have lost touch with the earth, our heaters and air conditioners robbing us of the drama of seasons, our cars keeping our feet from pacing the land, our concrete and our shoes and our carpet delivering us from the feel of unprocessed earth. *We live on top of the created world,* I think to myself, *not in it.* And this van, this great wheelchair with a radio and a bed, we sit in it and roll at unthinkable speeds across a desert that would have cost our forefathers a season. The earth cinched tight at the invention of the wheel. *It's like a time machine,* I think to myself. *It moves us through an age of work in a short week.* But as we are passed by yet another car, twenty years more modern, I remember the primitive nature of our transportation. Everything is referable, I suppose. The van chugs and has the old, arthritic feel that wants and perhaps deserves sympathy. To have been formed by caring Germans, all around green and mountain, and now, after so many years of service, not to retire, but sold to rough brutes who travel dry deserts like cowboys. How the thing must loathe its masters.

"I figure we've got another three hours before we get to Albuquerque, and then several more before Flagstaff." Paul's voice comes half coherent through the slapping of wind. The air swirls through the van and has the gritty feel of beach sand. Metal on passing cars shines in bright, bleached-out glimmers.

"You getting sick of the desert?" I ask.

"I don't mind it that much," Paul counters, talking loud over the road noise. He steadies the wheel with his knee, pulls his shirt over his head, and throws it over his shoulder. "We've got pretty good desert back in Oregon. It's not quite this dry, but it's similar."

"I thought it rained all the time in Oregon," I say.

"It rains on the other side of the Cascade Range but not in central Oregon. Portland and Eugene get all the rain. During the winter, the Willamette Valley is like a rain forest, but go a hundred miles east, over the Cascade Range, and it's all desert." Paul's expressions brighten as he talks of his home.

"I never knew that. I pictured tundra during winter and rain all through summer."

"You're gonna love summers in Oregon," he says. "They are perfect. Eighty or ninety degrees, dry, blue skies and clear streams. It's like living in a Mountain Dew commercial . . . Hey, did I ever tell you that a friend of mine was in one of those?"

"A Mountain Dew commercial?" I question.

"Yeah. My friend Henry. Have you seen the one where there's a bunch of people on a dock and they swing on a rope over the water?"

"Yeah, I think I've seen it."

"Henry is in that commercial. They filmed it up at Blue Lake, right near Black Butte."

"How did he get in one of those?" I ask.

"They just brought a film crew into Sisters, pulled off the side of the road, and started looking for people for the commercial. Henry was at the Thriftway and they stopped him coming out the door. He said he had a candy bar in his hand, and when he finally understood what they were asking, he squeezed the candy bar till chocolate busted the wrapper. He shook the guy's hand and got chocolate on it. They gave him two hundred bucks to come swing on the rope. He said it took them all day and then they had dinner and hung out with the film crew. One of the guys on the crew had met Robin Williams on the set of *Good Morning, Vietnam*."

"That is sweet," I say. "Two hundred bucks to swing on a rope and get on television." I ease back and rest my arm out the window. "I'm pretty sure that is what God is wanting me to do with my life. I'm pretty sure He wants me to be a rock star or an actor."

"Is that right?" Paul says.

"Yes, it is," I say, even before he finishes his comment. "A rock star or an actor. Me and this Henry are going to have to get together when I get to Oregon. I figure a Mountain Dew ad will be a pretty good place to start." I've got a sly grin on my face and am pulling in about twenty pounds off my gut, tensing my muscles and snorting like Barney Fife.

"I could just see that, Don. You would make a great Mountain Dew guy. They could pan the camera across the girls on the beach and slowly swing over to focus right on your hairy back, just when you turn around to address the camera, your belly preceding, falling over your belt."

"Exactly. You're seeing it now. People dig normal guys," I say.

"Is that right?"

"Yes, it is," I say. "Hairy backs are the next thing. Chicks know a man when they see one."

"You're making me a little queasy, Don."

"Don't get jealous on me, Paul. This is going to be a long trip and I don't need that kind of conflict."

"I hear you. I'll try to stay cool. It's just tough, what with your hairy back and all. Knowing you are going to be a shirtless rock star or Mountain Dew guy and I will probably end up a nobody." Paul makes a pouty lip.

"Don't let yourself think like that. I'll never forget the little people. The little people are the ones that make it happen. When I get my first movie award, you know, the little gold trophy thing, I will stand at the podium and say, 'I want to thank the little people, even very little people like my old friend Paul.'"

"You would do that for me? Stand up there and mention me by name?"

"Sure I would. You'd do the same for me."

Paul sits in quiet for a while, a sly grin on his face.

"Actually, Don, I probably wouldn't," he says. "I probably wouldn't mention you by name if I got the award."

"You wouldn't."

"I don't think so, man," Paul says. "I mean, you've got to thank the producer and the director and other actors and Regis and Kelly and family and all that. I would probably just say, 'I'd also like to thank the little people,' and leave it at that. Just a blanket statement that would cover everyone. That way nobody gets offended."

My mouth is open a bit, an expression as if to scratch my head. Turning to look at Paul, I offer agreement. "I see what you're saying. If you thank one guy, you've got to thank them all, and if you leave someone out, you'd hurt feelings. I guess I'd do the same thing as you in that case."

"What do you mean?" Paul says.

"I'd just thank the necessary people and not list any of the little people."

"You can't take it back," he says.

"I'm telling you, I wouldn't thank you."

The van slips a funny nudge forward and then suddenly slows. Paul hits the pedal and . . . nothing. We are coasting. In the middle of nowhere, we are coasting slower and the van is obviously going to roll to a stop. The pedal squeaks as Paul presses it to the floor. Though the engine is running, there is no register in the RPMs.

"You upset the van, Don. You were being selfish and upset the van. Now look at what you did."

"I had nothing to do with it," I say with a laugh. "You didn't move the gum, did you?"

"Didn't touch it." The wad of gum is still stuck firmly against the plastic light. Paul steers the van onto the shoulder. Rolling to a stop, he kills the engine and it ticks with heat. Several cars buzz by and rock the van with a gust. The desert is silent. There are a few cacti and scattered smatterings of rocks and red boulders, but no gas stations, no stores, just miles and miles of Mars.

"I've got an idea," I say, very calmly, melancholy. "Let's jump a train. You could be Big Pauly Paul and I'll be Smack Daddy Pop. We'll meet up with some Crips and Bloods."

"That's real funny, Don. It's the linkage. That's all it is," he says.

I keep talking: "Maybe if we hike across the desert we'll find a train. I want to ride in the caboose."

"It's the linkage, Don. No big deal. Lay off it."

Paul leans in and checks his side mirror for an oncoming car. He opens the door and rounds the front of the van, walking toward the back of the van, past my door but not meeting my eye. I open the door and follow. His look is somewhat frustrated as he jerks open the engine compartment.

"We just need to tighten it up a little." My words come as something of a condolence.

"Yeah, it looks like that's the problem."

I nod my head. He leans down on one knee and has his hand in the engine compartment. He pulls it out abruptly, shakes his fist, and blows on it.

"Needs to cool down," I say.

"I can get it." He puts his hand back in. I lean down with him. The linkage has loosened considerably. Both carbs are closed tight.

"I can fix this one. Ben left enough cable to rig it. But the other is worn pretty good." Paul points to the other linkage and he is right. The original cable is fastened at exact length, and the attachment is loose. We are going to have to rig it like the last one. New wire and all.

"Should we just clip the old one off?" I ask.

"Probably," he says.

"We'll need more wire," I say.

"Look around for a piece of cable, would you?" he asks.

I stand up to look down the long highway. It goes back several miles before it disappears.

"I'll dig around in the van," I tell him.

THE VAN'S GOT A BROKEN FEEL TO IT. IT'S AS IF IT wants us to appreciate it when it runs, so it stalls on purpose, forcing us to stop and think about the bad treatment we've given it, and to stop comparing it to more modern machines. I mostly ignore the vibes as I look for some wire. I've got the big door open to let some air swim around.

There's no wire in this van, I say to myself. The glove box has all the same stuff as before, and no wire. I search the floor, and under the seats, and under the sink, and around all the boxes of groceries (which are beans and rice mostly, with about seven or eight little bottles of Tabasco sauce).

"I'm gonna walk the shoulder a bit. See if I come up with something," I say.

"Yeah. We are definitely going to need a piece of wire for this other one," Paul shouts from behind the van.

The shoulder is clean. Hot and glistening. Vapors swirl in the distance. The shrubs look anchored, as though you could pull on them all day and they'd never give. They are few and scattered, dotting the cracked sand for miles. *There's not going to be any wire out here,* I think to myself. I break a piece of sagebrush in my fingers. It's got that pine tree smell. Smells good and clean, like bottled-up Colorado. A semi rolls in from the distance, comes in like wind, and blows its horn as it passes. We're parked tight on the shoulder. The gust blows past. Stirs up dirt. Another semi and then a car, and I see, out a bit, a little something glimmering that doesn't look like glass or road. Walking up to it, it's just a strip of plastic and I toss it off the shoulder.

PAUL'S HANDS ARE TIGHT AROUND THE LINKAGE connector. He's got one hand pushing it in close to the carburetor and the other working the linkage tight, threading it and wrapping it. He's done it twice now and pulled it out a third time to start over. He looks at the other carb and sees it loose, and sort of blows a little sigh and shakes his head. He lowers his head, presses with one hand, and begins to thread with the other. Hearing a semi come up, he tilts his head into his arm and closes his eyes. The truck bellows past and spits some stinging sand across his back and all around the engine and his arms. He shakes it off and goes back to his work.

LOOKING BACK, I SEE THE VAN AND REALIZE IT IS closer to the road than I thought it was. Paul is invisible behind it. A car comes up and slows a little, making his way half into the other lane and then quickens to pass the van at full speed. The shoulder is uncommonly clean, as though fate had swept it, knowing we were coming to a stop right here. Three days ago there was probably a lot of trash along this road. There was probably a good piece of wire too. Some street sweeper, or more likely a collection of prisoners with yellow jackets and garbage bags, cleaned the place up. Just our luck.

I say a little prayer, asking God for some help.

Trouble leads to question and question leads to prayer. It's funny how I usually don't care about faith until life falls apart, until I find myself in the middle of some kind of jam. So I pray a little and not too much later I get an idea, a fix for our trouble. The idea puts a jolt in my step and I head back toward the van.

"You fond of that stereo?" I ask.

"What's that?" Paul says.

"How much do you care about that stereo in there? Can you live without one of the speakers for a while?"

"Good thinking, Don."

I get to work ripping the paneling off the passenger door and disconnect the speaker from its wire. Removing the stereo from its hole, I'm able to pull the wire all the way through and I've got a good four feet wrapped around my hand when I round the van. Paul has the first linkage fixed pretty tight and together we manipulate the other. I cut the wire and he connects it and begins to thread an end through the linkage connector. "You ought to stretch it out first," I suggest.

"Yeah." He undoes a little of his work and pulls the wire to stretch it. I hold the connector firm and he threads it through again.

"Work the pedal, would you?" he says.

Working the pedal shows Paul's fix is good. He has me hold it and rock the gas so he can test the strength. He wants it to hold for the rest of the trip. "Looks good," he mumbles.

"What's that, Paul?"

"Start it up!" he shouts.

The van starts. The gas that was in the carb quickly fires. New fuel funnels through. It moans, backfires, and drinks the fuel like lemonade. Pressing down the pedal revs the engine louder. I get the thing screaming and hold it. Paul closes the engine compartment and comes around to the driver's window. He's standing out in the road and giving me a look about revving the engine.

"Sounds like it works," he says with the same look.

"What's that you say?" I've got the engine so loud I pretend not to hear.

"Sound's pretty good. Maybe you should lay off the gas," he shouts with a smile.

"Give it gas?" I say and press down the pedal.

He thumps me on the side of my face. "No," he says. "It works. No more gas."

I let off the gas and lean back in the seat. He goes to open the door but I lock it. He reaches through the door and unlocks it and goes to open it and I lock it again.

"Need a ride?" I ask.

"That might be good." Paul smiles, grabbing quickly at the lock so he can open the door.

"You drive," I say, shifting over to the passenger's seat.

"That's right. You haven't slept, have you?" Paul climbs in and places the toolbox between the seats.

"No. I haven't slept. I'm fading too." The stereo is up on the dash so I stuff it back into the hole, poking the wires behind it. "That other speaker should still work," I say.

"Maybe time for a little Skynyrd." Paul's got a grin and he's reaching over to the glove box. I quickly raise my feet so they're firmly against the dash, blocking his attempt.

"I see how it is." Paul grins and nods as he forces the gearshift into first and releases the clutch. He checks the rearview mirror and pulls us onto the highway. "I see how it is," he says again.

7 FLAGSTAFF

WHEN WE NEAR THE CITY IN THE EVENING, FALLING stars dive and duck behind tall buildings. Flagstaff rests on the side of a mountain and so it is serene. You can see the dark peak rise like a thunderhead. We are on a black stretch of road that enters Flagstaff from the east. Signs mark the giant meteor crater just thirty miles out. You can pay a fee, during the day, and stand on its rim, or go inside the museum and watch films about space and that sort of thing. Paul and I pass the signs without so much as a word. We are heading toward a bigger hole in the ground than this. Streetlights on the outskirts of town stand guard like old Roman soldiers. Fire engines are chasing smoke signals from someone's tragedy. This city is cut from a different cloth than other cities: people living in community, not so much on top of the earth but in it, close to its mountains and to the great canyon, some seventy miles beyond. These are desert people who have come to live in the thick of trees collected on this mountainside. The whole thing reminds me of a tiny island in the ocean, and I begin to think of the van as a boat, puttering toward shore. Many cities, these days, seem to have people living on the surface of life but hardly in its soil, diluting the deeper questions of life in television monologues and reality shows, amusing ourselves to death, as Neil Postman would say. But this city feels different. It feels like these people have come up with different answers to the *why* questions, and they created a little commune that became a city, and they share their answers only with each other, answers about desert ghosts, about the sun being a god, about messages encoded in stars.

But then I come to Flagstaff with presuppositions. Without having been here, I can say with confidence that half these people believe in UFOs. One in one hundred has been sucked into a spinning-sphere ship and carries vague memories of little green men taking skin samples from his buttocks. They have scars to prove it and will show you if they've had enough beer and the bar is nearly empty. There is also a growing college crowd who've bought into the idea of simplicity. They drive fashionable Jeeps, wear the same khaki pants every day, and have dogs named Sigmund or Maslow. In each of their apartments you will find, somewhere, a painting by Georgia O'Keeffe. They curse cement and consider New York and Chicago thorns in the side of Mother Nature's flesh. They are tan, good-natured, and don't wash their hair.

I don't know that this town would accept me. You don't dust Houston off your boots in three days. Paul, however, would fit just fine. As far as I know, he has never been abducted by aliens, but they would forgive that. He is courteous and would stare for hours at their Georgia O'Keeffe paintings, nodding as they pontificate about her use of color and form. I, on the other hand, would simply say she uses too much brown and makes me thirsty.

Paul is better than me in this way. He can appreciate the person inside the persona. To him, people are more important than ideas. He does not laugh at jokes that deprecate others. His is a true, empathetic, kind character. We've similar histories, Paul and I. Both of us grew up in broken homes; both encountered faith at an early age; both share enthusiasm for taking chances. Still, he is advanced further in altruism, which I have always considered to be a kind of emotional genius. What I mean is that most of us are always worried about what others are thinking, the concern finds its way into our words and actions and dreams and feelings, and Paul seems to be above it, or below it, I don't know, just disaffected. He doesn't worry about much of anything, which strikes me as a kind of miracle. How does a person stop caring about the opinion of others enough to enjoy them without manipulating them? How does a person stop caring about money to pay rent, about where his food will come from, or whether or not he has a good retirement package? When with Paul, one is confronted with the notion that life may be much easier than the rest of us believe it is, that most of the things we worry about are not worth worrying about, that a low bank account or unfashionable clothes won't give you cancer. And this is precisely how it sometimes feels to me, that a low bank account or low social status will give me cancer.

I tend to think life is about security, that when you have a full year's rent, you can rest. I worry about things too much, I worry about whether or not my ideas are right, I worry about whether or not people like me, I worry about whether or not I am going to get married, and then I worry about whether or not my girl will leave me if I do get married. Lately I found myself worrying about whether or not my car was fashionable, whether I sounded like an idiot when I spoke in public, whether or not my hair was going to fall out, and all of it, perhaps, because I bought into Houston, one thousand square miles of concrete and strip malls and megachurches and cineplexes, none of it real. I mean it is there, it is made of matter, but it is all hype. None of the messages are true or have anything to do with the fact we are spinning around on a planet in a galaxy set somewhere in a cosmos that doesn't have any edges to it. There doesn't seem to be any science saying any of this *stuff* matters at all. But it feels like *it* matters, whatever *it* is; it feels like we are supposed to be panicking about things. I remember driving down I-45 a few months ago and suddenly realizing the number of signs that were screaming at me, signs wanting me to buy waterbeds, signs wanting me to watch girls take off their clothes, signs wanting me to eat

Mexican food, to eat barbeque, backlit, scrolling signs wanting me to come to church, to join this gym, to see this movie, to finance a car, even if I have no money. And it hit me that, amid the screaming noise, amid the messages that said buy this product and I will be made complete, I could hardly know the life that life was meant to be. Houston makes you feel that life is about the panic and the resolution of the panic, and nothing more. Nobody stops to question whether they actually need the house and the car and the better job. And because of this there doesn't seem to be any peace; there isn't any serenity. We can't see the stars in Houston anymore, we can't go to the beach without stepping on a Coke bottle, we can't hike in the woods, because there aren't any more woods. We can only panic about the clothes we wear, panic about the car we drive, sit stuck in traffic and panic about whether or not the guy who cut us off respects us. We want to kill him, for crying out loud, and all the while we feel a need for new furniture and a new television and a bigger house in the right neighborhood. We drive around in a trance, salivating for Starbucks while that great heaven sits above us, and that beautiful sunrise is happening in the desert, and all those mountains out West are collecting snow on the limbs of their pines, and all those leaves are changing colors out East. God, it is so beautiful, it is so quiet, it is so perfect. It makes you feel, perhaps for a second, that Paul gets it and we don't—that if you live in a van and get up for sunrise and cook your own food on a fire and stop caring about whether your car breaks down or whether you have fashionable clothes or whether or not people do or do not like you, that you have broken through, that you have shut your ear to the bombardment of lies that never, ever stop whispering in your ear. And maybe this is why he seems so different to me, because he has become a human who no longer believes the commercials are true, which, perhaps, is what a human was designed to be.

It makes sense, if you think about it. I mean we stood out in the desert this morning, and the chemicals in my brain poured soothingly through the gray matter, as if to massage with fingers the most tender part of my mind, as if to say, this is what a human is supposed to feel. This is what we were made for, to watch the beauty of light fill up earth's canvas, to make dirt come alive; like fairy dust, making trees and cacti and humans from the magic of its propulsion. It makes me wonder, now, how easily the brain can be tricked out of what it was supposed to feel, how easily the brain can be tricked by somebody who has a used car to sell, a new perfume, whatever. *You will feel what you were made to feel if you buy this thing I am selling.* But could the thing you and I were supposed to feel, the thing you and I were supposed to be, cost nothing? Paul seems to think so, or at least he acts as if this is true. He doesn't want to stay in a hotel room and catch up on the news. He doesn't want to rifle through the sports page and make sure the team he has associated his ego with is doing well. I don't think he is trying to win anything at all. I just think he is trying to feel what a human is supposed to feel when he stops believing lies. And maybe when a person doesn't buy the lies anymore, when a human stops long enough to realize the stuff people say to get us to part with our money often isn't true, we can finally see the sunrise, smell the wetness in a Gulf breeze, stand in awe at a downpour no less magnificent than a twenty-thousand-foot waterfall, ten square miles wide, wonder at the physics of a duck paddling itself across the surface of a pond, enjoy the reflection of the sun on the face of the moon, and know, *This is what I was made to do. This is who I was made to be,* that life is being given to me as a gift, that light is a metaphor, and God is doing these things to dazzle us.

THE MAIN ROADS IN FLAGSTAFF BREAK OFF INTO tributaries that climb the hillside; streets are lined with two-story brick offices, pubs, and retail shops. It is not as busy as I thought it might be. It is ten o'clock in the evening and the streets are vacant, save the occasional cars and lone walkers. The air has cooled considerably. We've probably lost thirty degrees in two hours. All the way in, we were gaining altitude, so the coolness is due to elevation as well as evening. Trees are dense at this altitude. Pine and evergreen. Mountain air. This is how I imagine Colorado or Montana, but not Arizona. I imagined Flagstaff as a desert town, but it isn't. There are shade and streams and small parks. We opt not to stay in Flagstaff, but to keep driving toward the canyon. I am trusting Paul will be able to drive the short distance, because I am too tired to hold a thought, much less navigate the winding road.

We round a bend and weave through town to find an exit road that cuts deep embankments in the side of the mountain. The road hugs the hill and we navigate tight curves banked by a wall of dirt on one side and pine on the other. Two lanes and no shoulder. Flagstaff fades and disappears into the trees and behind us. Patches of snow rest amid pine needles. The temperature has actually cooled enough to allow snow to stick and stay. Our headlights sweep along the tree line as we round another curve. The lights peer deep into the forest and I can see the white-backed snow humps in with the brown and green. "Are you seeing the snow, Paul?"

"Yeah."

"It's amazing," I say.

"Have you ever seen snow, Don?"

"A little. It snowed once in Houston, but it wasn't cold enough to stick. It only snowed for a few minutes. I was just a kid."

"Well, there's your snow." Paul says this with a smile.

"There it is."

I've got my eyes looking for snow like a child would for a deer after one had jumped across the road. I'm fixated by the idea of snow. People in Houston dream about it during winter. We celebrate Christmas with shorts on and get about five or six days a year that actually drop below freezing. Winter is just summer with an ice cube and a straw. As a kid I'd always dreamed about living in a place where it snowed. I picked Maine on a map because it was as far north as you could go and still run for president.

Every few curves we see a small house tucked into the woods. People living the simple life. They chop their own wood and grow their own carrots and beets and spend evening hours peering their beady eyes through Radio Shack telescopes, hoping to get a look at Luke Skywalker.

Paul slides the van off the side of the road a bit, our tires rubbing against the abrupt pavement. He pulls back on the road, overcompensating into the opposite lane. He steps on the brake and slows the van, and it rocks toward the left front. He pulls back into our lane and shakes his head as if to wake himself.

"Did you fall asleep?" I ask.

"I don't remember," he says, sort of smiling, but more out of relief that we didn't wreck than from a joke.

"We should pull over and sleep. We can see the canyon in the morning," I tell him. Paul starts looking for a dirt road and eventually pulls off into a field. I get out and feel the silence in the high desert, noting the stars against the horizon where hills fade to black in slow mounds. I notice a pile of snow a hundred feet away and walk over to examine it, coming to it slowly, a celestial carcass, like some angel shot out of the sky, falling to earth to glisten and melt.

8 FLOATING BODIES AT HOOVER DAM

THE AREA AROUND THE GRAND CANYON IS SURPRIS-
ingly flat. Dense with pine trees, the ground not taken by forest is brown with desert sand. A Disneyland atmosphere
surrounds the place. Rangers have tried to give the area a park
feel (and it has some of that), but it is mostly a tourist trap and
one more state decal stuck on the back of an old couple's
retirement vehicle. There are lawn chairs and picnic tables and
crying babies held by mothers who juggle diaper bags and
strollers. Fathers wear khaki shorts, white tennis shoes, and
blue socks. They lead their families around the canyon edge
like tour guides, explaining how many millions of years it took
for the river to carve this hole in the earth.

Paul and I are set back twenty dollars apiece at the entrance.
We pay the sum in exchange for permission to enter the park.
We decide not to pay the additional thirty dollars required to
camp. With the van, we agree that we can sleep anywhere and
will head back into town if we need to. Our first stop within
the gate is the canyon edge, where the aforementioned scene
plays out before us. No amount of hype or brochure sales copy
can prepare a person for the breathtaking depth of the canyon
itself. From twenty feet away, we see an abrupt drop in the
landscape. As we near the edge, the depth is all-consuming.
There seems to be no bottom. No words are spoken here, and
the sound of children fades to the background as a breeze
whistles through sagebrush and a fiery red cliff drops under
our feet. It is a top-of-the-roller-coaster feeling as I imagine

myself plunging headlong over the rail. Enough emotion to take a step back and catch my breath. Regaining my senses, I lean over the edge and focus my eyes to find the bottom. Perhaps the Colorado River that Ben Bonham told us about will come to view. But it doesn't. What I see several miles down is a flat surface, a peninsula edged by another drop. A canyon inside of a canyon. We are not at the park's most popular overlook, but at a trailhead for those planning a hike all the way down.

"How many miles do you figure it is to the bottom?" I ask.

Paul looks down at a few hikers, looks again at the peninsula, and shrugs his shoulders. "I guess we will know soon enough."

"Do you think we can start today?" I ask, half unsettled at the tremendous depth. I feel a weakness in my legs and am altogether unsure whether I have the stamina to find the bottom.

Paul notes the reservation in my voice. "I don't know if we need a permit or anything. We can go to the information center and find out. We'll do fine, Don."

"I'm looking forward to it," I say.

Paul turns and walks toward the van. A child licks his ice-cream cone, and an old couple pass binoculars back and forth. One is talking to the other about a certain shrub or tree that the other has spotted. "To the right," he says, as she swings the black tubes too far. "Not over there," he says, "here, honey." He points but she doesn't see, too busy fidgeting with the focus lever.

I near the trailhead and eye its steep switchbacks weave under each other. They are thin trails with no protective guardrails. One of the hikers gets caught by a gust of wind and leans back against the rock wall until it passes. One false step could send her into a freefall that would last thirty seconds or more. The trail becomes so thin to my eye that I lose it in the camouflage of red rock and sand.

Paul is more eager to hike the canyon than I am. He didn't

look at it for more than a minute before turning away. The look on his face and the surety of his step tell me that, come rain or snow, we will hike to the bottom of this hole.

The information center is a cave of a structure. It is walled with river rock and has a wood porch like a cabin in the mountains. A big building with a big parking lot, RVs line the road for several hundred yards before we find an open space. Families with matching sunburns stream in and out of the building. One family on the large porch gathers around their leader, who wrestles with the creases of the park map. It is all he can do to keep the map unfolded. It wraps around his arms like a fishing net.

Inside the information center, everything is dark. While not overly warm outside, the sky is bright and so our eyes adjust slowly to the brown décor of the large room fit with cement floors, ceiling fans, and brochure-lined walls, all of it smelling like mosquito repellent.

Paul bypasses the brochures and the rock exhibit, making his way to the counter where a young girl in a brown uniform stands with a fake smile.

"Can I help you?"

"Yes. We were needing a trail map for the canyon."

"Are you going down?" she asks.

"Yes," one of us says.

"Do you have your permit yet?"

"Well, I didn't know for sure if we needed one," Paul remarks.

"You do," she says.

"We do," I say, lifting my eyebrows. I pull out my Blockbuster video card and set it on the counter. She looks at it confused, then back at Paul.

"You will need a permit," she says.

Paul turns and looks at me and then turns back. She's still got that same smile going, and he's softly bouncing his fingers on the counter.

"Do you know if there is a cost for that?"

"The permit?" she clarifies.

"Yes," Paul answers.

"There's no cost. But you can't get a permit here. Permits are issued in the trailhead office."

"The trailhead office," Paul echoes. I pick up my Blockbuster card and set down my Bally's Total Fitness membership card, along with my driver's license. The girl looks at the cards and I lift my eyebrows and, after looking at me confused, she looks back at Paul.

"Yes, the trailhead office," she says.

I crack a smile as Paul walks the girl through every step of her job.

"Where is the trailhead office?" he asks.

The girl turns and grabs a three-ring notebook with a dozen or more pages, each page held in a protective glossy sheet. She flips slowly through them and sets her finger down firmly when she finds what she's looking for.

"Here it is," she says as she turns the notebook around so Paul can see. I look over Paul's shoulder at the map.

"This X is the permit office?" Paul asks.

"That's the place."

"Now, where are we?"

"You . . . you . . . are here." And she places her finger only an inch from the permit office.

"So," Paul begins, "it looks like we should just go out the door and, well, it doesn't look like it's very far."

"Well," she says, "if you go out this door"—she points and looks to the left—"it is right there. It's a brown trailer."

"It is right outside the door?" Paul asks in disbelief.

"Yes," she says, and I audibly chuckle. She doesn't notice my laugh, and then I see a sheepish look come over her face. She turns and points out the window. "Duh, I'm so silly," she says. "You can see it outside the window. That's it right there."

"Right there," Paul clarifies as he points to a brown trailer.

"That's it," she says and her smile turns big.

"Duh," I say with a gentle smile. Paul steps on my foot to get me to stop.

"I mean," I begin apologetically, "we should have known that."

"Oh, no. It's my job," she clarifies.

"Duh," I mumble and Paul steps on my foot again and the girl smiles real big.

"Have fun in the canyon," she says.

"We will."

I let Paul go a few feet toward the door while I remain at the counter. "Paul," I shout, "do you think we need a map to the door? It's awful dark in here." I turn back to the girl and she smiles and points to the door.

"Over there," she says.

"There," I clarify with a confused look and a point.

"He's got it," she says and looks at me like I'm stupid. "It's right there. He found it," she says.

"Thanks. Duh, I'm so silly sometimes."

"That's all right," she says, turning to the next person in line.

"I can't believe you did that." Paul holds the door open and greets me with a grin.

"I was just playing with her."

Paul eyes the brown trailer across the parking lot. "That's it. Let's go get the permit."

The interior of the trailer is wood paneling and brown trim. There is a tall man in a uniform behind a counter. Otherwise, the trailer is empty. Paul greets the uniformed man.

"Hello. We want to get a couple of permits for the canyon."

"You are in the right place," the man says. "Did you make a reservation?"

"No. We didn't know we needed one."

"Most people make reservations before they come. We can only have so many people in the canyon at a time."

"Do you have any openings?" Paul asks.

The man pulls out a three-ring notebook and files through pages. It is a thick book and filled line by line with signatures.

"I don't know if we can get you in anytime soon," he responds.

"When's the soonest?" Paul asks.

The man looks back at his notebook, scanning down the page with his finger. He flips the page and scans down the backside. Paul sighs and gives me a hopeful look. I set my Blockbuster card on the counter but Paul picks it up and puts it in his pocket before the man sees it.

"I can get you in on Easter morning. You will have a permit to camp at the bottom that night. Indian Springs campground will have a space for you the next day."

"Indian Springs?" Paul questions.

"Indian Springs is the campground about halfway up. I can put you at the bottom on Sunday night. You will have to hike out the next day and come to Bright Angel. All I can give you is one day at Indian Springs. Then you'll have to come out."

Paul lifts his eyebrows and sighs. "If that's all we can get, we'll take it, I guess."

"That is all I can do for you."

Paul looks over and asks me what day it is. "Wednesday," I respond.

"You'll have to stick around for a few days," the uniformed man says, clarifying the importance of not breaking the rules.

"Fine with me." Paul glances my way.

"Yeah, that's fine." I shrug.

The man turns the notebook around and hands Paul a pencil. "You guys come back and check with me if you decide to leave. Plenty of people would like these permits."

He pulls out a pink piece of paper and hands it to me. It has a list of numbered guidelines. "Don't veer off the trail," he begins. "Pack out your trash, don't approach animals, carry plenty of water, don't wash your gear in the river, only make camp in a designated area, use no radios or other electronic devices that create an excess of noise."

The list goes on for a while and the man reads each rule carefully. He then hands us permits to sign.

"Keep your copy with you at all times," he says. "Does either of you have a heart condition?"

"Heart condition?" I ask, puzzled.

"A heart condition or any other medical problem that might get you into trouble."

"No," Paul says.

"No," I answer.

Looking directly at me, he begins his warning: "Last week a man had a heart attack about halfway up from Bright Angel. There was nothing we could do for him. Rangers carried his body to the rim. If you get into trouble at the bottom, we will not send a helicopter down for you. There is no place for us to land. So, our policy is to float your dead body down the river and fish you out at Hoover Dam."

The man turns to Paul, straight-faced, and then gives a wink. "Just kidding," he says. "Still, a man did die last week. But if you get into trouble, we can bring you out on a donkey. But you have to be dead first. And your parents will have to pay for the donkey. That's the only way you get a free ride out."

"Kidding?" I ask.

"I'm not joking this time. If you aren't sure that you can make it to the bottom and back, don't go. This is a difficult hike. There is nothing easy about it. Nine miles in and ten miles out. An elevation loss and gain of over five thousand feet. Every year we have people die on those trails."

"We will be careful," Paul assures the man, folding his permit and putting it in his pocket.

We turn toward the door and my legs feel numb. I've got butterflies in my stomach. Houston is very, very flat. I've never been above one thousand feet before, much less from five thousand to zero and back. Or whatever the elevation is.

"You boys have a good hike," the man says as we walk out the door.

"Well, bud, we're in." Paul raises his hand for a high five.

I meet his hand and give a good grin. "Can't believe it," I say. "We are actually going to do this."

"It is going to be great, Don. You are really going to love this hike. Your first big nature experience." He sees my grin turn down a little. "Think of it, the canyon walls, the red rock, the river flowing right by our camp, the stars from the bottom of the canyon."

"Can't think of a better place to die," I say.

"That's the spirit!" Paul says, turning to walk toward the van.

A body floating down the river, I think to myself. The sound of the turbines at Hoover Dam, my crying mother, the bloated-blue figure wearing the Grand Canyon T-shirt that sickens the onlookers at my funeral.

"I'm pumped, Paul. This is going to be good," I say through a fake grin.

"You bet it is," he says, looking back.

9 DANCING

IT IS DIFFICULT TO RECALL, MUCH LESS RECAPTURE, the excitement of an adventure's beginning when you find yourself in the boring middle of it. Paul and I have been waiting for three days. Tomorrow morning we will hike into the canyon. My earlier reservations about the intensity of the hike have been allayed by a burning off of anxiety, the twiddling of thumbs. And today we are off on short hikes to and from the day-use area. The canyon splendor has bewildered the depth of my imagination. We've seen every overlook the park allows. This gargantuan hole they call Grand has no less depth from any angle. To the human eye, it is bottomless.

The waiting has not been all bad. Paul, the cook, has been standing over an enormous pot of beans and rice for an hour and I have written postcards to family, friends, and Ben Bonham, the last of whom will receive a detailed description of the canyon edge, specifically worded to remind him and his wife of the beauty they twice knew.

A park ranger came through the day-use area and attempted conversations with several families. He spent a little time with us and answered questions about the route we've chosen to hike. Ours will be a loop down the Kaibab Trail to where we will camp on the canyon floor. On Monday we will leave Kaibab and take the Bright Angel Trail halfway up where there is a meadow and another camping area called Indian Springs. We will stay at Indian Springs two days and then finish the ascent on the third day. All in all, being only nineteen miles and over three days' time, the hike doesn't intimidate the way it did a few days back. The ranger also told us about the sunrise service tomorrow morning. "Sunrise over the canyon is beautiful," he says. Apparently it is an Easter tradition and hundreds of people attend every year.

Imagining the service reminds me again that life is more than clothes and cars and a new flavor of toothpaste, that it is community and creation and beauty and humanity. And I think I am starting to prefer the latter to the former; by that I mean I am getting used to not having any music or television and not pulling over and buying something as a way of feeling some kind of change. There is a serenity in life, after all, and once a withdrawl is felt at having left the lies behind, a soul begins to feel at home in its own skin. The first day at the canyon there was a lot of withdrawal. I actually walked over to the gift shop and contemplated buying a little license-plate keychain with my name spelled on it. I talked myself out of it because I don't actually have any keys, but part of me just wanted to smell the smell of new rubber and have something new as a way of feeling different about myself. But I didn't buy it. I hiked back to the canyon edge and watched the sun go down over the massive stretch of brown, and then I sat on a bench and watched lovers stroll along the guardrail and felt a quiet peace as the coolness gave way to coldness, which got me off the bench and had me walking along the canyon rim, praying, I think, and thanking God for beauty and for rest and thanking Him for something better to believe than commercials.

I was raised to believe that the quality of a man's life would greatly increase, not with the gain of status or success, not by his heart's knowing romance or by prosperity in industry or academia, but by his nearness to God. It confuses me that Christian living is not simpler. The gospel, the very good news, is simple, but this is the gate, the trailhead. Ironing out faithless creases is toilsome labor. God bestows three blessings on man: to feed him like birds, dress him like flowers, and befriend him as a confidant. Too many take the first two and neglect the last. Sooner or later you figure out life is constructed specifically and brilliantly to squeeze a man into association with the Owner of heaven. It is a struggle, with labor pains and thorny landscape, bloody hands and a sweaty brow, head in hands, moments of severe loneliness and questioning, moments of ache and desire. All this leads to God, I think. Perhaps this is what is on the other side of the commercials, on the other side of the curtain behind which the Wizard of Oz pulls his levers. Matter and thought are a canvas on which God paints, a painting with tragedy and delivery, with sin and redemption. *Life is a dance toward God,* I begin to think. And the dance is not so graceful as we might want. While we glide and swing our practiced sway, God crowds our feet, bumps our toes, and scuffs our shoes. So we learn to dance with the One who made us. And it is a difficult dance to learn, because its steps are foreign.

I begin to think of my time at the canyon in these terms, as learning to dance in a new way, the first few lessons had me feeling clunky and awkward, but soon they will give way to a kind of graceful sway, and I won't stop at gift shops or hunt for a television, but like Paul I will be able to stand over a pot of boiling beans for hours and feel completely content, as though there was nothing in life that I was missing out on. It gives me a little joy to think about things this way, and I smile at a couple as they pass me along the guardrail, and I pull a bit of pine needle off a tree and roll it in my palms and smell the mintlike scent of creation as I let the green shards spill from my palms to the path along the rim. And I think to myself, *There is nothing I am missing. I have everything I was supposed to have to experience the magnitude of this story, to dance with God.*

10 EASTER DESCENT

SEVEN MILES FROM GRAND CANYON NATIONAL PARK there are sleeping pines that line the dark highway. They break their fences to reveal stretches of moonlit desert back toward Flagstaff. On this particular stretch of road there is a hotel, where families sleep soundly in the early morning darkness. Behind this hotel there is a van, a Volkswagen with two tired, sleeping passengers. They cover their heads in blankets at first light and each thinks to himself how he should wake the other up. But the lazy sun slowly climbs the lazy sky and the lazy passengers go back to sleep beneath the sleeping pines and care not about Easter sunrise or creating memories or witnessing, once again, the great metaphor of God, the sun coming up over the horizon, rising once again, as though from the dead.

• • •

ON THE ROAD FROM THE HOTEL TO THE CANYON WE ARE able to pick up a Flagstaff radio station. KTLY, an oldies station, plays the Beatles on Sunday morning. One of the first bands to utilize stereo technology, the Beatles produced their early records so the lead vocals are committed to one speaker and the music and backup vocals to the other. Short one speaker, we have a built-in karaoke machine. Paul and I are unsure in our singing. Is it "Help me if you can I'm feeling down, and I do appreciate you being round," or is it "Help me if you can I'm feeling down, and I do appreciate you coming round"? My

93

money is on "coming round." Regardless, the words "Won't you please, please help me" come in clear from the driver's side, and Paul and I are tapping our palms against the dash, coming in strong when John, Paul, George, and Ringo offer their voices to the right side.

The disc jockey has a middle-aged voice. "This is Geoffrey Clark and you're listening to All Beatles Sunday on KTLY Radio, 102 FM, Flagstaff, Grand Canyon. That was 'Please, Please, Help Me,' and now, one of my personal favorites, a really groovy tune called 'Paperback Writer.'"

We picked up some resealable bags from the national park grocery store a couple days back, and once we reach the parking lot at the trailhead, Paul begins filling a few of them with day-old beans and rice. We've got bananas and apples and several tea bags and hot apple cider mix, as well. I ask him if we have some steak, and he shakes his head no. I ask about milk shakes, and he shakes his head no.

"You probably want to put that in the top of your pack," Paul says after handing me a bag of brown mushy beans.

"Do you think we've got enough water?" I ask.

"Four canteens should get us to the bottom. There will be fresh water there, and I've got purification tablets if there's not."

I place one change of underwear, two pair of socks, and a T-shirt into my bag. Pushing them deep, I make room for my copy of *Catcher in the Rye* and a book of letters and poems by Emily Dickinson. My sleeping bag is not one of those fancy, light ones that campers have nowadays. It's cotton and wool and doubles the weight of the pack when I fasten it to the frame. I tie my metal cup to one of the side straps, and my toothbrush and toothpaste fit neatly in a side pocket.

"Do you have toilet paper?" I ask.

Paul doesn't look up but pats a side pocket on his pack. "Yeah, I've got some in here." He is pulling on a strap, tightening his sleeping bag to the top of his pack.

"Do you have any to spare?"

"Got plenty."

A couple of hikers lift their packs, tighten their straps around their waists, and stroll past us. I watch them out of the corner of my eye as they disappear behind a boulder and then appear again a good fifty feet down the canyon. They round a corner and disappear again.

"How are we going to get back to the van when we come out?" I ask.

"Well, we will just hike back to this trailhead when we come up from Bright Angel. We can probably hitch a ride if we want."

"Yeah, that sounds good," I say.

Paul opens the big sliding door on the van and rummages around.

"What are you looking for?" I ask.

"Just looking. Want to make sure I got everything."

I bought a Swiss Army knife for the trip. It has a fork, a knife, a toothpick, and a corkscrew. They had one with a spoon but it was twenty dollars more. I put my knife in the backpack but then decide I want to carry it in my pocket.

"Is this your hat?" Paul asks. He's holding a Panama-style Maxfli hat that he found beneath the bench in the van.

"Yeah, that's my golf hat."

"You play golf?" he asks.

"A little. Hand it here. I may as well wear it down."

I pull the hat firmly over my head. It has a tight elastic band so it fits nice and comfortable. I lift my pack by the frame and swing it around to my back. Feels like lead. It's so heavy, with the water and books, I stagger a little.

"Looks like you've got a heavy load there, Don."

"Yeah," I agree.

Taking the pack off, I remove my Emily Dickinson book and *Catcher in the Rye*. I also remove an apple or two, thinking that I will just make do with the food that I've got. The food is making the pack heavy. I have five meals with snacks and reduce this to four and no snacks, save two apples. It is not wise to hike so long without enough food, but the beans and rice are potent enough to fuel a racehorse, so I use that excuse to put one of the bags back into the van.

Paul slides the door closed and rounds the van to lock the doors.

"I guess we're ready," he says as he lifts his pack over his shoulders.

"We really are a couple of characters, aren't we?" I suggest, looking at our reflection in the window of the van. Paul has an old army pack he picked up at a surplus store on Galveston Island, and I've got this old pack from the seventies that is bright orange. Like a vest on a road worker, the pack is so bright it might very well glow in the dark. Another couple passes us with expensive gear and clothes, and Paul and I just shrug our shoulders.

"I don't think I'll be losing you in the canyon," Paul says, patting his hand against my bright backpack.

We round the boulder and stand side by side at the edge of the trail. There are clouds building in the distance, but the sky around them is deep and blue. It climbs as endlessly as the canyon descends and we experience one last bit of awe before we depart. I take a deep breath and pull at the shoulder straps of my pack.

"All this beauty makes a person realize how insignificant you are," Paul says.

"How insignificant I am?" I question. "You're the insignificant one."

He grins real big as he realizes how his words sounded. "I didn't mean it like that," he says.

"No, I know what you meant, bud. I was just thinking kind of the same thing. I was looking at all this depth and it came to me how very shallow you are."

"Ha, ha," Paul chortles. He takes a few steps down the trail and then turns. "You know, Don, I was just looking at this little flowery cactus here and thinking how nice it looks, and it made me realize how ugly you are."

"Is that right? How ugly I am," I say, kicking some dirt toward my friend.

OUR FUN TURNS TO WORK FAIRLY QUICKLY AS WE wind down the switchbacks. Some descend thirty and forty feet in only a few paces, but the canyon offers splendor at every turn. It is a wonder they carved a trail into the canyon at all. It is onerously steep. At times the trail thins to three or four feet, with nothing but drop as a border. The mind gets used to the danger so that a hiker can set his stride only inches from the cliff, making pace, not caring about his fall. It gives me a sense of pride as I narrowly navigate the trail and keep steady with Paul.

I start thinking about the wonder of the canyon, how mountains get all kinds of attention because they are so high, but canyons are no less magnificent, only overlooked because they don't stand out to the eye. After all, it is no more a miracle there is a towering pile of dirt and rock than an absence of it. And who cares that there is no view from the bottom? Half the time you can't see anything from the top of a mountain anyway and they are terribly difficult to climb. In terms of analogies, canyons are sorely neglected. A canyon can be used to describe hell or confusion or all sorts of important spiritual realities. Without canyons, mountains would have no point of reference, for example. A canyon is, after all, an upside-down mountain. Except they most often have rivers at the bottom, and mountains have no rivers on top. Just snow and little flags that represent different hikers from different countries, and little frozen bodies clinging to frozen flags.

The Grand Canyon, as Paul tells me, is not the deepest canyon in the United States. I didn't know that. The deepest canyon is on the Oregon-Idaho border. It is Hells Canyon, and drops more than six thousand feet from rim to river. Paul tells me it is a gradual slope with a road that goes to the bottom so it doesn't have the dangerous view this canyon provides, and that is why nobody recognizes it as spectacular. I cannot imagine anything deeper than this, I tell him.

The trail does not give in its slope. My toes are sliding into the front of my boots and my heel has not felt shoe in an hour. Looking up, the canyon rim does not seem so far. We've hiked a mile or more and still the bottom of the canyon is not in view. We only see the first ledge that hides the river. And there is no telling how far the river is from the first ledge.

"Doesn't seem like we've gotten anywhere, does it?" Paul says as he looks up at the rim.

"I was thinking the same thing."

As we hike, Paul gets ahead of me by a switchback and then another. I'm growing tired and my toes are really getting to me. My right big toe rubs against the side of my boot. I can feel the skin getting tender so it slows my pace and Paul gets a little farther ahead. His pace is slowing, too, but he still gets away. He's four switchbacks down and I can see him when I come to the edge and look directly down. I walk through the pain, trying to ignore it. I grimace as I step and there is a rocking in my stride. I move a bit more quickly to catch my friend. Coming within one switchback of Paul, I see he has a drag in his step. No smile. No grimace, but no smile. He's not having it as tough as I am, but it sets me at ease to know I am not a complete wimp. This hike is actually difficult, even for Paul. He rounds the switchback and I notice he gives a nod to someone underneath my trail. He engages in a conversation and I wind down the corner to see two hikers sitting in the mouth of a shallow cave. One is dipping his Swiss Army knife into a jar of peanut butter. He has a piece of bread on his knee. The other hiker is leaning against the rock and looks exhausted. His legs are stretched out over the boulder in front of him.

"How long have you guys been hiking?" the one without the knife asks.

Paul looks over and shrugs his shoulder. He turns back. "About two hours. Probably two hours. How about you guys?"

The guy with the peanut butter handles his bread and doesn't look up. "We left the bottom about four hours ago. Maybe more."

"Four hours," I clarify.

The one on the right rubs his leg. "Don't worry. It takes a lot longer coming up than going down. You guys should be there in three hours."

"You said that right," the other adds. "Coming up is a bear."

As we leave, the guy with the peanut butter pulls his knife from the jar. He has the knife that includes the spoon. It has a bigger blade, too, and it makes me wish I had paid the twenty extra bucks to get that one. Peanut butter, however, doesn't sound very good. Too thirsty. We leave the two hikers to their sandwiches and round another switchback, walking now into a brisk, dry wind.

"How are your feet?" I ask as Paul drags his steps in front of me.

"They're getting to me a little. How about yours?"

"Mine feel fine. Feel like a million bucks."

"Is that right?" Paul inquires.

"Sure. Feel like I could run a marathon." My smile gives away my lie.

"Is that why you were making that grunt noise back there?" he asks.

"What grunt noise?"

"Back there when you leaned against that rock and started crying for your mommy."

With that, I give him a good kick in the backside. He jumps a few steps and kicks a little dirt back on me.

"We'll see who's crying mommy," I say.

Paul gains a few paces and then turns, looking at my feet.

"Seriously," he asks. "How are you holding up?"

"My toes are killing me, and I've got a blister starting on my right foot."

"I've got duct tape if you need it," he says.

"Duct tape?"

"Yeah, it's great. Put duct tape over your blisters and it's like having second skin."

"Just one more use for duct tape," I add.

"The stuff is great, isn't it?"

"I used to fix all the vapor hoses on my Datsun with . . . whoa . . . hey now." A gust of wind catches my pack and I lose my footing. Coming to my knee only an inch from the cliff, my body and most of my weight look over to see a few pebbles bounce down the rock face. They move in slow motion and twist and turn and catch ledges all the way down. At least a thousand feet. Paul grabs my pack and pulls me onto the trail.

"You all right?"

"I'm good," I say and get back to my feet, being careful to stay away from the edge. "The wind caught me like a sail."

"It almost had me too," he says. "We've got to watch these corners."

My heart is racing. I can still see the pebbles falling through the air. I shake it off and begin again, slowly and cautiously. Step by step.

I can feel the dirt on my knee drying up and it is tight, like a bandage wrapped over a scar. The wind continues to threaten and every few switchbacks it presses against me and rocks me a little. Paul is having trouble too, but manages it well and walks through the wind with a determined look. He gains a switchback and then I lose him around the corner. Too tired to catch up, I move slowly and can really feel the pain now. The blister on my toe is screaming, and my knees and shins are beginning to get tight. I thought hiking down would be easier than up, but it occurs to me I am using muscles I've never used before. My legs are having to stop my weight from falling and they are weak and can't take much more. Rounding the corner, Paul is a good distance ahead. A couple hundred feet down maybe. He shows no sign of stopping for a break, so I try to pick up my pace. It is no use. Moving slowly helps the pain. I grimace with every short step and begin to count the hours since we left. It must be three hours now. We left at around ten and it has to be one or two o'clock. I left my watch in the van, thinking I wouldn't need it, so I'm not sure of the exact time. Still, the canyon looks deep, and judging up from down, we are only about halfway. This is going to be a tougher hike than I imagined.

● ● ●

WE'VE BEEN AT IT FOR FOUR HOURS NOW. PAUL IS A good three hundred feet down. He's slowed his pace, but is still increasing the distance from me. Every step sends a jolt through my legs. I can feel the raw flesh on my toe. The skin folds up and then down every time I take a step. It is a terrible pain. My knees feel arthritic and my mouth is cotton dry. I'm too weak to get water and there is too far to go to stop and take a break. Besides, if I stop, I won't get going again. This isn't a pain that is eased by resting. My pack is heavy and bends my back straight. It rubs weight against me and I feel it slide left and right as I rock my body down the path. Who cares about the ledge? Who cares about the cliff? Quicker to the bottom, that's what I say.

FOUR AND A HALF HOURS, I'VE LOST PAUL BUT I HAVE seen the river. Back a few switchbacks, I got my first glimpse of it and it looked like heaven. Except it looked like hell, too, as it was so far away. I must be inside the second canyon. The one that isn't visible from the top. There is some grass down here and the path is wider. It has cooled off significantly and the air feels good. There is a thundercloud building overhead and it gives welcome shade. No rain, but good, cool shade. I plod the trail, keeping my head down and eyes fixed on the dusty path. My mouth is still cotton dry and I can't gather enough spittle to moisten my tongue. Everything is aching. I've reduced my pace to that of a turtle. I'm depleted, almost completely out of energy. I wonder if I would have grown up in Colorado or Montana if this would be so hard. If a trail this well maintained goes this deep into the canyon, it's not like it hasn't been traveled a million times.

The path takes a bend and becomes a narrow ledge that overlooks a small green valley. The rocks are no longer brown; they are gray. I follow the brown trail down the gray rocks as it makes a wide, deep loop and ends up below and opposite me. There is a narrow creek, a little stream that feeds some plant life, giving the valley color. My eye is so pleased at this sight, this very different sight, that I am energized and lift my feet a little above a drag as I take in the view. I haven't seen green in five hours. And water. Look at it. Listen to it lightly tap against the rocks. Following the stream with my eye, I see the trail where it meets the creek and there sits my old friend Paul. He has his pack off and is eating an apple and wearing a smile with bright eyes.

I really pick up my pace here, showing off for Paul. Making out like I'd not had such a rough go of it.

"We made it, bud," he greets me as I come toward him on the lower part of the trail.

"This is it?"

He holds up a finger. "Only one more mile. And it's an easy one."

"How do you know?"

"A ranger told me."

"Where is he?"

"He went back to the campground."

The stream gurgles next to us and the air lifts off the moving water, cool and damp.

"How long have you been here?" I ask.

"About twenty minutes." Paul throws his apple core into the grass on the other side of the stream. "How are you feeling?"

"Like a million bucks," I say. "How about you?"

"I'm thinking about going for a little jog later."

"A jog, huh?"

"Yep," he says.

"Well, I suppose we should crank out this last mile. If I stop, I'm not going to get started again."

"Yeah, I'm game for that," Paul says as he lifts his pack. "You want water first?" He's got a canteen open and he hands it to me. Without answering I take about five swigs. Big swigs that fill my belly and suddenly it feels like I've eaten Thanksgiving dinner. I'm full and feeling a little queasy.

"You sure you don't want to stop and rest?" he asks.

"I'm fine."

The texture of the trail has changed. It is more sand than dirt. White sand, and at places it becomes thick like a beach. My feet drag into it and sink an inch or so. Paul has these red tennis shoes on, and when he steps, the sand goes over his heels and spills down into his shoe. When he lifts up his foot, I can see that he has covered a blister with duct tape.

"How's that duct tape working?"

"Hurts like crazy," he says. "You got blisters?"

"What do you think?" I say.

We both drag and rock and sway with grimacing expressions. The trail swings away from the stream and, once again, begins descending.

"It's a lot cooler down here," I say. "I wonder if it is because we are close to the river."

"I don't think so. I mean, we are close to the river, but it feels to me like a cold front moved in while we were hiking. That cloud up there. I bet you it's got cold weather in it."

"You think?" I ask, making conversation with short breaths, holding back the pain in my legs.

"I think so," he begins. "We dropped a lot of altitude today. It should actually be warmer down here than it is up there. And instead it's gotten cooler. I think it is a cold front."

"Makes sense, I guess."

Just as the pain is about to do me in, the trail offers a view of the broad, milky brown Colorado River. The river has no beach, only canyon walls. And I realize this is it. *The bottom of the Grand Canyon.* Only a few hundred feet down. Paul and I stop to look down at the river carving through the rock. It is wide and brown, full like pure muscle, the textures on its surface moving quickly along the rock banks. The river snakes its dark, flat belly around a bend and it is something to see. It is slapping its sides against the canyon wall like a dragon caught in a fishing net. The trail bottoms out where the stream that we were near empties into the canyon. We follow the trail as it begins to climb, up to a ridge where an enormous steel-cabled bridge crosses the river. It's only as wide as a sidewalk, but sturdy as a plank of thick steel blasted into both sides of the rock. They must have built it to withstand a flood. It is a good fifty feet off the water and they have burrowed a hole through the rock to get to it. Paul leads through the dark opening and rounds the corner where we are met by a grated walkway that is walled by tight-cable handles. As we step out on the bridge, the Colorado is visible directly below us, through the grate. We make our way to the middle and stop to take in the view. Below the bridge, to the right, there is a little beach where another stream empties into the river from the north side. This must be Phantom Ranch, the campground we are staying at tonight. A few white-water rafts are pulled onto the beach. These are enormous rafts, with built-in coolers in the middle.

They look like they could seat twenty people or more. The bridge sways and the river blows air through the grate as though from an air conditioner.

"I think we made it," I say.

"Looks like we did." Paul turns and takes tired steps down the other side of the bridge where the trail drops immediately onto the beach. The tall, narrow gateway that is the river basin lifts hundreds of feet above me, framing the sky.

I make my way behind Paul and the pain darts through the tendons in my legs. All I am thinking about is getting to our camping space and sitting down. The pain increases with every step. A ranger stands at a wooden gate down near the beach. He welcomes us and points us toward Phantom Ranch, which is another hundred feet up a side canyon.

The camping space is small and marked with rocks that separate us from our neighbors. It slopes toward a large creek and there is a big rock right down on our own beach. The water rushes over it and makes a soothing sound. I drop my pack to the ground and have a seat on the picnic table. Then I lie down. My muscles tighten and throb. They relax; then they tighten and throb again. My head is spinning and my belly is still filled with sloshing water. Even though I am still, I can feel it sloshing. My body rocks the way a body rocks when you've been in the ocean all day, and you still feel the waves lifting you long after you are on dry land. I can feel the blood running through my veins. I feel it pulsing in my legs and in my feet. I feel it in the arteries around my sore heels and around my toenails that for more than five hours were pressed forcefully against the front of my leather boot.

Paul sets his pack down on the ground and rests his back against it. Then he slides down and uses it as a pillow. As he takes off his shoes, I can see he's got a little blood coming from his heel. It makes me wonder what my heels look like. I don't have the energy to take off my boots. Just want to lie here and watch that thunderhead roll over. It rolls soft and slow, cutting through the thick sky like a barge into a sound. The cottonwoods frame the sky and the creek plays gently with the rocks and I ache and sway and the blood runs through my veins.

11 PHANTOM RANCH

THERE IS A BUZZ, OR RATHER A MOAN, ABOUT PHANTOM Ranch. Hikers are in pain to the right and the left. In the site next to ours there is a girl with an enormous backpack. She has taken off her boot and is peeling her sock from her foot like a second skin. Her foot is poultry-white and swollen. She massages it with her hand and grimaces. She's a small girl and I feel for her. Her pack is twice the size of mine. She unstraps her sleeping bag, pushes the backpack off the table, and unrolls her bag to slowly lie on top. One booted foot and one bare foot hang off the table and she rests on her stomach and uses her arms as a pillow. She makes me think I've not got it that bad.

Paul is doing what he can to make camp. He finds a soft piece of ground and unrolls his sleeping bag. He takes his little stove out and fiddles with the propane knob. Getting it right, he strikes a match and the blue flame shuffles through the black burner.

"You want some cider?" he asks.

"Not right now," I say softly, looking around at the other campers.

There are a couple of pros in the site behind us. They've carried a big tent in and are efficiently putting it together. They are wearing all the right clothes. Their packs are large internal-frame packs and they've brought the gear necessary for a long stay. Their stove makes Paul's look tiny. It has four burners and a large propane tank fastened to the side.

Across the creek is the trail we hiked in on. Five or six campers are making their way up the trail. They must have come in on rafts because they show no sign of being weary. They are laughing and getting along.

"You hungry at all?" Paul asks.

"Yeah. A little. Haven't eaten since this morning."

"Do you want to warm your beans on the stove?"

Paul and the stove are ten feet away. Much too far to walk. And in order to get over there, I'd have to come down off this table. I'm not sure I can do that.

"Nah. I'll just eat it cold," I say.

"A real man," Paul says.

Leaning my pack against the table, I can see down into the pouch where my clothes and food are. I pull the beans out of the side pocket and grab a spoon from the same pouch.

"You want Tabasco sauce?" Paul has a little bottle of Tabasco and he throws it over. "The stuff is potent," he warns.

I pour about half of the little bottle into the bag.

"Don, I'm telling you, it's hot."

"I know what I'm doing."

"That's right. You're a Texan."

"Let me show you how it's done," I say.

Paul is right. The stuff is hot. This isn't picante sauce. This is flaming hot. I try not to let on, but Paul has a good laugh as he watches me suck air.

"No problem," I say and then cough. "Whoa. This is good stuff."

"I think your tongue is on fire, Don."

I reach down for my canteen and drink it to the bottom. The water offers no relief.

"You want some more water?" He holds up his canteen and I go over to get it. He holds it so I can't get to it and I'm coughing through a painful laugh.

"'I know what I'm doing,'" he mocks.

"I'm fine. Just thirsty." I pin him down with my knee and

grab his canteen. I take the water and hold it in my mouth, in my cheeks, and run it over my tongue.

"Texas boy had some trouble with that." Paul chuckles.

"No. No, it just went down the wrong tube."

Paul rolls his eyes. I return to my bag of beans and dip my spoon ever lightly into the food like a chip in a bowl of hot sauce. *milk best for hot*

Having eased my hunger pains, I lay myself down on my bag next to Paul. We talk about the day, about the hike, and about tomorrow's departure. We will leave just after sunrise. We'll get a jump on it, we say. Leaving early will have us at Indian Springs campground just after noon so we may get in a day hike before sundown. I don't tell Paul, but I am not excited about a day hike. I imagine I will be in a lot of pain tomorrow morning, and another hike once we arrive at Indian Springs, right now, seems out of the question. But tomorrow is tomorrow and tonight all I can do is rest.

A ranger comes around and tells us there is a gathering up near the cabins. A little show that the rangers put on. Paul looks over and raises his eyebrows. I shake my head that I am not interested and he seems to lose interest with me.

"I don't think I will be going anywhere till tomorrow morning," I say.

"I'm all for that."

"You know, I'm really not looking forward to tomorrow's hike. I'm in a lot of pain. It's going to be tough."

"We'll go slow," Paul says. "We've got all day so we can take our time."

The sun is under the canyon rim and what is left of light is shaded by the thunderhead. It rolls over, thick and gray, threatening rain. Visible from Phantom Ranch is just a sliver of heaven. The cloud breaks here and there and reveals a little blue. It is a deep blue, an evening blue with the showing of a few stars that struggle against the lingering sunlight. From our camp we can see where the gathering is going to be and the rangers have a fire glowing. I can't make out the flames, but the canyon wall is dancing with shadows and light.

The rafters pass our site on their way to the gathering. They laugh and make conversation and walk with a certain skip in their steps. One tells a joke and they laugh and another adds to it and they laugh again. They go on like that all the way up the trail and over the crest to where the shadows are dancing on the wall.

12 BRIGHT ANGEL

PAUL IS OUT OF HIS BAG AND SO ARE MOST OF THE other campers. I don't feel like moving. I test my legs to see how sore they are, and even the slightest movement sets a shot of pain through my thighs and into my back. My feet ache and my calves ache. I roll over just to get some kind of motion going through my body. I finally roll out of bed and do a lame push-up to get onto my knees. I arch my back straight and use the picnic table to stand.

By the time Paul returns from brushing his teeth, I have two socks on each foot and am dealing with my boots and their tightness over the socks.

"Little nippy this morning," Paul remarks. "Did you get cold last night?"

"Didn't notice till I got up," I say, honestly not having thought about it until he mentioned it.

"Cold front must have moved in," he reports.

We make talk about the weather for a while and then Paul gets serious about hitting the trail. He's moving with a weariness but has determination in his motion like he's working through the pain.

"If we get moving we'll warm up," he counsels.

"Yeah," I say under my breath.

My ankles are weak and my knees are stiff. Not as bad as I thought they would be, but stiff nonetheless. I bend my knees and walk around camp, rolling my bag and tying my gear on my pack. Paul hands me a banana and I peel it slow, taking my time.

We sit on the picnic table and take one last look at Phantom Ranch. We hadn't been there long, hadn't really met anybody or participated in anything, other than moaning and sleeping. This is a place for rafters, for sure. I doubt anybody who actually hikes down here would be interested in a puppet show about Darwinian evolution.

"How do you suppose they got the wood down here to build those cabins?" Paul wonders.

I hadn't thought about it, but I offer something to make conversation. "Helicopter," I say.

Paul looks down the creek toward the Colorado. "I bet you they brought the wood in on the river."

"There's white water on that river, isn't there?" I ask.

Paul looks up and studies the canyon walls. "It's too narrow here for a helicopter. They had to use the river. I bet they used the river."

"Helicopter," I say, studying the walls. "Do you think we could catch a ride? There's probably another supply coming in soon. We could make like construction workers and hitch a ride."

Paul sticks his thumb out like a hitchhiker and looks up at the sky. I do the same. We look and look but no helicopter. I lift my thumb way up in the sky and make a pouty face. "Hello, helicopter," I say. We have a good laugh as two hikers come up the trail and make strange, subtle glances at us.

"Will you carry me?" I say to one of them, who walks by in silence.

"You feeling okay?" Paul asks, breaking the joking mood.

"Better than I thought I would."

"That's good," he says.

"Yep."

"You ready to get going?" he asks.

"Yep," I say, lying down on the picnic table. Paul takes another look around the place.

"Why do you suppose they call it Bright Angel Trail?" Paul asks. "Do you think it's an Indian thing?"

"Probably," I say. "It seems like everything around here is something Indian, you know."

I'VE EMBRACED PAUL'S MENTALITY ABOUT WORKING through the pain. My weak ankles strengthen and I find stride to keep pace with him as we begin the ascent. Within minutes my breathing is full. My lungs are at capacity. He isn't moving so quick and part of me believes he is going slow to be considerate. No matter, this is fast for me. At least this first hour.

This trail is different from Kaibab in texture and color. The rock is gray here, where Kaibab showed red and brown for the entire descent, save the last few hundred yards. The cliff on the right side of the trail is not so steep. As we climb, we go deep into the canyon wall. We are following a flood course of some sort. I imagine this little gorge as an enormous creek bed that empties into the Colorado. It carries nothing but rock now, but there are grasses and shrubs deep in the crevasse. There is a little water in there somewhere. There must be a small trickle, because I can hear it as I round certain corners far from the surface.

I think to myself about the weight in my pack. Last night Paul and I talked a bit about all the stuff that we carry with us, all the weight we walk around with, emotional baggage, thinking we need stuff we don't need. We weren't getting very deep or anything, but I keep thinking about it, and how much stuff I walk around with, about how life is a dance and God just meant for us to enjoy life, not get bogged down in sin and religion. Just be good, it seems like, is the point of life; be kind to people; don't hate anybody; forgive people because we all make mistakes. I know there are always going to be exceptions to this kind of thinking, but it seems like life would be better if we could just let go of the thought we need more and more stuff to be happy, more and more of the approval of others.

Coming down the trail is a family with bright smiles. I give trail and they thank us as they amble by. One of them, the lady, asks us if we're heading all the way to the top or just to Indian Springs. Indian Springs, I tell her. Not much farther. Just around the bend, she says. They move on and I look back at Paul as if something isn't right. We've been hiking for three hours. We couldn't be there already.

Paul steps out in front. "Didn't take long."

"Not at all. I thought Indian Springs was halfway to the top."

"Thought so too," Paul says.

"Seems like we just got started."

"We did. It's still morning." Paul looks up at the sky, finds the sun, and makes a shadow on his eyes with his hand. "It's about eleven."

"Really? Eleven o'clock, Paul?"

He takes his hand down and grabs at the straps under his arms. "Yes, eleven o'clock."

I look up with my hand, making a shadow on my eyes. "About eleven seventeen. Right about eleven seventeen if you ask me."

I'm worried about not splitting the hike evenly. If we've only done three miles today, tomorrow will have six for us. And if we've only risen a couple thousand feet, then we have the other thousands for tomorrow. That's a long walk. I'm about tuckered out now, and today was an easy day. I don't let the fear get in my eyes, though. Not for Paul to see. We're having a good time all around. Even with the toughness of the climb. And it is true that I am being a wimp about all of this. I do wish, though, that I was in better shape.

I follow him around the bend to see green and trees. Indian Springs. I don't know what I imagined, nothing really. I never pictured it, but certainly didn't expect this. Patches of grass, shrubs, a big restroom, and picnic tables with concrete covers.

It's a Texas roadside park right here in the canyon. They brought it in on helicopters, no doubt.

We come into the campground from the rear. There is a well, with a bucket on a rope, built from river rock with a stream running beside it. Willows line the stream and tall grasses stand in bunches. A broad space built in a valley, the National Park Service has lined the trails with rock and the stubble grass grows in with cacti in the places they don't let hikers walk. There must be thirty or more campsites, each with a picnic table and a cement structure slanted above it. There are no cabins. Only one building and it's a large outhouse with a girl door and a boy door. Paul chooses a picnic table farthest from the trail.

"This all right with you?"

"Fine," I say, still looking around the place.

● ● ●

WHOEVER SAID, "EAT, DRINK, AND BE MERRY," HAD more than beans and rice, that's for sure.

What is it they eat in Arizona anyway? In Texas we eat barbeque and it's good. Restaurants such as Luther's and Central Texas Bar-B-Q. They cook their meat in huge black greasy pits made from old barrels. Two-hundred-gallon barrels. In Louisiana they eat crawfish and boudin. They have deep-fried donuts in the French Quarter and drink coffee and listen to poor men with worn shoes play "When the Saints Go Marching In." But what about Arizona? Mexican food, I guess. Southwest cuisine. My mouth is watering even now. Scrambled eggs on flour tortillas. Picante sauce with fried onions on a big, thick ceramic plate that screeches when you run your fork across it. I'd love a plate of that right now. I'd love some thick, buttery pancakes with maple syrup running off the top, and some bacon, thick pieces of smoked bacon.

Paul shifts his weight and notices the ache on my face. "You thinking deep?"

"Deep?"

"You've got a deep look on your face," he says.

"No."

"No what?"

"Not thinking deep," I say.

"What are you thinking about?"

"Food."

Paul sits up. He lets out a gasp, an agreeing moan like he's got an empty stomach too. "We've got beans and rice. A banana?"

"Later. I'm daydreaming about real food right now. You know, real food. Truck stop food or Mexican food."

Paul lifts his tired body out of the dirt and wipes the dust from his shorts as he sits beside me on the table. "If you could have any food right now, what would it be?"

"You're not helping. I'm really hungry."

"Think about it. What food would you want?"

"Chicken fried steak," I say. "But I don't know."

"Sounds good. That's one thing I'm going to miss about the South, Don. The food. There isn't any food in the world like Texas food."

"You can say that again. I've never been much outside of Texas, but I can tell you that there is no food anywhere like we've got it . . . anywhere."

"Any food, Don. What would you have?" Paul asks again.

"You listen to Lyle Lovett much?"

Paul shrugs his shoulders. "What does Lyle Lovett have to do with anything?"

"I'm getting there. He sings this song called 'Nobody Knows Me Like My Baby.' You ever heard it?"

Paul shrugs his shoulders again. He doesn't answer but looks out at the field of grass and sand and lets his eye climb the tall wall of rock where he finds a skeletal tree frozen against the sky. His eye stops on the tree and I can tell by his look that he's calculating the distance to the top.

"It's a good song," I say.

"What does it have to do with food?"

"You'd have to hear it to understand."

"You're gonna tell?"

"Well . . . it goes . . . and I don't remember the words exactly, but it goes, 'I like to sleep late on Sunday, I like cream in my coffee, I like my eggs over easy, with them flour tortillas.' He says *them* flour tortillas. He doesn't say just flour tortillas but he says *them* flour tortillas, you know. With that Texas dialect."

"He's a Texan?"

"Yes, from Houston. Went to Texas A&M and his roommate was Robert Earl Keen Jr."

"Who's that?"

"Doesn't matter. Listen to how the song goes . . ."

"He sings a song about food." Paul looks frustrated as he ponders the distance to the tree in the sky.

"No, it's not about food. It's a love song," I say.

"A love song about sleeping late and eating eggs. Your kind of love song, Don."

"Listen to how it goes. He sings, and it's real slow, by the way. Just him and this real slow guitar part and he goes, 'I like to sleep late on Sunday, I like cream in my coffee, I like eggs over easy, with them flour tortillas. And nobody knows me like my baby.'"

Paul rests easy and lets his eyes come off the tree in the sky. He puts his eyes on the field of grass and sand and thinks to himself.

"See how the song is?" I begin. "It's about this girl. His wife maybe, I don't know. But she knows everything about him. About how he likes to sleep late on Sunday and have breakfast with flour tortillas and about how she's the only one who makes his coffee right. It's a love song like that."

"Sounds like you're hungry for more than food, Don." He says this with a laugh. A narrow laugh.

"I don't know, but for about an hour I've had that song on

my mind. Maybe because it's the only song I know that has food in it."

"You miss Kris?" Everyone back home called Kristin "Kris." Paul is referring to the girlfriend I broke up with.

"Little. Last night I missed her a little."

Paul gets a sly look on his face. A to-the-point, sly look. "She ever make you breakfast like that? Like that song?" He knocks my leg with his fist.

"Kristin?"

"Yeah. She ever make you breakfast?"

"No. And I know what you're getting at."

"Just asking."

"She's not really like that."

"Didn't mean to pry," Paul says.

"Don't worry about it. You weren't prying."

"You think she's the one, Don?"

"You mean *the* one? The one and only?"

"Yeah," he confirms.

"No."

"I guess that's why you broke up with her."

"Yeah. I guess." The sweat on my legs and arms is beginning to chill. I'm wishing for a jacket or a sweatshirt. "You know, Paul," I start, "I think she was going to break up with me anyway."

"What makes you say that?"

"Little things. She would say little things. Do little things. I don't think she was really into it."

"How long did you two date?"

"Not long."

"How long?"

"About six months or so."

"That's pretty long. Some folks figure it all out in that amount of time."

"I really liked her, you know. She just wasn't in it. I think I dropped the bomb first. But she was about to do it anyway."

That last sentence is said with tenderness. As if to release some small ache. Paul's expression gives sympathy. But he doesn't know it is more the pain in my legs than the pain in my chest that is causing this melancholy. Kristin is Kristin. A beautiful girl. I miss her, I guess. But she and I were never meant to be. She was in between boyfriends and was too pretty to go without. I was there like a number in a bakery. She pulled the ticket, glanced at it, and waited to exchange me for some loaf of bread or cake or pie or feeling that she was beautiful. But I gave her the slip. Came right out of her hands before she could claim the prize and I bet you, I bet you a million dollars, she doesn't even remember that number. She'll just pull another ticket, glance at it, and wait for them to call out her number. She won't remember the things I said and won't realize I had never said them to another girl. She'd heard them before and it all ran together like bad poetry. You could see it in her eyes when I talked to her. You could hear it in the way she said thank you when I complimented her dress or the color of her eyes.

It's funny how you think you need something but you really don't. I mean I remember feeling like if I didn't have this girl I was going to die. But I am not dead, and I feel fine, and I think half the time when I like some girl I am really looking for some kind of redemption, some kind of feeling that I matter or am valuable or am needed, and I don't think there is a problem with that, but it just makes you realize how much we use each other sometimes.

I heard once that real love doesn't ask what is in it for me; it just gives unconditionally. It just tries to take the weight out of somebody else's pack, lessen his load, and if it gets reciprocated, that's great, but that isn't what you did it for. It makes me wonder if real love, not the crap that we trade on the street, but real love, longtime, old-couple love, is another metaphor. I mean, I was thinking about it the other day and I couldn't think of a purpose for love in terms of Darwinian mechanisms. It seems like there is a reason for sex, for lust and all of that, but what about love? How does love, like beauty and light, help the Darwinian process? And I wondered if love itself, the real thing, the Lyle Lovett kind, wasn't another metaphor for God.

"You know what I'd want? If I could eat anything right now?" Paul breaks the silence and I come back to the surface. "I'd like a big bowl of Raisin Bran. With big, plump raisins and cold milk," he says, kind of licking his lips.

"That does sound good, Paul. Raisin Bran."

"You never answered my question, Don," Paul says after a minute of silence in which both of us were thinking about cereal.

"What was that? What meal would I want?"

"A meal. Any meal. What would it be?" Paul says.

I rest back and look up at the tree in the sky. There is a flagpole, too, way up at the Grand Canyon Lodge. You can barely see it, like a toothpick with a red rag flapping at its top.

"Any meal, Don," Paul says.

I sit there for a minute, thinking about it. "I'd like eggs over easy," I say. "With them flour tortillas."

13 REWARD

MY FEET ARE FROZEN. I ROLL MYSELF OVER TO MY backpack and pull out every article of clothing. I shove the underwear and T-shirts to the bottom of my sleeping bag and wrap my toes in the fabric. After a few minutes I realize it isn't helping. This is a deep blue cold. You can see it in the depth of the black sky and feel it in the still silence of the desert. All of Indian Springs snaps of cold. There is no light on the horizon. The sky is so heavy it drips dense shadows down the canyon walls. I look over at Paul and he's deep into his sleep. He is zipped up and snoring and though his breathing is not loud, or even bothersome, it irritates me because he is sleeping and I am not. He told me I'd be cold tonight. He said my bag was a "fair-weather" bag and the temperature would likely fall below freezing. He was right.

The cold didn't come gradually. It woke me about an hour ago and I've been in pain ever since. My head feels as though the blood in my brain is beginning to thicken, and if I loosen my jaw, my teeth begin clattering against each other. I won't be falling asleep again. A fetal position helps my hands, and when I raise my shoulders over my neck I can feel some warmth. And I am shaking now.

"Paul," I say and pull at his sleeping bag.

He rolls over and runs his hands up the inside of his bag to find the zipper.

"What is it?"

"I'm freezing out here," I tell him.

Paul opens and closes his eyes slowly. He checks the sky and looks around camp in a daze. "You're cold?" he questions.

"Freezing."

"I'm sorry."

"That's okay. But I need you to do something."

"What's that?"

"Sleep on my feet."

"What?"

I press my feet under his bag. "You have to sleep on my feet. I can hardly feel them."

He checks the seriousness in my eyes and says nothing. Just rolls over and lays his legs over my feet. I go back into my bag without humiliation or embarrassment. This is beyond anything social. I have to get warm.

• • •

THE CANYON WALL SLIDES THE SUN'S SHADOW SLOWLY down the rock face. I chart its progress, knowing that with the morning sun will come a little bit of warmth. But it is slow, slow, slow; sliding down the canyon wall like syrup. I set my head deep into the bag and hold my arms around myself to find warmth. Paul has moved off my feet, but I don't wake him because he was no help.

I figure I slept about an hour. Maybe two. Every minute was counted with a thousand clicks of my teeth. The sleepless night has set a sting in my dry eyes. My nose is dry too. I move my fingers to check the fabric of my bag, wondering where it is on me and where it isn't. After another half hour or so, I finally fall asleep.

• • •

I EASE MY ACHING BODY FROM MY SLEEPING BAG AND stretch my back. I reach for the sky and yawn. Rolling over, I set my hands against the ground and stand. I feel the bones in my back and my ribs separate from each other. My legs are stiff and my feet are jolted within by sharp points of pain. My belly is empty and past hungry. Paul is sitting out in the dirt about twenty yards away, out in some sunlight.

"You were right about the cereal, Paul."

"What's that?"

"The cereal. Being the best thing to eat right now. I could go for a big bowl of Raisin Bran and cold milk. I might even take that over the eggs and tortillas."

"Now you're coming around." Paul gets up and leans forward to stretch his back.

"You know," Paul begins, "it's funny. Two weeks ago when we talked about things we wanted or our aspirations, we would have talked about houses or boats or cars. Now that we've been on the road for a while, everything is reduced to a bowl of cereal." Paul develops a smile as he stands straight again. "Isn't that just beautiful? Cereal. There are people in this world who are killing themselves because they want more and more of nothing. And the only thing you and I want in this world is a bowl of cereal. That just shows you how the things we think are important really aren't important."

"And a boat," I say.

"What's that?" Paul asks.

"I wouldn't mind a boat," I tell him. "A nice, big sailing boat with a wooden hull. I'd like to eat my cereal on my boat."

Paul rolls his eyes and shakes his head at me.

● ● ●

PAUL HAS HIS BAG ROLLED UP AND IS FASTENING IT TO his pack. "We should get going. It's getting late."

I break my blank stare and realize that I am not packed. Paul looks eager to hit the trail. "How are we going to get the van?" I ask. "It's a long way back to the other trailhead, that's all I'm saying."

"We'll hitchhike," he says, still fidgeting with his backpack. "You ready?" he asks.

"I need to pack my stuff. I will be ready in a minute."

"I am going to go brush my teeth in the stream. Want to come?" Paul pulls his toothbrush from his pack and taps it against the back of his hand, getting the dirt off it.

"I think I am going to get some journaling done," I tell him. "Would you mind if I took some time to do that?"

"Are you going to write for a while?"

"I don't know. I want to get a few thoughts down before I forget them. It may take a while, but I can probably do it tonight, once we get back to the van and all."

"No, don't worry about it. If you want, I can start hiking and you can follow a little later."

"You mean on the trail? You want to go separately?"

"Whatever you want. If you want to write, I could get started." Paul shrugs his shoulders. "Whatever you want, Don."

"Yeah, I might as well do this now. I'll meet you at the top."

"Cool." Paul takes off with his toothbrush and I go over to my pack and pull out my pen and notebook. While rummaging around, I know the reason I want to wait here. It's because I don't want Paul looking back to check on me. The trail to the top is pure switchbacks, six or seven miles of stairs, essentially. I am pretty sore, pretty out of shape, and that is going to take me all day with these legs and these blistered feet. I'm kind of faking it about the journaling thing. I mean, I wouldn't mind writing some stuff down, but the truth is I just want him to go so I don't have to feel like I'm having to keep up with him.

"I will probably go ahead and get the van. Is that cool?" Paul asks as he walks back into camp.

"Sure. I shouldn't be far behind you."

"You're just going to stay here and write?"

"I can do this later, Paul. I figure you are going to want to hike faster anyway, though, so I thought this would be cool."

"Nothing's wrong?" he asks.

"Dude, no. No way." I get up from the table and go over by Paul. I feel uncomfortable, as it is obvious he thought I was shrugging him off.

"No," I say. "I just wanted to get some stuff written down. Besides, I'm not looking forward to being the slow poke up that hill, you know. You are going to be a mile in front of me before you reach the top anyway. I'm saving myself some face by sticking around."

"Cool," Paul says.

"It's cool," I confirm.

"It's cool, Don. But you haven't eaten or slept and this is the worst part of the hike. You are going to have a tough time. I'm just telling you."

"I hear you. I'm going to get out of this canyon. Stop trying to be my big brother. I'm older than you, remember?"

Paul loads his pack on his back and gives me a grin and a pat on the shoulder. He ambles down the trail with a jug of water sloshing, dangling off the center of his pack. I follow him with my eye as he disappears behind a rock and then appears again. He isn't wearing shoes. He doesn't have any shoes on!

"Paul!"

"Yeah!" he shouts.

"Your shoes?"

"My feet are bleeding. No shoes today."

"You aren't going to wear shoes?"

"No shoes. See you at the top," he says.

He turns and continues, hitting the first switchback in a brisk stride. He rises like a man on an escalator and turns in fluid motions to the up and the up of each switchback. In no less than a few minutes, he is a hundred or more feet in the air and he won't be slowing down for some time. Probably won't even stop for water. Paul is just about the most athletic guy I know. It's funny, you know, because with most guys I wouldn't feel comfortable telling them I was afraid of being too slow up the canyon, but Paul, even though he is an athlete and could have gotten some social points by putting me down, just didn't care. It's funny how the guys who are really good at something never make you feel like crap about not being good at whatever they are good at, you know. I sit back down at the table and pull out my journal. It's all blank. I hate journaling, to be honest. I put it right up there with talking to yourself. I told myself I would do some journaling on this trip, and I might as well start. I write some stuff about missing Kristin, about the sunset in Oklahoma, about fixing the van with some speaker wire, all stuff I doubt I would find very interesting twenty years from now. I start wondering what it is I will want to read about twenty years from now. I tap my pen against the page and think for a second.

I FIGURE YOU MIGHT FORGET WHAT KIND OF PERSON *you were back when you were on this trip. I want you to know you weren't a bad guy. But you fell into thinking a lot of money and a lot of stuff and a lot of social collateral would get you somewhere. And I don't know who you are now, and what you've done with your life, but try to remember, God doesn't expect you to accumulate a lot of stuff. You were really happy here in the canyon, you know, I promise it's true. I guess I just want you to remember there was a time when you did a pretty difficult hike, and you decided that you didn't need to carry a bunch of stuff on your back because the climb was hard. And I don't know who is around you, whether you met a woman or have some kids, but I really hope you have shown them this stuff, that life is going to be okay, that you just have to enjoy it. If you can't buy a nice car for your family or anything, don't worry about it. Just go into your kids' room and kiss them on the forehead, okay, 'cause there is all kinds of beauty and it doesn't have anything to do with having some stuff. Also, don't kick yourself around. If you can't climb up out of a canyon real quick, just do it slow. And also just remember that this guy Paul is one of the most incredible people in your life. There was a time when he showed you a lot of grace. I don't know what else to say. You're a pretty good person, you know. God made a whole beautiful earth and decided to put you in it, to experience all of this beauty. You can't do that watching television all the time. Nothing else. I have to go climb out of a hole. Maybe you do too. All the best. Feel like I'm talking to myself, for crying out loud.*

THERE IS AN EXHAUSTION THAT STRIKES DEEPER THAN muscle and flesh. It is a bone-deep exhaustion and is all new to me. The trail continues remarkably steep, but there is traffic on the footpath. Lively children walk briskly with their parents in tow. I sit down on a rock in a crag and look down over the canyon, marveling at the beauty of it all, and how far I have come.

I have taken more rest without Paul. It should have taken me about four hours to get this far, but I figure I have been climbing these steep switchbacks for about six. Paul would have trudged quickly. Without his quick step to keep me accountable, I struggle. My water is more than half gone. It sloshes in my stomach like a baggie of goldfish. I could throw it up if I wanted. I could tighten my stomach and throw up right here on the path. My whole head seems to be swaying and throbbing. My face must be blue or green. Women have pity in their expressions and men walk by quickly with eyes averted. Amazingly, I was passed a while back by a fellow I met years ago in Tennessee. I recognized him coming, but didn't have the breath to address him. He literally grazed my shoulder. I turned, but he was gone before I could process that it was him. He did not recognize me and I can't say I was eager to make contact.

Strapping my canteen to my pack, I shoulder my load and

step back onto the trail. My feet drag and slide. My footprints must be long but I am too tired to look and see. The traffic gets heavier with each switchback and the Disneyland atmosphere that surrounded me a couple days ago is coming back to mind. So many happy families on their vacations. Fathers and mothers and grandparents. The presence of older people tells me that I am nearing the rim. A group of elderly people come down the trail in leisurely strides. The women wear big hats and guard the sun from their eyes with cupped hands. The men grab at their women's elbows when I near, carefully protecting them from a dangerous fall.

I am utterly exhausted and ashamed at my inability to conquer this canyon with dignity. I am passed by nuns, who offer water. One tells me that I am almost there. I nod. Almost there. If only there were here. If only I could drag the rim to me, rather than me to the rim. I am not above crawling the last quarter mile.

Finally I see the trailhead. It is close. I stop and lean against the canyon wall to eye my heaven. The trail rises before me and beyond it is the sky. Thirty more steps will have me out of this hole. I make like somebody with some decorum and walk the last switchback with no drag in my step, the noblest action I can muster. And coming over the ridge I see the Grand Canyon Hotel big and brown across a lawn. And there is Paul. He has a grin across his face like a man whose wife has delivered a baby. He sits on the beam of a wooden fence and greets me. I walk the last few steps and shake his hand. My good friend Paul, I say to him, and I can see that he sees the relief in my eyes, and all the fear of the last two hours, wondering whether I would make it. I lean against the fence and look out over the Grand Canyon. A canyon I now know intimately and have hiked all the way to the river and back. Paul sets his hand on my shoulder and tells me that I've done it. That it wasn't easy, but I did it. None of that matters to me now. Perhaps it will tomorrow or the next day. I am only glad to be done with it.

"I got the van," Paul says.

I acknowledge him with a grunt and am glad to know we don't have to hitchhike back.

"Had time to stop at the store," he says.

"Is that right?" I whisper.

"Got you a little something while I was there."

I hadn't noticed that Paul was holding anything, but he sets it in my hands. I look down into the tin cup and eye the golden flakes. Paul reaches into a grocery sack and pulls out a small carton of milk. I hold the tin cup in disbelief and watch the milk flow around the flakes. The raisins lift and swirl. The flakes float to the top and he drops a spoon into the cup. Paul smiles at me and pats me on the back.

"This is your reward," he says.

My smile is so big that tourists notice. I think there may even be a little moisture in my eyes. I don't know if I have felt this much joy in ten years. Paul laughs as I take the first bite and suck on the spoon as I pull it out of my mouth. Paul takes a swig from the carton of milk and we look out over the canyon, the red walls and shadows and pines, the crags and caves, the switchbacks that descend all the way to the river.

14 MIRACLES

As far as I know, Hoover Dam was engineered by a guy who later made vacuum cleaners. He no doubt felt sorry for the people of Nevada. They live in so much brown. He surveyed the land and decided on a spot to dam the Colorado and give the people of Vegas a place to swim. Later, perhaps, he ran for president. Lake Mead is big and blue and holds up large party boats with striped canopies and barbeque grills that make the boats look like they are on fire when the smoke billows out from under the canopies and lifts gray signals into the desert sky.

I've been driving for a while. Neither of us tired, Paul has been telling me how it goes with a rattlesnake bite. We may do some more hiking, he says, and one of us could get bitten. It's a good thing to go over it. He tells me I have to take a razor blade and cut all around the bite, taking a good quarter inch of flesh in the operation. He says I shouldn't think about the pain, that I should just take the blade, stick it in deep, and carve it out like a small melon. If I do it quickly, apparently, it won't hurt as bad at first. And I am to remember I am saving my own life. Then, apparently, the cut has to bleed. It isn't always necessary to suck the blood out, he tells me. I can just let it bleed if I get a good, deep cut going. Most of the poison will bleed out, and while I will feel like I'm dying for a few hours, there is a good chance I will live through it.

All of this is comforting, I tell him. Because I would hate to die of a snakebite.

"Water moccasins are a completely different story," Paul says.

"What's that?" I ask.

"Water moccasins. They are completely different. You can't just cut and get the poison out. It's not that easy."

"I see," I tell him. "That should be important here in Nevada."

Paul goes on a bit about the variety of snakes in this region compared to the South and the Northwest. He says there are no water moccasins in Nevada because there is no water. Save Lake Mead, which is hardly swamplike. There are rattlers out here, however, he reminds me. We are bound to see one pretty soon, he says. I just drive and watch the road. He has his feet up against the glove box. Red tennis shoes with white stripes. Canvas Adidas. He has an elbow out the window and the warm, midday air blows his hair into a swirl, slapping against his forehead. He keeps wiping a hand across his face to soothe the itch, all the while talking about snakes.

The road we've chosen is bare. We are coming up from below Vegas. We chose this route because it looked scenic on the map. We thought we might camp out here and hike off into some valley. But so far, the terrain looks rugged and the only good cut through these hills and canyons is the road we're on. The hills are not tall, but steep, so I have to down-shift as low as second as we climb. Then back to fourth. Then second again. As we crest a hill, I push the stick out of second and find no resistance in the transmission. I slide over to fourth to drop it in, but the stick is loose. It doesn't go. The van whines in a high rev and races as I press the gas. I pull the stick hard to jam it into fourth, but it won't go. It feels like the transmission has dropped out.

"Paul."

"Yeah."

"We've got trouble."

"What is it?"

"No gears. No fourth gear."

"Try third."

"No third. No gears at all."

I spot a small pull-out at the bottom of the hill and navigate the van over the shoulder and down a small dirt inset that parallels the road. Coming to a stop, clouds of dust roll over from the back of the van and down the windshield before dissipating. Again, I try the gears. Nothing.

"Is it the clutch?" Paul reaches over and feels the stick.

"No. The clutch is fine. There wasn't any grind to it at all. I just lost it completely. It can't be the clutch. It's the tranny. Something broke."

"All right," Paul says, unsettled. He slaps his hand against the dash.

I kill the engine and open my door. Nevada is quiet as though it is hiding something. The wind whispers suspiciously. Stepping out of the van, I feel the ache in my knees and muscles. But I can pace it out in a few steps. Paul, without saying a word, gets out of the van and rounds to the driver's side. He presses the clutch and motions the stick to first, second, and all through the gears.

"There's too much play," he says.

"There are no train tracks out here," I announce.

Paul rests his weight and drops his limbs like he's frustrated. "This is crazy. Did you feel it going out?"

"Didn't feel anything. I went to downshift and it wasn't there."

"That's not possible, Don."

"That's what happened." I lean against the van with one hand and hold a thumb out for a ride. No cars are on this back road. We haven't seen one in about twenty minutes. Paul has a frustrated look, both arms laid across the curvature of the steering wheel. He's shaking his head at me now. Thinks I'm acting silly in a serious moment. I point my thumb up a little higher.

"I'm gonna get us out of this jam," I reassure him. "There's no reason to panic."

"I'm not panicking." Paul shakes his head. "And you're an idiot."

"Why am I an idiot?" I put my hand in my pocket and look my friend in the eye.

"Because you are," he says, shaking his head.

"I went to put the thing in gear and the gear wasn't there. That doesn't make me an idiot. It's your stupid van. Maybe you've been driving it like an idiot for the last year."

"You're pissing me off, Don," he says, looking over at me.

"You're breaking my heart, Paul," I tell him.

I step closer to the driver's window. He doesn't look at me. He keeps his eyes fixed as if there were some speck of dust on the windshield that had, in the smallest possible print, a word that, if spoken aloud, would solve all of his problems.

"Frustrated?" I don't look at him. Don't really expect him to answer.

"What do you think?" he says.

"Things could be worse."

"I don't want to hear it, Don."

"You know, Paul, when I was in the orphanage . . . did I tell you I was in an orphanage?"

Paul shakes his head. There is a beginning of a grin on his lips but he looks away and holds his frown and then looks back at the window.

"When I was in the orphanage," I start in again, "me and the girls used to sing this little song. Paul, I'd like to sing it to you. Maybe you'd like to sing it with me. You'd like that, wouldn't you?"

"I don't want to hurt you, Don. I really don't."

I sing very softly . . . "Tomorrow," I sing. "Tomorrow, I love ya, tomorrow, you're always a day away."

I stop singing because I have forgotten the words. Paul is looking at me without a smile. No frown, but no smile. He reaches over and pats my head. I grin like a dog.

WE'VE BEEN SITTING IN THE DESERT FOR NEARLY AN hour. We haven't seen a single car. I stand up to break the boredom, pick up a rock, and throw it out into the brown, toward a cactus. I kick a few rocks across the road, which stirs up some dust that blows across Paul's lap.

"Sorry," I say. He doesn't move, just wipes the dust out of his eyes, then lies down, looking up at the sky.

"You getting tired of me, Paul?" I ask. He doesn't say anything.

"I don't care," I tell him. "You can say it."

"Yes," he says. "I am getting tired of you."

"What are you tired of?"

"Everything's a joke. Some things aren't funny and I feel pressured to laugh so you won't feel bad. Do you know how annoying that is?"

"No."

"Trust me. It's annoying. And you're slow."

"Slow?" I ask.

"Slow, Don. You're fat and slow."

"Tell me how you really feel," I say, sitting back down, gathering some dirt in my hand, and letting it slip through my semiclosed fist.

"What about me?" Paul asks. "What are you sick of?"

I sit there and think about it for a minute. "Nothing," I respond. "You don't annoy me at all, Paul. I want to be just like you." He just looks at me like he knows I am lying.

"You're a jerk," he says softly. "You're never serious for a minute."

"You're a walk in the park," I tell him.

FOR A CHANGE OF SCENERY, I CROSS THE STREET, SET my foot on the bumper of the van, and climb up the windshield, to the top of the van, being careful not to break the wipers with my boot. From the top I can see a bit farther. There is nobody out here.

"Don!" Paul yells. He's looking up at me.

"Yeah."

"I'm seriously discouraged."

I look down at Paul. He raises his legs and folds his arms around his knees.

"I don't know what to say, Paul. I can't think of a way out of this mess. We may be here for a while."

"Yeah."

"A car will come," I tell him.

"It's been an hour."

"Did you ever see that movie *Trapper John, MD?*"

"What?"

"That movie on television: *Trapper John, MD.*"

Paul looks up with his hands cupped over his eyes. "It wasn't a movie. It was a television series."

"But you saw it, right?"

"A few times." There is a long silence. "Why do you want to know whether I saw that television show?"

"I feel like Trapper John, MD."

Paul shakes his head. "Why? Why do you feel like Trapper John and why does it matter?"

"He had an RV and he used to go out in the parking lot and sit on top of his RV and bake in the sun."

"Yeah. So what?"

"I feel like that. Up on the van and all. Makes me feel like Trapper John."

"That's great. But for your information, it wasn't Trapper John who had the motor home. It was the other guy. The guy with the curly hair. The younger guy."

"I thought it was Trapper John."

"Nope."

"Are you sure?"

"Yep." Paul sighs. "What does this have to do with anything, Don?"

I look down at my miserable friend. For a second, I think I'm the crazy one. There is no reason for me to be fooling around. We have no water, so we need a ride. And there have been no cars for the better part of an hour, like Paul said. The sun is in midsky, so we've got a half day of sunlight to get us more and more thirsty. And how do we fix this thing? We don't have money for a transmission and there's no telling what is eaten up under the van. It is basically useless. We will probably have to hitch the rest of the way. Neither of us is going to call home for help. I know that without asking.

Paul looks up and meets my eye. "Do you want to pray?"

"Whatever," I tell him, not really wanting to pray.

Paul lowers his head like a little kid in Sunday school and rests his chin on his knee. He closes his eyes and speaks fairly loudly. His words are soft and low: "God, we are stuck in the desert and the van doesn't work. We don't know what to do. We don't know whether to leave it or what to do. I guess we need a ride or something." I'm looking out over the hills, watching some heat rise off the dunes in the distance. "We need a mechanic, God. That's what we need. If You could send us someone to get us on our way, to help us with this transmission, that would be great." Paul stops praying. He stands up and starts walking out into the desert.

"Paul." He hears me but he does not turn.

"Paul!"

He turns toward me with a frustrated look. "Yeah?"

"Look." I point over the horizon. He can't see it yet, but there is a car coming.

"Is it a car?"

"Yes."

He walks quickly to the other side of the road and stands gazing. He's half in the road.

"Be careful," I tell him. He steps back onto the shoulder.

Over the hill comes a station wagon. Brown in color, it matches the landscape. The wagon slows a little as it nears, but speeds up again as the driver realizes we are not a wreck or anything worth looking at. He drives by at about thirty or forty miles per hour and hardly looks our way. There's a man at the wheel, and a woman in the passenger's seat with a few kids in the back. As he passes, the children turn to look at us through the back window. His brake lights flash and then come on solid.

"He's stopping," Paul says.

I slide down the windshield and catch the bumper with my boot. The reverse lights on the wagon come on and the man backs up onto the shoulder. Dust kicks out on either side as the station wagon weaves backward. It's a brown wagon with brown wood-panel trim. A real gas-guzzler from the early eighties.

He is a bearded man with a red baseball cap. His beard is untrimmed and his wife looks troubled that he decided to stop. The children are quiet in the backseat. One looks over at me without any expression, then turns back to face forward. The other two do not look. They do not even look at Paul, who has begun a conversation with the man. Paul steps away from the door as the man reaches through the open window to pull the outside handle. A closer look at the car reveals it to be quite the jalopy. A rope fastens the hood to the bumper and another of the same sort fastens a suitcase to the roof.

The man steps out of his car and pulls up his sagging pants. Running his hand across the front of his shirt, he tucks it in. He has a tattoo on his forearm of a woman without clothes. She probably had a good figure at one time, but she looks faded, oblong, and tired of being attached to him. The man is talking to Paul about the van. He's asking what Paul thinks is wrong with it. Paul tells him it's the transmission and the bearded man just shakes his head and looks out in the desert and shakes his head again.

"Sounds really bad," he says. "Well, you boys are in luck. Probably haven't seen many cars out here, have you?"

Paul confirms that we haven't.

"Not many people get out this way. You could have been here for hours if it weren't for me stopping to help. Not a lot of people would have stopped, you know."

"Thanks," Paul says.

"Don't mention it." The man removes his cap and runs his hand across his thick hair and puts his cap back on. "I'm a mechanic," he says.

"You are? I mean, huh, is that right?" Paul leans against the van and looks away.

"Can you help us?" I ask, trying to get the man to get to the point and ask for money, which is probably the only reason he stopped in the first place.

"Well, I've got business in Arizona, and it really does set me back to stop here. I've got an appointment and all, you know."

"I see," I say. "Well, you better get going, then. We wouldn't want you to miss your appointment." Paul looks over at me with a cold look, telling me with his eyes to keep quiet.

"Well, now, wouldn't want to leave you boys stranded. Like I said, there's nobody going to stop for you out here. You were lucky I stopped. Certainly didn't have to."

"Like I said before, we don't want to keep you. We'll figure something out. You can go on."

"I can take a look at it real quick, if you want. I normally don't do this for free, but I can help you out, I guess." The bearded man stands there with his hands in his pockets and rocks back and forth on his heels.

Paul looks at me as if to question whether we offer him money. *If we do,* I think to myself, *we will really be running short of cash. Simply can't do it.* I don't even think the thing can be fixed anyway. The last thing I want to do is give the man twenty dollars to tell us there is nothing he can do and then tell us he can't give us a ride because his wagon is full. So I tell him we don't have any money. I clarify and tell him we can't spare any money and then I ask him if he is still willing to look at it. Feeling guilty, he kneels down, lies on his back, and slides under the van. I shake my head and Paul gives me a little punch. We both get down on our backs and slide under the van with the man. Plenty of room under this piece of garbage, that's for sure.

The mechanic asks again about the problem and Paul says it won't go into gear. "Not even first gear?" the man questions. And Paul says we have no gears at all. "Happened all of a sudden," the man mutters and Paul confirms that is the way it happened. The bearded man runs his finger up along the underside of the tranny, looks down the long side of the underneath, and squints his eyes to see to the front. He moans a moan, which means he sees something, and then slides his short frame a few feet toward the front, about three or four feet from the transmission itself. He slides his fingers along a rod that runs the length of the van. He pinches the rod and pulls it up and back. It slides easily. He has found the problem. It isn't the transmission, he tells us. It's the shifter rod. There's a little plastic or aluminum piece that fits right here and it's gone.

"See here. These two rods snap together right here and that piece fell off. It has four teeth. Two on each side. Two fasten toward the front and two toward the back. You are getting all the play in the stick because it's not connected to the tranny. This is definitely your problem."

"Can it be fixed?" Paul asks.

"Yes."

"We need the part?" Paul asks.

"Yes."

"Where can we get the part?"

"Junkyard. That's the only place."

"There's no junkyard anywhere near here, is there?"

"No." The mechanic continues to study the problem. "Do you have a clothes hanger?" he asks.

Without answering, I slide out from under the van and

open the big door. I begin to sort through some of Paul's stuff when he surfaces and tells me he doesn't have a clothes hanger so don't bother looking. A voice from under the van tells us to ask his wife, so Paul goes over and asks her. She gets out of the wagon and opens the back to remove a clothes hanger from a stack of clothes that rests on an ice chest with "Miller High Life" printed on the side. Without so much as looking at Paul or saying anything, she hands him the clothes hanger and closes the back of the wagon. She returns to her seat.

Our mechanic unwinds the clothes hanger and threads it through the fittings on both rods. He pulls it tight and then threads it through again. I am watching him on bended knee with my head ducked low. He looks over and tells me to pull the stick down into second gear and leave it there. I do as he says, and he shouts from below to pull it harder. I press down hard and hold it with my other hand. I can feel him jerking against the stick, trying to pull it out of gear. Hold it, he shouts. I pull it back even harder. As he threads the wire through the fittings, the stick jerks up and back a few inches. Finally the motion subsides and he slides out from under the van. I let go of the stick.

"You will have to keep it in second gear," he says. "That will allow you to get going, but you will have to drive to Vegas pretty slow."

"Better than nothing," I say.

Paul shakes the man's hand and thanks him. He straightens his cap and tells him it was nothing. I thank him, too, and he tips his head at me.

"You boys have a good day," he says, wiping his hands against each other.

"Thanks," Paul tells him.

"Thanks," I tell him, reaching to shake his hand.

"It was nothing. Just keep it in second and you should be fine. Not too, too far, but you probably want to get moving." The man nods at us and gets back into his car, starting it and pulling it back onto the road.

We watch him disappear and then Paul gets in the driver's side. I round the van quietly and take my seat. Paul pulls us onto the road, being careful not to push the lever out of gear. After a few miles he tells me he is sorry for calling me fat and slow. Whatever, I tell him, putting my hand outside the window to catch some of the slow-moving air.

15 VEGAS

NEVADA HAS NO OCEAN. YOU COME OVER DUNE AND dune and no water washes up on no shore. Las Vegas is an island of lights and trickery, and the desert laps against it on four sides. Trucks are ships, barges coming in from foreign continents, a subtle, odd reminder that some other kind of life exists, some sort of normality. Desert winds wash tourists up on casino shores to gawk at the natives, entertainers, gambling addicts, magicians and scantily dressed women, showmen who can't sell albums anymore, vague memories of Elvis and Neil Diamond. It is an oasis for hard-luck cases who spend small fortunes on a shortcut to the American dream. P. T. Barnum, eat your heart out. This is a circus too heavy to travel. The show doesn't come to the people; the people come to the show.

We have come one hundred miles at thirty-five miles per hour. And on the outskirts of town we find a junkyard. I step to the counter and ask the man if he has a Volkswagen van. He tells me he has two but they have been gutted. There's nothing on them. But then he tells me it's a dollar to go in the yard and see for myself. I look at Paul and he pulls a dollar from his wallet. We walk with heavy heads down a ramp on the backside of the trailer that fronts as an office. We look out on a sea of cars on concrete blocks and wheel rims. Before us are the Toyotas and Nissans, all sorts of disasters and tragedies kept for their parts: alternators, bumpers, rotors, leather seats, rearview mirrors, stereo knobs, hubcaps. A man who works at the place points us toward the Volkswagen section, so we wander in and out of

Buicks and Fords and Chevys to the European imports where we find a line of Volkswagen Beetles, both new and old. Behind the first line of Beetles are two vans. They are ghosts of what they used to be and Paul and I just stand there looking at them in disbelief. They are nothing but shells. The evening sun shines through them. Nothing there, no doors, no wheels, no seats, no engines or wires for the electrical. They sit like metal boxes atop cinder blocks.

"Unbelievable," Paul says, looking back toward the Beetles, wondering, perhaps, if there are any more vans than these.

"Not much there," I say.

"Nothing," he confirms. Paul stands silent and puts his hands in his pockets. He turns to go.

"Where are we going to go?" I ask.

"Another junkyard. Maybe a Volkswagen dealership," he says without stopping.

"We could take a look," I tell him.

Paul is weaving back through the Jettas and Passats. He turns to look at me. "What for? There's nothing there. Let's go." He stops for a second. "You want to look. I don't want to look," he says. He walks back over to pacify me.

"I don't want to look. I just want to stand here and live in this sliver of hope," I tell him.

"I'll look," he says, and walks over to the first van stooping to his knees. He lays himself on his back and slides under the van. I go to the other van and do the same. Underneath, the van is gray and empty. There are no brake lines, no muffler, no gas lines, no nothing. Just the bottom of a box. I could set my fists against the bottom and bench-press the thing off its cinder blocks, it seems so light. But then I see the shifter linkage, and a sense of hope stirs: a butterfly circus in my stomach. I follow the linkage with my hand and eye the connector. "Paul!" I shout. He doesn't answer. I turn over with a giant grin. "Bud, you won't believe this." Paul is lying beneath the other van with both his hands clasped and resting on his belly. He's wearing a smile like mine. "Paul!" He doesn't answer. He just lies there looking up at his own shifter linkage. Then he laughs. "No way," I say. "You've got one too."

"It's here," he says. And so we lie there on our backs for several minutes, just admiring the little piece of plastic, about two ounces worth, that holds the entire van together. After a while Paul starts pulling on his, wondering how to get it off. I go back to the office and borrow a screwdriver and a pair of pliers and we manage to disassemble the linkage off of the van Paul was under. We pull the thing out and have a seat on the floor of one of the vans and tinker with it until we can get it off.

"We need this too," Paul tells me, handing me a small clip.

When we go back through the trailer, the man at the desk takes a look at our part and shrugs his shoulders. He motions to us to go without paying. Paul and I spend another frustrating hour under our van, unwinding the coat hanger, then cussing at the clip and the plastic part that doesn't seem to fit until it slides, in one gentle motion, into its fitting, for no other reason than it is tired of hearing us complain.

16 CALIFORNIA

STILL IN THE PARKING LOT AT THE JUNKYARD, PAUL looks around the place and asks me if I am getting hungry. I tell him I am. He says we've got beans and rice and we could warm the pot and eat that. I fake like that would be an okay idea. He says it doesn't sound all that good to him, but we could do it.

"Doesn't sound that good to me, either," I confess.

"Any ideas?" he says, lifting his eyebrows.

"How much money do we have?" I say, knowing we haven't spent hardly anything in the last few days.

"Not enough to justify anything lavish."

"Maybe we could go to a grocery store. We could make sandwiches or something," I say.

"We really don't have enough money for that," he says, pulling out his wallet.

I go over and get my sock out of my small box of stuff. "For sandwiches?" I question, pushing my hand into the sock and pulling out a wad of ones and fives.

"We can only spend about five dollars per day," Paul reminds me.

"Five dollars each?" I ask, hoping he will forget.

"No," he says. "Five dollars between us."

I recommend that we hit a grocery store anyway. Some stores have day-old bread and maybe we can stir up enough for some meat or lettuce or anything that isn't beans and rice. He agrees and we get back into the van and start driving through the suburbs of Vegas. The sun is setting now and the color over the mountains is surprisingly beautiful. All the dust in the air, perhaps from the city itself or maybe from trucks coming over the pass or dry fires out in the mountains, is sharpening the sunlight and dividing it into bright orange rays pointing straight at the city and white light coming off the top of the range like some kind of suspended atomic explosion. Winding through the streets of Vegas, we start thinking again about food. Paul starts talking again about the perfect meal. He has changed from Raisin Bran to pancakes and sausage, and even though it is evening, pancakes and sausage sound perfect. A meal like that would hit the spot, I tell him. Paul spots a grocery store and steers the van into the parking lot. Five dollars, he says. All we can spend is five dollars. I confirm that I agree, but I think to myself that I am not past shoplifting.

We walk into the store and are embraced by a gentle, air-conditioned breeze. It's cold in here, Paul says. The aisles, one after another, seem to be filled with old people squeezing melons. I can't believe all the food, all the options. Chips and salsa, bean dip, candy bars, whole chickens, cooked and glazed with salt and butter, macaroni and cheese, a whole deli with huge vats of potato salad and teriyaki chicken, a deep-fried section with burritos and corn dogs right next to an entire aisle of beer. The only real food I've eaten in two weeks was a small cup of cereal and four bowls of the same cereal about an hour after the cup. The only thing Paul has eaten is a cup of cereal.

I grab a shopping cart and lean my weight over the handrail. I push it along like a kid. As we go through the chips and salsa aisle, I toss two bags of Doritos in the cart. Paul looks at me and shakes his head. I grab a set of Tupperware dishes from the housewares aisle and also one of those little dishwashing tools with the spongy head. When we get to the bread, Paul begins comparing prices. I run my arm along the shelf and dump eight loaves into the cart. Paul laughs and shakes his head again. He picks out a loaf of bread and heads toward the back of the store where they keep the meat. Along the way, I stock up on toilet paper and the current issue of *People* magazine. I also grab three cans of Alpo dog food, as they are running a special. As I round the back of the aisle, Paul is standing in front of the meat.

"Lunch meat is too expensive," he says.

"How much?"

"Too much. We can get a jar of peanut butter for the same price. Peanut butter will last a whole loaf of bread and meat will only get us about two sandwiches."

"Well, let's get peanut butter then," I say, taking two boxes of buy-one-get-one-free cereal from an end cap.

"All right." Paul turns his back to the meat and wanders lazily, with a defeated posture, along the back of the store. He grabs a turkey roasting pan and places it in my cart. I grab two cans of Spam and a no-stick frying pan. Paul doesn't notice the end cap of bleach as he turns down the peanut butter aisle. I mumble under my breath something about what a great deal that is. I grab three gallons and set them in the child's seat so they don't squash the eight loaves of bread.

Paul starts reading the label on the peanut butter. He places it back on the shelf and grabs a cheaper brand. The one with the bland label. He asks me if I want chunky or smooth and I ask him if they make a brand with chunks of steak. "They stopped making that years ago," he says. "You want chunky or smooth?" he asks again.

"Chunky," I say. "What about jelly?"

Paul turns and walks down a few feet to the jelly and looks for something cheap. "This stuff is expensive. The peanut butter was three dollars and it's another three for the jelly. With the bread, we are over budget by two dollars." He puts the jelly back.

"We can't have peanut butter without jelly," I tell him.

"We can't afford it," he says, shrugging his shoulders.

"Two dollars?" I question.

"What happens when we run out of gas?"

"The dude gave us the Volkswagen part for free," I remind him.

"The part was never in the budget in the first place," he reminds me. "We should only be spending four dollars because we spent a dollar at the junkyard."

"What about this turkey roasting pan?" I say. "We can't afford that either. Put the jelly in your pocket, Paul."

"You want to steal it?" he asks.

"Yes. I want to steal it."

"Okay," he says.

"Okay," I say.

"Okay," he says, and puts the jelly back on the shelf.

"Hey, I've never gotten a look at this budget you keep talking about."

Paul points his finger at his head. He says it's all in his mind and it's very clear.

"I see," I tell him. "I've got a budget, too, you know."

Paul looks down at my cart. "I see your budget."

"I'll put the dog food back," I tell him.

"What about the frying pan?"

"It's a keeper." I place my arms over the contents of the basket so he can't take anything out.

"Well, we can't afford peanut butter and jelly. Something has to go. Will it be the peanut butter or the jelly?"

"We can't refrigerate the jelly, so let's keep the peanut butter."

"My thought exactly," he says.

Paul heads toward the checkout counter with just a loaf of bread and a jar of peanut butter.

"Wait!" I tell him.

"What?"

"We can't just eat bread with peanut butter." I am looking pretty miserable.

"We'll warm up the beans and rice," he says. "We'll have peanut butter and beans and rice." He begins walking toward the checkout again. I follow him with my cart, adding a jar of jelly to my cart along with a can opener and a potato chip clip that looks like a giant clothespin.

"How much money is the bread and peanut butter going to cost us?" I ask.

Paul is searching for the shortest line. "The bread is one dollar and the peanut butter is three bucks."

"That leaves us one dollar."

"Yeah."

"What can we get with that?" I ask.

"We can save it for tomorrow. We will have six tomorrow. Just think, if we do this every day, we may be able to afford a watermelon or something big."

Paul finds a short line at the nine-items-or-less counter. I stand behind him with my cart. He looks it over again and asks how I'm going to pay for all of it. I tell him I have a coupon. The lady checking out customers tells me that this is a "nine-items" or "twenty-dollar" counter. Paul tells her that I have a coupon. She says unless it's less than twenty dollars, I need to go to another line.

"Sorry, bud," Paul says.

I ask the lady if I can get any nine items in the store for twenty dollars. She looks confused. I clarify: "Ma'am, this sign says nine items or less or twenty dollars or less, cash. Does this mean that I can choose any nine items and only pay twenty dollars for the whole batch?"

"That would be a good deal," Paul says to the lady. She looks at both of us confused. She explains the details of the rules and clarifies that the items have to add up to less than twenty dollars or there have to be less than nine total items.

"That is so confusing," Paul says.

"It is confusing," I say. And the lady just stands there in disbelief.

"You can understand my confusion," I tell her.

"Not really," she says, shaking her head.

I head off with my cart in tow behind me and disappear behind an aisle, reappearing without my cart, stopping at an end cap for a bottle of ketchup.

"You put all those groceries away that quickly?" Paul questions and the lady looks at me frustrated.

"They are in a better place now," I tell Paul.

"What are you talking about?" the lady says.

"It's taken care of," I clarify, giving her a wink.

"What's this?" He's looking at my bottle of ketchup.

"Ketchup."

"What for?"

"The beans."

"Beans."

"Yes. Your beans suck, and I need something to help me get them down."

"What did you do with that cart full of stuff?" the lady asks.

"We have several bottles of Tabasco, Don," Paul tells me. "We don't need any ketchup."

I give Paul a desperate look. "Give me this," I say.

"Where is the cart of stuff?" the lady asks again. I set the ketchup on the belt and tell her we just want the bread and ketchup and peanut butter. I tell her she has nice eyes, and she shakes her head and slides the ketchup over the scanner, picking up the phone to request a manager. She hangs up the phone and Paul wonders out loud what sort of shampoo she uses.

• • •

PAUL OPENS THE SLIDING DOOR AND PULLS THE POT of beans from under the sink. He sets the bread down on the floor and takes a spoon and stirs the thick gravy so it breaks off into chunks and then becomes slightly fluid. I look down into the pot and think to myself about pancakes and biscuits and gravy. I take a slice of bread and spread peanut butter over the top with my Swiss Army knife. One piece, folded over and thick with peanut butter, is enough to cover the roof of my mouth and the back of my teeth. Paul does the same, leaving the rice and beans to sit and age. We have two peanut butter tacos and then Paul gets the idea to add ketchup to his third sandwich. I watch him, not in disbelief, but in wonder. He takes a bite and rolls it around in his mouth. He lifts his eyebrows and nods, handing me the bottle of ketchup. I spread peanut butter over another slice of bread and then squeeze a dab of ketchup along the crease. I fold the bread over and ketchup bleeds through the side and out the top. It's not all bad, I say. Paul nods his head and tries to swallow.

• • •

I FORCE PAUL TO STOP AT A CASINO, AS I HAVE NEVER seen one from the inside. He reluctantly pulls over at the last one on the edge of town. Inside, we find scores of old people sitting around green felt tables and tossing chips into different squares, throwing dice, and laying down cards. Sexy girls walk by, asking us if we want to order drinks, and we keep motioning to them that we don't. Paul follows me around as I wind in and out of tables, wondering out loud how to play each game. At the back of the casino we find Al Capone's car, shot up with bullet holes. Paul and I walk around the thing, trying to lean over the rope to see inside. I picture the fat mobster seated in the back, bullets flying through the door and window, right into his body. I wonder out loud what it would feel like to get shot.

After an hour or so, we both get bored. It wouldn't bother me to have stayed in Vegas, to see a show or something, maybe just walk the strip, but Paul hates anything you have to plug in, and Vegas is an entire city that doesn't exist when the grid goes down.

Leaving Las Vegas for California has you on a long, straight stretch of highway that climbs straight up into the mountains. Paul has the pedal flat against the floorboard but the van doesn't have the muscle to keep up. Trucks are grinding slowly around us. Everyone has their engines racing and we can smell brakes from cars and trucks heading down the opposite lanes. I turn around to see the lights of the city growing distant.

After an hour or so, we pass a road sign that announces California eleven miles ahead. I never realized how big those signs are. The sign must be half the size of a billboard and the letters are made of hand-sized reflective pieces of plastic.

Having passed so many miles through the desert, the road seems to exhale as it hands us to the western edge. There is an official border post in California. Like no other state, California stops cars and pays frumpy men to peer through windows and make sure we aren't smuggling fruit in from Nevada. The crossing is wide, allowing three cars through three booths. Light traffic has us one car back and the guard is asking questions to the woman in the car before us. We are on a mountain pass, and the van is heaving heated pistons and ticking. We climbed five steep miles to the border and the van had a rough go of it. The car in front of us pulls ahead and the border guard motions us forward. Paul pulls the van to the lowered railing and the uniformed man leans into the driver's window. He speaks as he looks around and he asks if we are carrying any fruit or vegetables. Paul tells him that we aren't. He asks our reasons for coming to California and Paul tells him we are traveling around the country. The man nods and tells us to enjoy our time on the West Coast. He hits a button and raises the gate and we pass into the golden hills of California, now covered in darkness.

Inside the van, warm night air riffles the pages of a book on the back bench. The pages are open and are folding into each other and slapping around, ruining the binding. I step back to close the book and set some weight on it, when I first catch the scent of gasoline. Gasoline like a gas station, really strong. I close the book, set a blanket over it, and return to the passenger's seat. Looking over at Paul, he has his hand on his mouth and a finger resting along the bottom of his nose. It occurs to me that he had already noticed the smell of gas. He looks over but doesn't say anything. I place my hand outside the window and cup the air, guiding it in through the window. While an engine light is a problem you can ignore, the smell of gas is not. We could explode or something.

"You think that's us?" I ask.

"What?"

"The smell. Smells like gas."

"I smell it," he says.

"So you noticed it."

"Yeah, a ways back," Paul says.

"Do you think it's coming from the van?" I ask.

"Yes."

"You do?"

"Yes."

"How do you know?" I ask.

"Because we've been losing gas on the gas gauge."

"I see," I say.

Why Paul would drive for several miles knowing the van smells like gas, I have no idea. I wonder if he realizes there are two of us on this trip. I just sit quietly and wait for the van to explode into flames.

Paul eyes a gas station and steers down the off-ramp, stops at a stop sign, and crosses the street to the station. He pulls alongside the pump and kills the engine. Through the dusty windshield, I squint and see a line of liquid that trails all the way down the off-ramp and makes a small puddle at the stop sign and wraps around to the back of the van. We are literally dripping a stream of gasoline. Unbelievable. I point it out to Paul and he just shakes his head.

We get out and Paul opens the engine compartment. The van is hot and ticking. The back of the van smells like grease and gas and if anyone within ten feet were to light a match, we would surely explode, sending a line of fire all the way back to the border, which honestly makes me want to do it, just to see a stream of fire ignite all the way back to Nevada.

"We might as well pull it off to the side and try to fix it before we put any gas in it," Paul says.

"Yeah," I agree, still looking back at the stream of gas.

Paul starts the van with a cringe on his face. He's worried about igniting all that gas. He quickly throws it into first and crosses the street to park alongside a roadside restaurant. Paul goes around back and opens the engine compartment and I open the sliding door and grab the toolbox. Paul uncovers both carbs and sets the lids on the ground with the appropriate nuts stored in the bowl of the lids. I tinker around with some wire, stretching and pulling levers, looking for a place where gas could be leaking. Paul lies down on his back and slides underneath. He runs his fingers along the bottom, searching for some broken line.

"It's dark under here. Can't see anything," he says.

"Pretty dark up here too," I say.

Paul keeps running his finger along the bottom of the engine.

"I smell it but I can't see it," he says.

"We may have to wait until morning."

"Sleep here?" he questions.

"Any other ideas?"

"No."

Paul stands up and stretches his back. He takes a look around the place, at the mountains in the distance and the last glow of the moon. Trucks buzz by and the place has a lonely ear to it. I picture in my mind the stream of gas going up in a flame, flowing up the on-ramp, cars slamming on their brakes or driving off the highway and down the hill, tumbling over each other, crashing and rolling, toppling over into the gas station.

17 MILK SHAKES AND PIE

TRYING TO SLEEP, BOTH OF US ARE RESTLESS. IF WE weren't leaking gas, we'd be driving. I think I have learned to sleep inside the shake and rattle of the van, but sleeping in a parking lot, not knowing exactly when we will be able to leave, has both of us staring at the ceiling.

Paul has his hands under his head. He's thinking about the gas leak, wondering where the problem is. He turns on his side and faces the opposite window, then he shifts back over, sets his hands under his head, and stares at the ceiling again.

"What are you thinking about?" I ask, already knowing the answer.

"Nothing much. Just the van."

"You getting pretty frustrated with it?"

"Getting frustrated?" he questions.

Paul pulls his blanket off of him and sets his feet on the back of the driver's seat. He takes his feet down and rolls over to his side, sits halfway up, and rests some of his weight on his elbow.

"I can't figure out why the carburetor would start leaking gas for no reason. It doesn't make sense," he says.

"Something probably rattled loose. We just need to find it and fix it. I'm sure it will be obvious to us in the morning."

"Hopefully you are right."

Paul's face catches the passing glow of a headlight that sweeps through the van. The light is accompanied by the low growl of a motorcycle. Without looking I can tell that it is a Harley. I stretch my neck to peer out the window and sure enough, a Harley has pulled up to the front door of the restaurant. A large man dressed in black dismounts and stretches. He releases a yawn, bends over to stretch his back, then leisurely walks into the café.

"You sleepy?" I ask.

"Nope."

"You want to get some coffee or something? Maybe decaf so it won't keep us up all night."

"Well, I've got some change in the ashtray. We could use that."

"I'm perfectly willing to dip into my sock of money for this one," I proclaim.

"Sounds good," he says, getting up and sliding off the bed.

A cowbell mounted atop the swinging glass door sounds as we enter the restaurant. Decked out in pink, the place was obviously decorated by a woman. Pink walls and pink curtains. There is a long bar with swivel padded-top stools and a step up to sit on them.

Paul and I stroll up to the bar and rest our elbows on the counter. An older lady with an apron comes over with a pad and pencil in her hand. She sets the pad and pencil down and hands us menus. She doesn't say anything, just smiles. Her nails are painted deep brown and she wears a large wedding ring. Her hair is blonde but should probably be gray, judging from the lines on her face. Her look is somewhere between Vegas and California. She's probably one of the ones who heads into town on weekends and gambles away her tips.

She rounds the counter and heads over to the man who came in on the Harley. He mumbles his order and she scratches it on her pad.

Paul searches through the menu for the coffee prices, but his eye comes to rest on the milk shake column. He can't get away from it. He sets the menu down and pulls a handful of change from his pocket. Counting it aloud, and shifting the coins from one pile to another, he finds two dollars with twenty-seven cents to spare.

"You're not getting coffee, are you?" I say. "You're getting a milk shake, aren't you?"

"Maybe," he says.

"You wouldn't let me have jelly and you're getting a milk shake."

Paul rotates a little metal holder on the bar and pulls several little containers of jelly out of the center compartment. He sets them on the counter and slides them my way.

"Jelly," he says.

I give him a smile of approval and place two of the containers in my shirt pocket.

"Let's get milk shakes, Don. We deserve it."

"I want coffee."

"You sure?"

"Yeah. I've got a hankering for coffee. I'll be fine with just coffee."

"Do as you wish."

The waitress comes back over and asks for our order.

"What's your special today, ma'am?" I ask.

"Ma'am?" she questions.

"Yes, ma'am. Ma'am."

"Well, if you are going to be such a gentleman, I figure I can knock fifty cents off the chicken fried steak." She says this with an endearing grin, which stays as she waits for our response.

"Now, do you make that chicken yourself, or some fellow in the back makes it?"

"A fellow in the back," she says matter-of-factly.

"Well, then I'm just not interested. I'd like to eat some of your food. You look like somebody who can cook."

"Well, I don't do the cooking here, honey."

"You don't cook anything at all?"

"I cook, but not here."

"I see." I ponder a bit. "Do you make the coffee?"

"I sure do."

"Well, then I'll just take a cup of coffee. That will be fine."

"I'll make you a fresh pot. How's that?"

"Perfect. Decaf if I could."

"I suppose." The lady looks over at Paul.

"Chocolate milk shake. Are you okay with that?"

"I'll take my chances," she says and laughs.

"Thank you, boys." She takes the menus and sets them in a slot between the countertop and the cash register. She speaks clearly through an opening in the back counter where the dishes are stacked. "Chocolate milk shake, Bob." Bob, a black-haired man with a white cooking apron, nods to confirm the order. The waitress clips the other fellow's order to a spinning contraption and turns it so the cook can see it. He wipes his hands on his apron and grabs the order, squinting and holding it away at arm's length.

"Where you boys from?" our waitress asks.

"Texas," I answer.

"Texas? What are you doing way out here?"

"We want to be in movies," I say.

The waitress laughs and leans over the counter, resting her elbows on the bar and holding her head in her hands.

"You tired?" Paul asks.

"Been here all day," she says.

"Long day. Must be tough," Paul says.

"It's not all that bad. I'm used to it. Been doing this for fifteen years."

"You've been here for fifteen years?" I question.

"Fifteen years," she confirms.

"That's a long time to work in one place."

She stands up and rests her weight against the counter. She smiles and says that we are certainly young. Used to be people would get a job and wouldn't leave. Today's kids, she says, can never stay in one place. We're always looking to get ahead and move up. Paul nods in agreement and the waitress turns around to start the coffee brewing. As she works, Paul eyes the pies in the pie case that separates the back side of the bar from the shelves where the dishes are stacked. He nudges at my elbow and points to the pies. He licks his lips. I look over to see a lemon meringue with a slice cut out and a pecan pie too. The pecan looks rich and brown. I can taste the pie on my tongue, and the thick, cool texture of the filling, and the light, fluffy brown of the crust. It's enough to make me want to jump through the glass.

The waitress turns around to see us staring at the pies.

"They look good, don't they?"

"Yes, ma'am, they do," I say.

Bob, in the back, tells her that her order is up and she turns to lower a bowl of soup and corn bread onto her tray. She rounds the bar and sets the bowl on the motorcyclist's table. Bob takes a metal cup and holds it upside down over a large glass mug. Paul's chocolate milk shake comes out thick and slides down into the mug. The waitress comes over and sets both the shake and the metal container on the counter in front of Paul. He kindly hands me the metal container and drops a spoon into it with a clink. There's a good inch of milkshake at the bottom and I gather it into the spoon and tip it upside down over my mouth. In one gulp, the milkshake is gone.

"That's good stuff," I say.

"Best milk shakes this side of the Mississippi," the waitress tells us.

"Best milk shakes anywhere!" Bob corrects her from behind the dishes.

The waitress lifts her eyebrows and shakes her head. "Bob owns the place. He's a bit partial. But the milk shakes are good. He knows how to make them."

"Sure does," Paul says, sucking the thick shake through a straw.

The waitress turns my cup over and pours my coffee.

"What's your name?" I ask.

"Betty," she answers with a smile.

"Nice to meet you, Betty. I'm Don."

Paul lifts his head and wipes his mouth with his sleeve. "I'm Paul," he says, smiling and shaking her hand.

"So you want to be in pictures, huh?" she says to us.

"Yes, ma'am. Come out here so they could put my mug on the silver screen. Just like James Dean."

Betty's eyes tell me she liked James Dean. "He was something else. You've got dimples; you just might make it."

Paul lifts his head up from his milk shake. "Don't feed his ego, Betty. I've got to travel with him."

"You hear that, Paul. James Dean. She thinks I look like James Dean."

"You look like my big toe, and you look nothing like James Dean."

Betty smiles and shakes her head. She turns and opens the pie case. She lifts a slice of lemon pie and sets it on a plate. Then she slices the pecan pie, lifts a piece, and sets it on the plate. She turns and sets the lemon pie before me and the pecan pie in front of Paul.

"What's this?" I ask.

"Pie. Don't worry. It's on the house."

Bob peers through the opening and eyes the pie. He gives Betty a look and shakes his head. "You're gonna put me out of business with all that charity, Betty!"

"Mind your own business, Bob. These boys look hungry. Besides, they're going to be famous someday. They're gonna be in pictures."

Bob smiles and moans as he cuts into an onion. "This is my business," he says.

"Thanks, Bob," Paul yells.

Bob moans again and keeps cutting his onion.

Just before Paul slices into the pecan pie, I snatch it out

from under him and slide the lemon pie along the bar. He doesn't hesitate. He just lowers his fork right into the white foam and yellow cream. I could have set a shoe in front of him and he'd have stuck a fork in it.

18 BREAKFAST

INSIDE, THE RESTAURANT HAS A DIFFERENT FEEL THAN it did last night. The place is buzzing with gamblers driving home after a night of losing money. Paul and I settle in at a booth along the back wall, closest to the restrooms. A waitress comes over and turns our coffee cups over, filling both of them. She asks about cream and I nod my head yes. She sets two menus down and I read through mine as if it were poetry.

Last night we were given a little business card on which Bob wrote "free breakfast" and signed his name.

Paul closes his menu and sets it on the table. He takes a little packet of cream, opens it, and pours it into his coffee. He opens a packet of sugar and pours it in and stirs his coffee with a sigh. He slides back in his seat and asks what I'm going to order. The Mexican, I tell him. The Mexican? he questions. Yeah, the omelet. The Mexican omelet, it comes with tortillas. I'm getting the combination plate with two of everything, he says. Then he adds that he's getting a side of hash browns. You're ordering a side item also? I question. Yes, he tells me. I hadn't thought about adding something extra. I search through the side items. The waitress comes over and asks if we are ready. Paul looks over at me and tells her that it looks like we need more time. No, I say. I'm ready. I want the Mexican omelet with a side order of biscuits and gravy. That's it. That's what I want. Paul tells the waitress that he wants the number two combo plate with a side of hash browns. The waitress writes it all down, collects the menus, and heads back to the kitchen.

Paul takes a sip of his coffee and sets his cup down on the table. He's looking around the place, sizing people up, it seems, wondering where they came from and where they are going, dividing truckers from gamblers from families crossing the desert in a move from somewhere east.

"Where are we going, Don?" he asks me, still looking around.

"Pardon?"

"Where are we going? Are we going to hang out in California for a while?"

"I don't know. What were you thinking?"

"Doesn't matter to me. But we are running low on money, you know. We may need to get to Oregon pretty soon."

"How long have we been on the road?" I question.

"About three weeks. Maybe more."

"That long?"

"It's been a while," he says.

The waitress comes toward us, balancing plates in her hands. Passing us, she sets the plates down on the table behind me.

"Smells good," Paul says.

"You can say that again."

"Smells good," Paul says again. I crack a smile. I start doctoring my coffee, cream and fake sweetener.

"You know," I say to Paul, "I've got this friend in Visalia, California. Is that near here?"

"Visalia. It's between Bakersfield and Fresno. It's not too far, on the way, really, if we decide to go up the valley. Who's your friend?"

"His name is Mike Tucker."

"How do you know Mike?" Paul asks.

"We met at a camp years ago in Colorado. He came out to Texas to visit me last year. It might be nice to swing by and see him. If we have time."

"Sounds good," Paul confirms. "Do you think he will mind?"

"Not Mike. He's great. He'll be glad to see us."

"Maybe you should give him a call. See if he would care if we stopped in."

"Yeah. I'll do that. I think I have his number somewhere in my stuff."

Paul goes out to the van and brings back a road atlas. We start mapping our route through Visalia, up into Oregon all the way to Portland, at the northern border of the state. Our waitress comes along with our food in her palms. There are also plates running up her arms. She sets a Mexican omelet before me and slides Paul's plate toward him. She carefully maneuvers the side dishes of hash browns and biscuits and gravy off her arms.

"You boys look hungry," she says.

"Yes, ma'am," one of us answers.

"You call on me if you need anything."

"Sure," Paul says. "Thanks."

She steps away and straightens her apron, checking the table for condiments. Paul asks for Tabasco sauce and she turns to another table and lifts a bottle, setting it on our table with a smile.

"Thanks again," he tells her.

Paul eyes his food and I eye his food. He eyes mine and I eye mine. He shakes his head and I pick up my fork and dive into the yellow omelet. There are bell peppers and cheese and onions, a dab of sour cream on top, butter glistening off its side. The omelet has a layer of salsa over it and all of it bleeds and runs together as I slice it with my fork.

There is no talking now. We focus on our breakfast and the world fades away. We slurp coffee between bites. I half finish my omelet before slicing into the biscuits and gravy. The white, fluffy cloud of bread, covered in gravy with chunks of ham and bacon, settles deep into my stomach. I feel the warmth of it sliding down and the carbohydrates going into my bloodstream.

After eating, Paul rests back and holds his stomach. I do the same.

NEITHER OF US WANTS TO FACE THE BROKEN VAN THIS morning, so we sit and talk. We talk about California and about John Steinbeck and Hollywood. I ask Paul if he's ever been through an earthquake and we make small talk about the comfortable weather in Los Angeles. Paul says he could never live in a city with that much smog. We both agree that we will steer away from LA on our trip. After Visalia, we'll head straight to Oregon to see these mountains Paul keeps talking about.

"Do you think you will ever go home again, Don?"

"What do you mean?"

"Do you think you will go back to Texas?"

"Where else am I going to go?" I ask.

"Anywhere. You can live anywhere. It's a free country."

"I don't know. Haven't seen anything that hits me yet."

"Could you leave Texas?" he asks.

"Maybe. It would be tough to leave my family and all. But I suppose I could if I found a nice place."

"You will like Oregon," he says.

"Yeah?"

"Yeah."

"Why is that?" I question.

"You've never seen true beauty, have you?"

"What do you mean?"

"Mountains and all. Streams and waterfalls. Forest."

"Sure I have, Paul. I've not been hiding in my room all these years."

"Where? Where did you see mountains?"

"Colorado. I spent a few summers working at that camp where I met Mike and some other friends, this girl Danielle who lives up in Washington State. We may have to stop there and see her."

"What is Mike like?" Paul asks.

"Mike is crazy. Tall, skinny guy, drives around in this old Toyota Land Cruiser."

"He has a cruiser!" Paul expresses with enthusiasm.

"Yeah, man. So tough."

"Don, *I* have a cruiser."

"You do. Where?"

"In Oregon. I have one back in Oregon."

"Where?"

"In the woods."

"Pardon?"

"Yeah, it's out off this forest service road where nobody will find it. When I bought the van, I hid it so I could go on the trip."

"You hid a car in the woods?"

"A cruiser. Not a car. A cruiser. Yes, I hid it deep in the woods and buried it in brush. Nobody will find it out there."

"You know, Paul, sometimes you seem like a bottomless pit of interesting stories."

"What do you mean?"

"You hid a Toyota Land Cruiser in the woods, bought a Volkswagen, and headed to Houston."

"Crazy, huh?" he says. "I had to hide it so nobody would vandalize it. Actually it's in pretty rough shape, so I don't think vandalism would have made a difference. But still, I don't like the idea of kids climbing around in it and that sort of thing."

"I see." I nod my head.

"So," Paul begins to change the subject, "do you know anybody from Oregon? Did you meet anyone from the Northwest at this camp in Colorado?"

"Why do you ask, Paul?"

Paul cracks a smile. "Free food, man. A place to stay when we get there. We are seriously going to run out of money. Aunts, uncles? We could do odd jobs or something, you know."

"Odd jobs?" I question. "We are on vacation."

"We are going to run out of money when we get there. You know that, don't you?"

"It crossed my mind," I say.

"Well, do you know anybody? This girl Danielle, is she family?"

"You are the one who lived there, Paul. Don't you know anyone?"

"That's different. It's home to me. I can't just go barging in on people I already know. They'll think I am irresponsible or something."

"I see. So it's okay for me to look irresponsible but it's not okay for you to look bad. Is that it?"

"Exactly."

"Very funny. But, no, I can't think of anyone in Oregon. I have a good friend named Julie in Seattle, and Danielle is somewhere in Washington, but it's a small town, don't even know where. But not Oregon."

"Seattle is too far north," Paul says. "We wouldn't go that far."

"We will eventually. I want to see Seattle eventually."

"Eventually, but we really should find a way to earn some cash so we can travel for another week or so. Seattle, maybe Canada," he says, lifting his eyebrows as if Canada is on par with France.

"What's the name of the town where Danielle lives?" he asks.

"She's in Ridgefield. Very cool girl. You would like her, actually. She's a granola like you."

"What is that supposed to mean?"

"Nothing, just that she likes nature and stuff."

"Ridgefield. Ridgefield is just north of Portland. It's practically Oregon," Paul says, shrugging his shoulders.

"Well, then maybe we can go see Danielle."

"Yes." After a few moments, "So . . . ," Paul says.

"So what?"

"So, is she, you know, good-looking?"

"Danielle?"

"Yes. What is this *granola* like?" He pronounces the word *granola* as if I had been speaking of some kind of disease.

"If you must know, it so happens she is good-looking."

"Well, let's go then. I've got to meet this girl. This granola friend of yours."

I try to settle Paul down a little. "Hold on, here. I'm not a matchmaker or anything. You never bothered to ask if I was interested in Danielle. You just automatically claimed her for yourself."

"You said she liked nature, dude. What are you going to do with a woman like that?"

"I happen to like nature too. I'm not all city."

"Let me get this straight, Don. You want to get involved with this nature girl, Danielle, and then marry her and take her to Houston?"

"What's the problem with that?"

Paul eases way back in the booth.

"I don't mean any disrespect. I truly don't. But Texas isn't nature. Texas is city and smog and humidity and heat. If you want to hunt and fish, that's fine, but if you want to climb and kayak and all, no luck. Texas is not for a girl like Danielle."

"You don't even know her. How do you know what she is like?"

"You said she is a granola. A Grape-nut."

"I never called her a Grape-nut. I just said she likes the outdoors."

"Like me," Paul says, pointing his thumb at himself.

"Yeah. She is, but that doesn't mean anything."

The waitress comes over with the bill. Paul interrupts his interrogation to hand her the little business card with Bob's message about our free breakfast.

"You know Bob?" she questions.

"Met him last night. Here at the diner."

"Well, he must have taken a liking to you. He doesn't give free meals very often."

"Yes, ma'am," I say. "He is a great guy. Couldn't believe that."

The waitress flips the card around in her hand and slides it into the pouch in her apron. "By the way, fellas . . ."

"Yes?"

"Bob's free meal doesn't include the tip."

"Oh," Paul begins. "We were going to leave you a big tip. My friend Don here is going to take care of it."

"Good thing," she says.

I smile. Paul smiles. I dig into my pocket and pull out a few dollars and lay them on the table. They are all crumbled up like child's money. The waitress looks with a grimace. I pull out another dollar and she nods and walks away.

"Thanks, Paul."

"Don't mention it."

"You ready to get out of here?"

"No. You haven't told me yet."

"Told you what?"

"Danielle. Are you interested? Is there anything there?"

"Let's go."

"No. Tell me."

"She's a close friend. A pen pal. But if you must know, no. There is nothing there."

"She's not your type, huh?"

"I didn't say that. She's great. A great girl. Just not my type."

"She's not as pretty as you said, is she?"

"She is, Paul. This girl is beautiful."

"What does she look like?"

"Let's go," I say.

"What's she look like?"

"Well, not that she'd ever be interested in you. But she's got brown hair and brown eyes. She's athletic."

"Like me."

"Whatever. She's very intelligent. She doesn't read Louis L'Amour books, that's for sure."

"She's smart?" Paul frowns.

"She is. Very smart. A literature major. Very intelligent. Good conversationalist. Her letters are like poetry."

"Are you serious? You're just pulling my leg."

"No, I'm not. That is how she is. She writes and reads poetry. *Like you.*"

"I hate poetry," Paul grumbles. I shake my head.

"Don't tell her that."

"What do you mean?"

"Better freshen up on your Byron."

"Who's Byron?" Paul asks, playing stupid.

"Lord Byron, Paul. The poet."

"Is he a friend of yours?" He's got a dumb look on his face.

"He's dead."

"Oh, sorry to hear it. Did you know him?"

"Yes. He was my uncle."

"Oh, and Danielle liked his poetry, huh?"

"Danielle loved his poetry."

"Too bad he's dead," Paul says, smiling.

PAUL WALKS LAZILY AROUND BEHIND THE VAN. HE picks at his teeth as he watches me tinker with the wing nut atop the right carb. I look back to see his expression of confusion at my work. I take the carb lid off and set it aside, just sort of staring at the inside of the carburetor. I grab a screwdriver and tighten this, grab a wrench and tighten that. I make little noises like I'm figuring it all out. Paul's expression is the same, and we banter back and forth with groans and sighs. I pull a hammer from the toolbox and begin to tap against the frame. Paul's eyebrows lift at this and he grunts as if to say he hadn't thought of that. I bang a little harder, and he clears his throat.

"You got that thing figured out yet, Don?"

"Sure do. I see the problem."

"What is it?"

"It seems to be the flux capacitor."

"The flux capacitor?"

"Yes."

"What's that?" he asks, still picking at his teeth.

"It's much too complicated to explain. You just stand there and look pretty. I'll take care of this."

He kicks me on my backside and I rock my weight into the engine compartment. Acting like I'm stuck.

"Sorry about that, dude. Didn't mean to put so much weight into that one."

"Don't mention it," I say, pretending to struggle inside the engine compartment with my arms and one of my feet. Inside, I notice a small hole in the top of the casing. And, believe it or not, there is a bolt sitting in a gully of the frame. It couldn't be this easy.

"Hey, Paul."

"Yeah."

"Look at this."

"I thought you just wanted me to look pretty."

"I'm serious."

Paul leans in and I shift a little so some sun shines on the hole. "You see this?"

"Yeah," he says.

"And this bolt?"

"Yeah."

"Do you think it goes in this hole?"

"Couldn't hurt to try."

I set the threads into the hole and screw it in. The hole smells like gasoline. This must be the top of the fuel filter. Just like a lawn mower. Paul goes around to the front and starts the van. I keep my head down to look for a leak, and nothing comes. I can't believe it was that easy. I close the engine compartment and take my place in the passenger's seat.

"How long did we work on that thing last night?" Paul asks.

"About half an hour. Maybe more."

"How come we didn't see that hole?"

"It was dark."

"I know," Paul begins, "but there is no way we could have missed it. And the bolt being right there and all. No way."

"What are you saying?" I ask.

"Think about it, Don."

"Think about what?"

"A meal. Maybe God wanted us here to meet Bob and Betty. He wanted us here to feed us a meal. You got your stinking eggs and flour tortillas. We were just talking about this in the canyon, you know."

"I never thought of it like that."

Paul lets silence come up around our ears. He sits and looks at the windshield and picks at his teeth with his toothpick. "I'm starting to, you know. I'm starting to think this is God working with us. Helping us along and all."

"Could be," I tell him.

"Could be?" he agrees. "It's just strange, you know."

"Who knows?" I say, shrugging my shoulders.

19 NIGHT GOLF

IN THE MOJAVE, WE FELT AS THOUGH WE WERE TRAVEL-
ing through the desert in an oven. Joshua Tree National Park
was on our left for miles, and I kept thinking about Bono and
the boys, hiking up the hills in black and white. We moved
out of the desert and turned north into the Sierra Nevada. I
confess California has taken me by surprise. Not having been
here, all I knew of the state was Los Angeles, the Lakers and
Hollywood, and smog and surfers. But there are mountains
here, an impressive range, and the brown of the desert gives
way to green, rolling green hills fed by creeks running over
boulders, splashing down through pastures where sheep
graze. The Sierra Nevada has towering peaks that would give
the Rockies a run. We slope slowly through meadows, the
mountains in the distance, the deserts behind us. Mike had
told me about the mountains in California, but I never imagined them to be so majestic.

We come down from the hills and into the valley. The interstate runs just west of Visalia, where we exit and head east
through orange groves and come into town at the ballpark,
probably the home of a farm team of some sort. Paul pulls the
van over at the park and I use a pay phone to call Mike, all the
while looking at the back scoreboard through the fence, trying to find a team name. His mom answers and I tell her that
we are swinging through on our way to Oregon and ask if
Mike is around.

"Who is calling?" she asks.

"An old friend of Mike's. Mike and I met in Colorado."

"I see. Well, he is at work," she tells me. "He will be home in half an hour or so. Would you like to come to the house? You are more than welcome to wait here."

"Sure, sounds good."

"Are you in town?" she asks.

I tell her where we are and she explains the back roads from the ballpark, not too far.

We drive slowly through neighborhoods and I wonder at how the people who live here probably get to thinking that neighborhoods are all that America is, house after house. And I wonder again at how much land we have in this country, how many empty miles of desert there are between here and the nearest city, how we are only living in tiny islands on a vast ocean of government property. Visalia is flat like Texas. Deep into the horizon, though, you can see the mountains, dark peaks rising like a wall, stopping the rain from getting to Vegas.

We arrive at Mike's place and Mrs. Tucker makes us a pitcher of lemonade and puts some chips out. I can see Mike in her face and her gestures, and when she laughs I get snapshots of Mike back in Colorado. I start thinking about how strange it is that we come from families, that a man and a woman have sex and make a human that looks a little like them, that is part of them in some way, and how nobody gets to decide who they get born to, and how much of life is outside our control. Paul and Mike's mom like each other quite a bit and start talking about spirituality, about the sort of things Paul has been thinking about on the trip, about how God answered his prayer with the mechanic, and how God has been good to us. I keep thinking about how much she looks like Mike, how when she chews food, she chews the way he does, and when she nods her head, she nods her head and purses her lips a little and how Mike used to do that when we'd talk about serious things. I start thinking about what it must have been like for Mike to have come out of her womb. We just come out of these women's wombs, all of us. We come out like little footballs, trapped in skin, bound to earth by gravity, crawling around learning what a ball is and how to say "Momma" and finally walking, stuck to earth without wings, called by a name our parents thought was cute or interesting. And that is who we are; this is our name and this is our skin and this is how we chew, and we are, in large part, what somebody else tells us we are, and we never stop to think of how crazy the whole thing is. We never stop to ask *why* all of this is happening to us, about the *why* as opposed to the *how*, like I was saying a while back.

"How are you processing all of this?" Mrs. Tucker looks over at me to include me in the conversation.

"About God and all?" I ask.

"About God and all," she clarifies.

"I think He explains a lot," I tell her.

"Explains a lot?" she questions.

"You know, why we are here, maybe, what all is going on, how you had Mike in your womb and chew like him." As I say this, she begins to look confused.

"What do you mean, Don?" Paul inquires.

"I don't know. I don't know exactly. Just the whole thing seems odd. I mean, that is the thing about asking *why*, isn't it? You start asking those questions and the whole thing falls apart. It is as though nothing means anything anymore. I mean, it is great if you can buy into it, if you can just say, okay, God has done all of this to dazzle us, and the mountains and the desert and all the bugs and animals are just there for us to enjoy, and that is great. I am thankful for that. But you almost have to look at it poetically, because when you break it down without God's explanation or God's reason for us being here, it gets pretty confusing and odd. I had this girlfriend once, and I loved her. She was just beautiful, but then suddenly I was kissing her and I realized her mouth was full of germs and she has to use the bathroom, you know, just like a guy, and I couldn't like her after that. I mean, I liked her and I wanted to keep making out with her, but it was like, man, you know, this girl is a human just like me, and there isn't any poetry in this. It's just sexual attraction and germs and body fluids and chemicals. I guess what I am saying is, God is helping me see things more poetically." Mrs. Tucker kind of laughs when I say all of this, and Paul pats me on the back. She asks us if we want any more chips and we tell her we are fine, so she rolls up the bag and puts it back in the cupboard.

"I noticed his Land Cruiser in the driveway, Mrs. Tucker. Is he on foot?" I ask.

"He's on skates," she says.

"Skates?" Paul asks.

"Well, what are those things? They aren't skates. They call them something different." Mrs. Tucker scratches her head and looks at the ceiling.

"Roller blades?" Paul asks.

"That's it. He's on roller blades. He only works a few blocks away."

"What does he do?" Paul asks.

"He's a waiter. He's been a waiter for years now. He was doing fine dining for a while, but now he's at this little breakfast place. He likes it better because there isn't as much pressure. At the fine dining place, he actually had a dessert that he had to set on fire in order to serve it. Mike was always afraid he was going to set a customer's tie on fire. He hated it when people ordered that dessert. If you ask me, I think the flaming dessert, or whatever it was called, is the reason he left. Hated setting that thing on fire." She pauses. "Are you boys staying here tonight?"

"I don't think so, Mrs. Tucker. We don't want to put you out or anything," Paul says.

"No, sir. You are not putting me out at all. People are always staying here. One of Mike's friends, Keith, slept on our couch for several months. We didn't hardly notice him. Don't worry about it."

"You had a fellow living in your front room?" Paul questions.

"Yes. He was living in his car for a while and Mike asked if he could stay here. Mike knew him from the local community college. A real smart kid. He lived out the rest of the term right here."

"I see," I say.

Mrs. Tucker puts the Tupperware pitcher of lemonade back into the fridge and steps in front of the sink, in front of the kitchen window.

"There he is," she says, spotting him. "He's coming up the road."

Paul and I step outside and walk down the short driveway behind Mike's Land Cruiser. Paul checks out the cruiser up close and I walk down to the street to meet Mike. He's coming up slow, tall and skinny with bright red hair. Mike is another good-looking fellow like Paul. He's always got some gal writing him or calling him, I figure. He's wearing baggy khaki shorts and a T-shirt. He has a backpack on and he's sliding like a fellow on ice skates. His weight slides left, then right, and he rocks his arms at his sides as he propels forward. About a hundred yards away, he comes to a stop, sets his hands on his hips. I stand at the end of the driveway with a grin. He gets a big grin on his face and laughs.

"I don't believe it. What are you doing here?" Mike skates up to me and gives me a bear hug. He wraps his long arms around me and pats my back like I was choking on something. "Man, Don. It's good to see you. What are you doing here?"

"Passing through. Had to stop and see you."

"You better have, man. I didn't know you were going to be in town."

"I should have called. We were just driving, you know, and, well . . ."

"You don't have to explain it to me," he says. Mike goes

over and introduces himself to Paul. It makes me proud, honestly, to have a couple friends as good-looking and interesting as Mike and Paul. They start talking about Mike's cruiser and Paul is asking all kinds of questions. Both Mike and I start explaining to Paul how we met and get to telling old stories. We go back in the house and Mike takes a shower and gets changed, commenting how much he smells like burned bacon every time he gets off work. We say good-bye to Mrs. Tucker and load up in the cruiser for a quick tour of Visalia. We end up at this Mexican place across town, a hole in the wall. Mike says he wants to take us out and neither Paul nor I argue. We lean back and sip Coronas and I catch Mike up on the last month or so, taking him all the way to the bottom of the Grand Canyon and back, and how Paul and I met back in Houston. The conversation comes to a lull and Paul asks what there is to do in this town and whether it was too early in the season to catch a baseball game. Mike just holds his hands out and looks around, as if to say, well, this is it. We've got a Mexican place, he says, and holds up his beer. We've got beer, he says. Plenty of options, Mike says. We've got a mall, kind of, and a downtown with a park or something. Both Paul and I are laughing at him. We can lie down at the end of the runway out at the airport and feel planes land.

"Sounds good," Paul says.

"I will be needing a few more beers," I tell them.

"Actually," Mike begins, "there used to be some kind of cargo jet that would land in the evenings, but I think they truck that crap up these days, so there aren't any jets landing at night anymore. We used to lie out there and feel the thing fly over. It's crazy. Your whole insides just vibrate like you're hooked up to an electric socket."

"You're kidding," Paul says. I tell Paul to tell Mike about how he once peed on an electric fence and both Mike and I about wet ourselves when Paul gets to the part about not being able to feel his johnson for twenty-four hours.

Another lull in the conversation prompts Mike to mention the possibility of night golf.

• • •

THAT EVENING, WE DRIVE NORTH OF VISALIA A LITTLE and Mike parks the cruiser in a parking lot across from a golf course. I'm in the backseat and Mike turns to tell me there are several golf clubs behind me. He tells me to grab the nine iron for him and to pick one out for myself and for Paul. I do as he says, handing Paul the seven and keeping the eight for myself. Mike hands Paul an empty plastic grocery sack from the glove box. He keeps one and hands one to me. Paul asks what we're doing and Mike tells him it's called night golf. I don't ask any questions.

It's just past midnight and Visalia is asleep. We sit in a parking lot and across the street is a fence that protects a golf course. Mike points out a spot along the fence that is hidden in the shade of a tree. Streetlights illumine most of the fencing, but that one spot is hidden in shadows.

"That is where we need to jump the fence," Mike announces.

"I see." Paul eyes the fence.

Without speaking, Mike jumps from the truck and runs across the street. He throws his body over the fence and sprints into the darkness. Paul and I sit in silence, looking deep into the shadows across the street. We sit a little more and then a little more. Paul has his golf club at his side; he looks it over and fidgets with the handle.

"I think he wants us to go and jump the fence, Paul."

"I think so," Paul says.

"Well," I say, "I think we should follow him."

Paul jumps out of the truck and runs in a zigzag across the street. He's playing the part of a bank robber. All his motions are exaggerated. He pretends to see a car and lies down on the road. Then he gets up, freezes, and puts his arms out, pretending to be a tree. He throws his club over the fence, puts his plastic bag in his pocket, and scrambles over the chain-link. I can see his shadow as he picks up his club and runs deep into the darkness. I study the thrill of it, sit awhile as a car is passing, and then run across myself, having some trouble, getting snagged at the top of the fence, ripping my shirt. I gather my club and bag and run out into the darkness. I find the edge of a pond and stand still to listen for my friends. I can't seem to hear them so I start walking out onto the open range.

Through dark trees and moonlight, I hear my two friends laughing. I walk in the direction of the voices and I find Paul.

"Psst. Don, is that you?"

"Yeah."

"Where have you been?"

"I don't know. Back there somewhere."

"What took you so long?"

"I didn't know where you guys were. Where is Mike?"

"He's over there." Paul points but I can hardly make out his hand. My eyes have adjusted slightly, but it is still too dark to navigate. There are clouds over the moon and stars, so everything is murky.

"What's he doing?" I ask.

"Same as me. He's picking up golf balls and putting them into his bag."

"Why?"

"He hasn't said why. But this is night golf and this is how it works."

"I see," I say. "So what am I supposed to do?"

"Pick up golf balls."

"Where are they?" I ask.

"They are everywhere."

"Everywhere?"

"Yes. We're in the middle of a driving range."

"Oh. I get it. But what are we going to do with the golf balls?"

"Hit them," Mike says. His voice seems to come from out of nowhere.

"Hit them where, Mike?" I ask.

"At each other."

"Pardon?" Paul questions.

"Yeah," Mike begins, "we get at opposite sides of the driving range, and we try to hit each other."

I cannot make out Mike's expression, but the tone in his voice tells me he is serious. Mike disappears into the darkness. I realize the importance of the moment and drop to my knees, scurrying for golf balls. My sack at my side, I scoop and fill, scoop and fill. The rush of adrenaline aids my speed. From a distance, and through the dark night, we hear Mike yell *incoming!* Paul dumps his bag on the ground and takes stance. I take my half-filled bag and run off into a dark corner of the range. I can hear Mike's club hit the ball. The pop splits the air like a gunshot and then, about fifty yards away, I hear Paul yap, giggle, and take a swing back at Mike. I devise a strategy to never hit from the same spot. The only way we can identify each other is from the sound of the club hitting the ball. If I stay on the move, there is no way they can figure out where I am. So, I drop a ball to the ground and hit it toward Mike. I hear the ball land and hear Mike laugh. I got close, I know that much. Rather than dumping the balls on the ground, I take my club and run fifty yards farther. I hear Paul hit another ball and it flies past me. The whistle of it tells me it's moving quickly. That would have been a painful blow. So I drop another ball to the ground and take aim at Paul. I'm about seventy-five yards or so away, so I loft the ball so as to land on his head. No sound. I wasn't even close. I move another twenty-five yards down the length of the driving range. As I am running, I hear Paul give a serious yap and moan. He's hit. He's laughing. Probably on the ground, rubbing the knot on his head. I drop another ball and hit it toward Mike. Another miss. Mike hits one toward me and it lands just in front of me so I have to jump out of the way. The balls are not visible until they are right on you. My eyes are able to focus a little better through the darkness and I can see the reflection of Mike's club as he swings. He's aiming at Paul again.

I start thinking about how Mike has the advantage over me and Paul 'cause he knows the range and is apparently a better golfer. I run back over toward Paul to see if he wants to team up. As I get close to him, he takes a swing and lands a ball into my side. I fall down in a moan and roll over saying I'm hit. Both Mike and Paul have a good laugh at that.

"Paul. Psst, Paul."

"What?"

"Let's work together."

"What do you mean?"

"Mike is better at this. Let's gang up on him."

"How?"

"Let's run around behind him and take swings."

"Where is he?"

"He's over there. Come on."

Paul gathers some balls into his bag and we run the length of the range, outside the boundaries behind trees. We hear Mike take another swing. He laughs as the ball leaves the ground. His club glistens for a second and I stop Paul from running, draw him near, and point toward the place I saw Mike. We are even with him, but he is a good fifty yards out, and he's still facing the place where Paul was standing.

"Lose the clubs," Paul comments.

"Why?"

"Let's get up close and pelt him."

"Just throw them?" I question.

"Yes."

Paul grabs a handful of balls from his sack, sticks them in his pocket, and does it again with his other pocket. Pretty soon we are both loaded with ammunition.

"Paul, you go around back and I will get him from the side. Don't throw unless you get a good view of him."

"You got it," he says, and with that, Paul runs around to the back of the range. I wait to hear him charge, and then run toward Mike. Paul hits him and Mike goes down. Paul pummels him from the rear as I hurl golf balls from the side. He yells uncle but we do not let up. Mike gathers his senses, stands, and begins to grab at golf balls. He throws one toward Paul and as he releases I can see the complete outline of his body. I take aim and fire, hitting him in the shin on a bounce. He goes down again and gathers a few more balls. He throws one toward me and hits me squarely on the thigh.

Paul yells charge and we move in close and fast. Soon enough, we are on top of Mike and pelting him with golf balls. Mike can't stop laughing. This goes on for a while and Mike finally calls a truce.

MIKE GETS ABOUT TWO HUNDRED GOLF BALLS LINED up at the edge of the lake. It must be four in the morning. Everything is completely quiet, and none of us feel like talking anymore. The moon has come out a little now, so we can see the balls fly straight up over the lake after Mike takes a swing. The ball seems to suspend up there somewhere for a while before dropping in and making a splash out in the middle of the water. Every once in a while, a cop car turns the corner by the clubhouse and slowly drives up the street. Each time we lie down on our bellies and wait for him to leave.

20 THE OREGON TRAIL

WE WERE OUT TILL SUNRISE AND AT SIX MIKE HAD TO work the breakfast shift. He tells us to come in for breakfast, but Paul and I have already eaten pretty well and need to hit the road.

"I can't thank you enough for letting us stay, Mike," I tell him.

"Dude, stick around," he says. "You've got nowhere to go."

"We're trying to get to Oregon. We should probably hit the road," I say.

"Oregon is only about eight hours away. Leave tomorrow."

I look over at Paul and he shrugs his shoulders. We are at the kitchen table and Mike's mom has made us coffee. Mike refills my cup.

"You're not putting me out," he says. "You always feel like that and it's not the case. What's the rush with Oregon anyway?"

"No rush, really. I've just wanted to see it and that's where we're heading, you know."

"Go if you want." Mike shrugs.

"I've got a better idea," I say. "Join us, Mike. Come with us."

"Yeah!" Paul says.

"I can't," Mike sighs.

"Why?" I ask.

"Work."

Paul chimes in again: "Come with us, Mike. Have you ever been to Oregon?"

"Never been," he says.

"You'll love it."

"Mike," I begin, "we're going up to Ridgefield to see Danielle."

"The girl we met in Colorado?"

"Yes," I tell him.

"The girl in the red dress?" he asks, perking up.

"Yes."

"What red dress?" Paul asks.

"Go take a cold shower, Paul," I tell him.

"She's a babe," Mike says to Paul.

"I knew it," Paul says. "Tell me about her, Mike."

"Look at this guy," Mike says. "Acts like he's got a shot."

"She's that pretty, huh?" Paul says.

"She's that good-looking."

"Yeah, yeah, tell me more," Paul asks.

Mike starts explaining to Paul how we met Danielle. He tells him how smart she is and that she's a great soccer player. "We were all really close that summer in Colorado," he says. "We were inseparable. We'd climb Red Mountain for sunrise. She was funny, huh, Don?"

"She was funny?"

"Used to watch old black-and-white movies or something. But, man, that red dress."

"I know," I say.

"What red dress?" Paul asks.

"She had this red dress on, our last day there, long and formfitting, you know. Man, she looked good. All of us were like, um, maybe she isn't just a tomboy, you know."

"No kidding. There's a woman in there, for sure," Mike adds.

"I've got to meet this girl!" Paul exclaims. "Let's get out of here. Mike, come with us."

"Can't," he says. "I have to work. You guys have a good time." Mike meets my eye and holds a fist over the table. I tap his fist to mine. "Say hello to Danielle," he says.

WITH PAUL AT THE WHEEL, WE DRIVE WEST TO Interstate 5 that will take us through Oregon and into Portland.

The van enjoys the flatness of the valley. We found our pace about one hundred miles ago and the van has not wavered, choked, or coughed in complaint since. We are sailing through America's bread basket, cabbage and beets and fruit trees and fields of grapes.

Paul tells me we should make Oregon by sunset, and then Portland before midnight, or shortly thereafter. I ask him if we intend to drive the night, and he shakes his head, saying he doesn't know if he can make it.

"Is this a pilgrimage?" I ask my friend.

"A pilgrimage?" he asks.

"Yes."

"What do you mean?" he inquires.

"Are we on a spiritual pilgrimage?"

"I don't know. I don't know what a pilgrimage is, I guess."

"I think it's when you are looking for the answer to something, or when you are trying to figure out God," I tell him.

"Are you trying to figure out God?" Paul asks.

"I don't know. I think I did, a bit, back in the canyon, but then you have to kind of jump into it, don't you? I mean, you have to see and believe the world is God's, that He is there and He made it for us. You have to see things poetically."

"What was all that crap you were talking about with Mike's mom? All that stuff about making out with your girlfriend?" Paul asks.

"I don't know," I tell him. "I don't really feel like being on a pilgrimage yet."

"You don't feel like looking for God?" he asks.

"No," I say. "I don't. I mean I know He is there, but what if I want life to be about something it isn't? What if I want life to be about getting paid and getting married or just being happy in the pagan sense?"

"Getting paid?" Paul asks, shrugging his shoulders. "I don't know. Just because you want life to be something doesn't mean that is what it is. What if life is about something else, and it doesn't matter what we think?"

"I know what life is about. But what if I don't like it?" I say.

"Tough, I guess. It is what it is."

"What if that sucks?" I ask.

"What if it does?" he says. "I guess there isn't anything you and I can do about it. It's like you were saying, you know, about having to take a crap and being born with somebody else's DNA and all, life is just what it is, and it isn't like we are given a lot of freedom."

"Gravity and all that crap," I say.

"Gravity and all that," Paul confirms. "Not a lot of options."

"And that sucks," I say, putting my hand out the window to cup the wind.

"What if it doesn't suck?" Paul says.

"What do you mean?"

"What if, you know, if we just give in to it, and say this is what it is, then it gets good, and it's fighting it that makes it so bad."

I think about that for a second but don't know how much I like it. It feels like we don't have a lot of options. And don't get me wrong, I feel like life is good, but it just feels like, as a human, we aren't given a lot of options. It feels like, outside a relationship with God, you know, life doesn't mean anything. Which is fine, but what if you just want a little break? And I know this sounds terrible, but what if?

"I think that sucks," I say after a few minutes. Paul lets everything be silent. He is putting his free hand out the window now, cupping the air.

"You on a pilgrimage, Don?" he asks.

"I don't know," I tell him.

"You on a pilgrimage?" I ask.

Paul doesn't answer for a second. "Maybe we're all on a pilgrimage," he says. "Maybe it's all one trip, one big road trip through the cosmos, through the nothingness. Maybe we're all going somewhere. Or really, maybe we are all being taken somewhere."

"Where are we going?" I ask.

"Maybe it isn't for us to decide, just to give in to it."

"What is *it*?" I ask.

"*It* is whatever God wants *it* to be," Paul says. "Maybe we are just supposed to trust that He won't beat us up when we get there. Maybe we are supposed to trust that He is good."

"Maybe so," I say. And after that we don't talk about it anymore. I start closing my eyes to try to get some sleep but it is useless. I lean back in my seat and look out over the miles and miles of farmland, all the green stretching back behind us, out toward the mountains, all the earth making all those crops, everything happening in its own time, a sustainable planet held together by some kind of mystery that physicists call Mother Nature, as if to pretend they aren't all believing fables. As if to pretend we aren't all believing fables.

"You tired?" I ask.

"Very tired. We didn't get much sleep last night."

"I know. I'm feeling a little tired too."

"You think you could drive?" Paul asks.

"How far is Oregon?"

"About three more hours. We should hit mountains pretty soon. They aren't too big, but we should start seeing them."

"I can drive," I tell him.

Paul pulls the van to the shoulder. He gets out and stretches, bending over and arching his back. He sets his hands against his sides and leans backward. I slide over into the driver's seat as Paul gets in on the passenger's side.

Steering the van back to the road, we rock and sway, bumping over the edge of the shoulder. I look over at Paul and only a mile down the road he is sleeping. I speak his name and get no answer. His mouth is open a little. He's out.

Fifty more miles has us in hill country and approaching

mountains. We've been out of Visalia for six hours now. If Mike was right, we should hit Oregon pretty soon. These hills are thick with evergreen. Redwoods line the road. The trees become enormous within fifty miles, tall and broad at their bases, and the ground has the look that it is permanently wet.

Another two hours down the road and Paul is still asleep. The interstate has woven through the redwoods and I've gotten some energy off the change in landscape, the shift to cool, moist air and the feel of Narnia. The mountains have given way to subtler slopes, but we go up and down all the same. Gradual climbs and quick descents. I start thinking again about what Paul was saying, about how we have to submit to whatever God has us on this journey for, about how we just have to agree that it is all His. And I know God made stars and friends and love and poetry to dazzle us, but there really is a part of me that wants some freedom, that doesn't want to have to do everything right or be religious anymore. It's not a serious struggle, but it's like I said about *how* and *why* questions, when you know the *why*, you are just kind of trapped, and when you only ask *how* and never ask *why*, you can be happy and ignorant. Even if God is taking the cosmos somewhere good, I begin to wonder what He does with folks who just want out.

AFTER ANOTHER HOUR, DRIVING INTO THE NIGHT, MY eyes grow heavy and my mind has trouble staying in the now. A forest kind of dark has laid itself over the landscape. There is moonlight in the sky, but it's having trouble sifting through the tall trees to find the road. I find myself having to be very intentional about staying in my lane when a car comes at us from the distance. I find myself justifying a quick closing of the eyes, catch myself thinking about my eyes being shut, then open them quickly, and shake my head to wake myself up. But it's no use. I'm fading.

For a change I weave between lanes, running my tires over the divider reflectors. The thumps give me a jolt and that helps a bit. I roll down the window and stick my head out like a dog. I sing to myself. I talk to Paul, who is asleep in the back now. I honk the horn. I talk to the trees. Something ahead catches my eye. I slow, pull the van to the shoulder, and park it like a car at a drive-in movie. A large brown sign stands some thirty feet in the air, reading "Welcome to Oregon." I pull the van off the road and park underneath it, get out, and smell the clean air. I walk into the forest a few feet and take a pee. I zip up my pants and stand real still to feel the silence. I walk back over to the van and slide the door open, climb over Paul, and lay my head on a pillow.

21 SINATRA

I FELL ASLEEP WITHOUT SHUTTING THE DOOR OR moving the van. The police officer pulls on Paul's pant leg and asks him to get out of the van. Paul calls my name and wakes me up. I slide to the edge of the bed and rub my eyes, looking around to remember where we are. Paul is looking up at the "Welcome to Oregon" sign and the officer is trying to get some questions answered.

"What are you two doing?"

"Sleeping, Officer, I think," Paul says, still looking at the sign. "I have no idea why we are parked right here, though."

"You two do some drinking last night?" he asks.

"No. I wasn't drinking. I was asleep."

"You been drinking?" the officer asks, looking into the van, lifting some blankets with his flashlight.

"No, Officer. I was driving last night and was pretty exhausted. I pulled over. It was dark."

"You didn't see that sign?" he asks, motioning toward the enormous contraption casting a shadow on all of us.

"I did. I just didn't know, you know."

"Didn't know what?"

"Didn't know where to park, I guess. I had to use the bathroom."

The officer looks deeper into the van, pushing some of our boxes around with the end of his light. He tells us all the things he could do with us if he wanted, that he could arrest us or give us a ticket, and quotes a bunch of laws.

"We didn't mean any harm," I assure him.

"Well, get back on the road," he says. "Can't stay here."

Paul stretches after the officer leaves. He grabs my foot and I kick him, moaning and covering up again with blankets. Paul rounds to the driver's side and I hear the engine start. The van jars through ruts in the grass and onto the road and I lean up to close the sliding door. *We're in Oregon,* I think to myself. It was too dark to get a good look at the place last night, so I uncover my head from the blankets and peer through the side windows. Paul's been talking so much about the place I feel like there must be something magical about it. I get up from the bed and take my spot in the passenger's seat.

I had imagined Oregon to be greener, actually. Not that it's not lush; it is. And it is certainly beautiful, but I guess I imagined a rain forest. Paul tells me Oregon can be divided into three major sections. There is the valley, which we are in; the mountains to our right, not visible through the thick trees; and the desert on the other side of the mountains.

"Like the Mojave Desert?" I ask.

"No," he answers. "More like high desert. There are canyons and rolling hills. Juniper trees, sagebrush, that sort of thing."

"Do you think we will get over there?" I ask.

"Sure," he says. "We may have to head that way."

"Why would we have to?"

"To get jobs. We are going to run out of money sometime soon. I don't know whether you noticed that."

"I thought about it. But I knew you had a plan."

"I see," he says.

"So?"

"So what?"

"What is your plan, Paul?"

"For jobs?"

"Yes."

"Well, for the past three summers I've worked at Black Butte Ranch. It's outside of Sisters in the Cascades."

"Sisters is a town, right?"

"Yeah. I told you about it. It's a great place except for the cone lickers."

"Cone lickers?" I question.

"Yeah. Tourists, you know. They come in droves and walk down the streets licking ice-cream cones."

"I get it. Cone lickers."

Looking at the map, I see that there seem to be only two major interstates through Oregon. Interstate 5, which we are on, heads north and south. It comes up from California and passes through Eugene, Salem, and Portland before heading into Washington State and through Seattle into Canada. Then there is Interstate 84, which runs east and west along the northern border of Oregon. There don't seem to be very many towns on 84. It goes all the way through Idaho to Salt Lake City, Utah.

Oregonians are all by themselves up here. I am used to Texas, where there are a dozen major highways that head to half a dozen towns with more than a million people. I feel like I'm traveling into the deepest remote parts of Alaska or the Northern Territory. There is a spot on the map, in eastern Oregon, where I can place my entire hand and not lay it over a town. There are only a few minor roads that head out that way and they all seem to dwindle off like weak creeks and streams. We're in the outback, I say out loud.

Paul rolls down his window and breathes the air. It's fresh air. Smells like forest, like it has rolled down off the mountains. You can smell nearby rivers and feel the coolness in the air.

"Tell me about Black Butte. What will we do there?

"I will work as a lifeguard. I've done it for years. About three summers."

"What about me?"

"Janitor."

"Are you serious?"

"Yeah. Janitor. It's good work, Don. They pay well."

"Whatever," I tell him. "How much money do we have?"

"Not much. About a hundred dollars. That will get us to Ridgefield, maybe Seattle if we want, then back to Black Butte. No more than that."

"I have about fifty dollars," I say. "That will get us a little farther."

"Food," Paul starts. "Don't forget about food. We have to eat. The fifty will pay for food."

"I forgot about that. Danielle will feed us. I'm sure of that."

"Did you ever call her?" Paul asks.

"I didn't. I meant to call her from Mike's, but we left in a rush and I was tired. I didn't think about it."

"Maybe you should call her. We don't just want to drop in."

As we get closer to a city, Paul exits the interstate and drives a few blocks into Eugene. I notice a coffee shop and think a cup of coffee sounds good. But then I see another. Two coffee shops on one street. We don't even have two coffee shops in all of Houston, much less two on one street. When we stop for gas, I wander over to a phone booth and call Danielle. It's long distance, so it costs me a dollar in quarters.

"Hello, is this Danielle?"

"No," a tender voice answers.

"Did I reach the Bjurs?"

"This is the Bjurs. This is Shirley Bjur."

"Are you Danielle's sister?"

"I'm her mom, but thanks for the compliment!"

"Hello, Mrs. Bjur. This is Donald. I met Danielle in Colorado a few summers ago. We keep in touch through letters."

"I know about you, Don. It's good to talk to you. Do you want me to get Danielle?"

"If that is okay. It was nice to talk to you."

"Nice to talk to you too," she says, and then sets the phone down. I hear her call for Danielle and hear Danielle answer and talk to her mom as she comes to the phone.

"Hello," Danielle says.

"Hey there."

"Hi." Pause. "Who is this? I'm sorry." She sounds confused.

"Don Miller."

"Donald!"

"Yeah."

"It's so great to hear your voice. Did you get my letters?"

"Which ones?"

"From Costa Rica!"

"Costa Rica?"

"You didn't get them?" She sounds upset.

"No. Were you in Costa Rica?"

"Yeah. I got back this morning."

"No way. I can't believe that. I almost missed you," I tell her.

"What do you mean?" she asks.

"I'm here. I mean not here, but close."

"Close to where?" Danielle asks. "Here?" she says as she realizes I am in the area.

"Yes. I'm in Oregon!"

"No way!" she screams. "Where in Oregon?"

"A town called Eugene."

"Don, Eugene is just down Interstate 5. You're pretty close. Are you coming up here? You'd better."

"Yeah, we're heading to Seattle maybe. I don't know exactly where we are going, but I'd like to come up and see you."

"Please do, Don, please come here. What in the world are you doing here?"

"A friend and I are traveling around in this Volkswagen van, we're seeing the country, and . . ."

"Like hippies!"

"Yeah. Like hippies. We're living like people in the sixties and all."

"You have to come here, Don. Are you coming?"

"Yeah. If that's an invitation, we're coming."

"It's an invitation! Come!" She is jumping up and down at this point. Her mom is in the background asking what is going on. Danielle is trying to explain.

"Well, tell me how to get there!"

I hang up the phone and walk toward Paul with a smile on. He has the van started and asks how it went. He asks if I told her about him and I tell him I forgot.

"You forgot?" he says.

"How far is Ridgefield?" I ask him.

"About three hours or so," he tells me.

"I told her we'd be there before sunset."

"We'll be there before that," Paul says.

"Well, we can hang out in Portland or something. You should get a shower if you are going to impress this girl. You're smelling pretty bad."

"I took a shower at Mike's!" Paul exclaims.

"Did you use soap?" I ask.

Paul laughs at that. He pulls the van back on the road and we weave toward the interstate. We pass yet another coffee shop.

"What is it with coffeehouses, man? They are everywhere."

"Welcome to the Pacific Northwest, Don. This is the coffee capital of the world."

"There's a shop on every block," I say in wonder.

"You haven't seen anything, Don. Wait till we get to Portland."

We are out of Eugene pretty quickly. Back into farmland. Oregon agriculture is not just fruit and vegetables; it's also Christmas trees. There are perfect rows of five-foot pines that stretch down flat valleys and up onto the hills. They keep their rows regardless of the slant of the earth. Beyond the hills I can see the outline of the mountains. I ask Paul if these are still the Sierra Nevada and he answers with an emphatic no. They are the Cascades. It's a volcanic range.

"Volcanic?" I question.

"You've heard of Mount Saint Helens," he says.

"Mount Saint Helens is around here?"

"Just across the border, really. Just up into Washington State about ninety miles. You can see it from Portland. But the big mountain around here is Mount Hood. It stands in the distance and is visible from the city. You can see it from almost anywhere."

I start wondering what it must be like to live in the shadow of a mountain. All of Houston lives in the shadow of downtown. Downtown is how we orient ourselves. It stands as our compass, a mountain of glass and mirrors. It strikes me as I think about it, how beautiful we find massive structures, either man-made or organic. I wonder if we find them amazing because they make us feel small and insignificant, because they humble us. And I remember feeling that way back in Colorado, that I was not the center of the cosmos, that there were greater things, larger things, massive structures forged in the muscle of earth and time, pressing up into the heavens as if to say the story is not about you, but for you, as if to remind us we are not gods.

SOON WE ARE OUT OF THE VALLEY AND INTO THE foothills. The interstate thickens with cars and buses, trucks and minivans. South of Portland, the land rises and turns green. Businesses rest in the shadows beneath clumps of trees.

Right of the highway, the earth dips into a river. It is a large river. I noticed it on the map earlier. The Willamette, it is called. The interstate follows along the river and then before us is downtown Portland. Despite its western status, it appears old and settled. The river wears the skyline like a crown.

We discuss our itinerary and agree on a shower. But where? I suggest we find a university and use the athletic facility. I am not one who can easily pass himself as an athlete, but a confident stride will usually get you anywhere and Paul tells me Portland State University is somewhere in the downtown area. We drive up and down one-way streets till we see tennis courts and a large adjoining building. Portland is a walkable city, every corner with another coffee shop; there must be fifteen or more on one street alone. The city blocks are half the size of blocks in Houston, so each corner holds a retail space and the foot traffic makes the city feel inviting. And people don't wear ties here, no suits, just slacks and a sweater or dress shirt. We are driving right through the middle of the business district and I literally don't see anybody wearing a suit. Paul tells me Portland is the world headquarters for both Nike and Columbia, and the place does have that granola athlete feel, that nonconformist but yuppie anyway kind of vibe. We ask a passerby if the university is near and he points us toward something called the park blocks. We wind through the streets till we find a long row of blocks designated for urban gardens and paths. At the end of the park blocks everything starts feeling school-like so we park the van.

We wander around campus for a while and find the athletic facility. With a confident stride, we march in through the doors, through the gym, and into the locker room. A man in a caged room hands us towels and we thank him and take showers. I hate being naked in front of anybody, but especially in an athletic facility. Paul walks into the open shower room and fidgets with the water. I am standing closer to the lockers, still in my pants. When nobody seems to be looking I pull off my pants and underwear and walk quickly to the showerhead. Paul starts trying to make conversation but I am not interested. I lather up, get my hair wet, rinse off, and head back to the lockers. Paul makes a comment about the small size of my johnson and I've got my pants on before I jab back at him a similar insult. Paul takes his time with the shower so I start walking around the place. I walk through the weight room and pick up one of the dumbbells, doing a curl with about forty pounds, then putting the dumbbell back on the rack.

Paul comes in after a while and makes a comment about working out before the shower, not after. We make our way back outside, and our fresh clean gives the world a new feel. I tell Paul that I don't think I got all the soap off my body and he laughs, telling me I could have taken longer than three seconds to rinse off.

The sky is bright today and this is uncommon, Paul tells me. The weather is all London until July, when it warms up and feels like Florida for about eight weeks. There are winters when the sun won't come out for two weeks at a time, but after July 4, there won't be a cloud in the sky for ninety days. It is perfect around here in the summer, Paul promises.

"What do you want to do now?" I ask him.

"You want coffee?" he questions.

"When in Rome . . ."

We wander down to a little coffee shop on the corner off one of the park blocks. It's called Coffee People and is filled with students poring over open books, wealthy businessmen, and homeless people listening to headphones. They are playing Frank Sinatra over the speakers.

The fellow in front of me orders a latté, which is all foreign to me. Coffee is something you order at breakfast, at a greasy spoon. The idea of dedicating a specific shop (much less fifty of them on one block) to coffee is going to take some getting used to. I struggle through an order, answering questions about how much room I want and whether I want foam and what size and so on and so on. I just stand there like a deer caught in headlights and the lady just says to give her a buck and she will take care of me. I hand her a dollar, which seems an extraordinary amount to pay for a cup of coffee, and she tells me to wait on the other side of the bar until my cup comes up. Paul and I get our orders and find a table at the back. He brings over a chess set that they keep in the place and we start setting up a game.

"What would make you most happy?" Paul asks, pushing his pawn forward two spaces.

"I don't know."

"Anything, Don. What would make you most happy in life?"

"Well, maybe a wife, some kids, a good job, I don't know. Why do you ask? What would make you most happy?"

"I have just been thinking how what we really want is for

people to love us. God, girls, friends, parents. It seems like life is all about that stuff, you know."

"Feels like it," I say, pushing another pawn up one space to back up my front pawn. "I feel like you are trying to say something."

"Yeah," Paul confesses. "I guess I am. Nothing deep, really, just that, you know, I know you have been thinking about things and I just feel like God put us here to enjoy Him, and He gave us free will so it is tough sometimes, because people use their free will selfishly, but I think also He created us to enjoy Him, that He is love, you know, and I would just hate to see you walk away from that. I mean, if He were love and all." Paul pushes his pawn forward and I spend a few minutes studying the board, trying to remember what all the pieces do. I move a knight over one of my pawns and tap my hand against the table.

"Thanks, man," I say. "I think I do that stuff, just make waves or whatever, just to bring attention to myself. I know it is all good, that God is good and all."

"I do that stuff sometimes too," Paul says.

"Do what stuff?" I ask.

"You know, just say things to bring attention to myself, stuff that is shocking or whatever."

I don't say anything to Paul but I know he never does that stuff. He is more self-aware than I am, more self-aware than most people.

22 KINDNESS

PORTLAND SITS A FEW MILES FROM THE COLUMBIA River, which serves as the border to Washington State. We leave the city to drive north through suburbs, the entire way both Mount Hood and Mount Saint Helens standing to the east. We cross the big river into Washington State and I begin wondering about apple trees, how all I know of Washington is apples. Paul explains how far it is to Seattle and then how Canada is only a couple hundred miles beyond that and it occurs to me how far north we actually are. I follow Danielle's directions precisely, and we are soon off the interstate and onto farm roads. There is agriculture on our left and right, a small general-store, and a burger shop renovated from a gas station.

We turn right, go for a few miles, and look for the sign that marks the road to Mountain View Christian Center, a landmark Danielle said would tell us we were closing in. Passing the church, we take a left at the next driveway. It is a long road that serves several homes, each with an acre or two. We follow the driveway and find a mailbox with the Bjur name printed on the sign. We turn right again and follow another driveway up a small hill where there is a large white house covered with windows in the front. The yard is landscaped with shrubs and flowers and is as pristine as a golf course. Paul parks the van and breathes deeply. I look behind me, through the back window of the van, as the door of the house slings open and out comes Danielle. She is more beautiful than I remember, her thin frame coming out of hips that slide left and right with each footfall, moving up her athletic torso to long arms and a head you dream about in your sleep. I look over at Paul and softly ask what he thinks.

"She's a looker," he says.

Danielle's hair is cut short. She is wearing a tie-dyed shirt, khaki pants, and combat boots. She is brown-bread tan. Her teeth are perfect. Her smile is perfect. Paul and I haven't seen a pretty girl in two thousand miles, it seems like. Or at least we haven't seen one that we could spend any time with.

"Hello! Hello!" she says, rounding to the passenger's side window, opening the door, and spreading her arms out for a hug.

"Hello, my friend. How long has it been?" I say to her.

"Three years, Don. It's been three years!"

Paul rounds the van and stands with his hands in his pockets. I introduce them, and Danielle offers her hand, which Paul shakes gently.

"You two come inside. You must be starving."

Paul plays the strong, silent type but I tell her we could eat a horse. Danielle says they don't have any horse but they do have turkey sandwiches.

"That will do fine," I tell her.

Inside we are greeted by Shirley Bjur, Danielle's mom. She's a petite woman and it becomes obvious where Danielle gets her beauty. Shirley is busy in the kitchen. We hardly walk through the door before we are ushered into a small breakfast nook and Shirley has plates on the counter, bread opened, and turkey and lettuce and tomatoes and mayo. She is talking nonstop, going on about how much fun Danielle had in Colorado and how she still keeps a few pen pals from those days and how much they missed her when she was in Costa Rica and how she and her husband had plenty of friends with a van like ours back in the day. Danielle and her mom are talking at once. One will ask me a question and the other will answer.

"Don, what are you guys doing here in Washington?" Shirley asks.

"Mom, I told you. They are traveling around America," Danielle says.

"America! It's a big country. Where all have you been?" Shirley inquires.

"They've been all over, Mom. Don lives in Texas, remember?"

"That's right. I remember, Don. You're a Texan. Tell me, do they wear big cowboy hats down there?"

"Mom, you've seen too many movies. Not everybody from Texas is a cowboy!"

"We went to Texas once," Shirley starts into a story. "Remember, Danielle, we were there when you were little. You and Elida argued and fought the entire way, remember?"

"I remember. Elida was being a brat!" Danielle exclaims.

"Who is Elida?" I ask.

"My sister." Danielle smiles. "I told you about Elida. Do you even read my letters?"

"Over and over," I tell her.

"Who is my little brother?" she tests me.

"I can't remember his name. I remember you guys adopted him from Colombia."

"Nate," she says. "His name is Nate, Don." She bonks me on the head with a roll of paper towels, sitting down with us at the table.

We eat turkey sandwiches and are bombarded by questions. Shirley attempts to include Paul in the conversation, but Danielle doesn't seem to notice him. She keeps asking about Mike and California and the Grand Canyon. She wants to know about Texas and how long we've been on the road and where did we sleep and did we go to San Francisco or Sacramento? Her grandfather lives in Sacramento.

Paul asks where Shirley's husband is and Shirley tells him he's up in the air. Paul takes this to mean that he's dead and offers his apology, but Shirley laughs and clarifies that he's actually in the air. He's on a plane flying home from Germany. He works for Hewlett-Packard. He doesn't have to leave town often, but when he does, he goes to China or Germany or some place that keeps him away too long.

Shirley begins to sweep the kitchen floor. "You two will just have to stay here until Randy gets home. He'll be glad to meet you. You need to stay for Elida and Nate too. They will be home from school in a couple of hours. You need to stay for dinner," she says.

"We don't want to put you out," I say.

"You have nowhere to go. You said that. You guys are just driving around. All I'm saying is, you are not leaving here till you get a good meal. And turkey sandwiches don't count."

"You're sure it's not too much trouble?" I ask.

"Not at all. Stay here tonight."

"Spend the night?" I question.

"Yes. You can have dinner tonight, and since tomorrow is Saturday, Elida and Nate and Randy will be here for breakfast and you can eat and be on your way."

"It sounds like a lot of trouble for you," I say.

"Where are you going to go?" she asks. "You are just going to go up the road a bit and sleep. Might as well do it here."

Danielle gets up and walks into the kitchen, resting her elbows on the counter, her face in her hands; she is smiling and nodding, agreeing with her mom. "You're staying here, Donald Miller. I'm not letting you guys sleep out on the road." She pouts her face as she says this. Man, is this girl beautiful.

"Whatever you say, ladies." I get up to stretch my legs and have a look around. "They're not letting us leave, Paul," I say to him, still seated in the nook.

"Sounds good," Paul says. That comment gives both Shirley and Danielle a chuckle.

WE TAKE A WALK TO THE END OF THE DRIVEWAY where a neighbor has goats in a pen. Paul names one of the goats Dimitrius but calls him Dimitri for short. Danielle thinks he's funny. It is here that we are interrupted by Danielle's sister, Elida. She races up the driveway in her Honda Prelude. She's got her hand on the horn all the way up the driveway and she's swerving left, then right. Danielle just laughs at her. She races toward us and slams on the brakes. Rolling down her window, she interrogates Paul and me.

"Who are you?" she asks. No smile.

"We're friends of Danielle's," I answer.

"Is that your hippie van?" she questions.

"It's mine," Paul tells her.

"Are you hippies?"

"No," I say.

"You, the blond." Elida points at Paul. "Are you dating anybody?"

"No," Paul says.

Danielle, who has been pulling petals off a flower, tosses them through Elida's window. Elida races her engine, tosses it into first, and squeals her tires. She waves her arm out the window and screams and laughs.

"She's crazy." Danielle laughs and throws her head back. "You're crazy!" she shouts as Elida makes the turn and disappears behind the house. Elida is as good-looking as Danielle, long brown hair, smooth skin, and filled out fairly perfect. *She must be in high school,* I think to myself.

"Let me introduce you guys to Elida." Danielle starts running back toward the house and we follow behind her. Elida is getting some books out of her car. She asks, this time with a smile, who we are. Danielle reminds Elida of Colorado and says she met me there and we've kept in touch through letters.

"You're the one from Texas!" Elida shouts.

"Yes," I tell her.

"Well, yeehaw!" She shakes her hip to one side and puts her

hand on her hip as she says this. I get butterflies and nerves when she cocks her head to the right.

Their personalities are distinct. Danielle will interest you in conversation and Elida will entertain you by goofing off. We head back inside the house and Elida and Danielle do this little song called "Sisters" where they put their arms around each other's shoulders and sing. It's cute. Shirley loves it. Now that Elida is home, Shirley changes from hostess to manager. Danielle needs to prepare dinner and Elida needs to go get Nate at school. Elida comments that she always has to get Nate and Danielle always gets the easy jobs. Danielle volunteers to pick up Nate if Elida will get dinner ready, but Elida says no, she'll do it. Shirley has to run to the airport to pick up Randy, who will be in at 7:00 p.m. He will be hungry, she says. So will Nate and the boys. We are now called "the boys."

With everyone in action, Paul and I decide this would be a good time to change the oil in the van. It will make us look manly and avoid the perception that we are bums who don't work. Soon, we are under the van and talking about the girls. Paul says he's in love with Danielle. I tell him to calm down. He asks me if there is anything there between her and me. I tell him no. I don't think she'd be interested, and besides, I think of her like a sister, and moreover, Elida is about the most beautiful thing I have ever seen. Paul says he doesn't think of her like a sister, either Danielle or Elida, but especially Danielle. He also says that Elida is too young for me and I am a pervert. It's like three years, I tell him. High school, he says.

I do most of the work on the van. Paul just lies there, underneath, with a wrench in his hand. He has a worried look and then a smile and then a worried look. Stop thinking about her, I tell him. He says shut up. I pull the bolt and let the oil drop down into a pan we borrowed from the Bjurs's garage.

"She doesn't like me," Paul whimpers.

"She doesn't know you yet. We just got here."

"And we're leaving. I'll never see her again." Paul sighs.

"You're serious, aren't you?"

"Yes," he says.

ELIDA, DANIELLE, PAUL, AND I ARE MAKING SMALL talk at the dining room table, looking through old photographs of Colorado, when Randy and Shirley come home. Randy looks tired, but not put out by our being there. You can tell that in a house full of girls, he is used to entertaining their company. And I even suspect he is glad to see some guys hanging around. He puts his bags down in the entryway and comes over to offer a handshake. He's fifty or so, graying but athletic. Danielle has his nose, a small, pointed nose they got from Norway or something. He joins our conversation but has very little to tell about his recent trip to Germany. The entire family had gone when the girls were younger and they are asking him if he visited any of the old haunts, but he hadn't. Pure business, he says, shaking his head. Visited a production plant and another production plant but that was about it. Over dinner, he begins nodding off at the table and Shirley suggests they both hit the sack early. She gets up with her plate and Randy pats her on the butt. Elida cracks a smile at that.

Paul, Elida, Danielle, and I have a great conversation about churches in the South. They've never seen a megachurch. Like Paul, they consider churches that have 1,000 members to be a large church. I tell them about First Baptist Church and Second Baptist Church, both of them with more than 20,000 members, and Lakewood with more than 30,000, all in the same city. And that's just the beginning. Spirituality is big business down in the South, enormous buildings and publishing houses connected to them, huge conferences and seminars and the whole bit. They don't understand how 20,000 people can all go to one church. There aren't even 20,000 people who live in Ridgefield. I tell them there are parts of it that are great, because you feel like you are involved in an enormous movement when you go to a church that big, and I think there is even something that comforts people about believing something that 20,000 other people in the room all believe.

"But it isn't very intimate, is it?" Danielle asks.

"I don't guess so," I say.

"I was thinking a lot about faith while I was in Costa Rica," Danielle says, shifting the subject within its theme. "Everything came to a head down there. I was really bent out of shape about church and Christianity. I knew I had to make a decision about what I believed."

"I didn't realize you were going through anything like that," I say.

Danielle tells us she did some serious thinking while she was there. She was very thankful for the other students (Christians) who were faithful to her even while she was asking some serious, and possibly offensive, questions about her faith. Everything was resolved, she says, when she had to get on a plane and discovered that she'd lost her wallet. They wouldn't let her on the plane without her ID. With only an hour to spare, she took a cab to the club where she had been the night before. She prayed all the way there and told God she was sorry and got really upset. She ended up finding her wallet in the booth where she had been seated, and somehow this helped her believe God was there.

"I know it sounds superstitious or whatever, but it was like God was saying, 'Hey, I know you are doubting me right now, but I'm here. Just trust Me.' It helped," Danielle says.

Paul says he had a similar experience in the junkyard in Vegas. He says he had been asking some serious questions, not about the truth of Christ, but about whether or not he was really living out and experiencing faith, whatever that looks like. He says finding the part in the junkyard was an "instrumental happening." That's what he calls it, an "instrumental happening." Then he tells the girls I am an atheist.

"An atheist, Don?" Danielle questions.

"No. I said I thought it sucked that God didn't make us born with wings or something and Paul seems to think I am having a faith crisis," I say. Danielle smiles.

"Wings, eh?" Elida says, looking very beautiful.

"Wings," I say.

She puts her cup of tea down and flaps her arms like a chicken.

Before we know it, it is 3:00 a.m. and we are all yawns. Elida says we can sleep downstairs, but Paul and I both shake our heads. We'll sleep outside, we say.

"Outside?" Elida questions.

"Can't sleep inside anymore. We've been in the van for over a month. We're used to the fresh air," one of us comments.

"Well!" Elida proclaims. "If you guys are sleeping outside, we're sleeping outside!"

"What?" Danielle questions.

"We'll all sleep on the lawn. I'll get the sleeping bags." With that, Elida disappears down the stairs. We hear her stirring around in a closet. Danielle tells us she's getting the sleeping bags out and pulling them from the garbage bags that Daddy keeps them in. There is a side door off the breakfast nook that opens out onto a deck that overlooks the front yard. Danielle steps out on the deck to see Elida unrolling sleeping bags. "Looks like we're sleeping outside," Danielle says with a smile.

• • •

". . . AND WHEN THEY WENT BACK INTO THE HOUSE, they saw the ghost of their aunt Edna. She was holding a knife and a pumpkin." Elida's voice is soft and quiet. She is almost whispering. "They look at Aunt Edna and she begins to sway in the wind. She says [Elida's voice gets deep], 'You never should have slept in the pumpkin patch.'"

Danielle can't help but interrupt: "Elida, Aunt Edna is not a scary name. And your story has no point."

"It's a scary story," Elida says.

"For three-year-olds!" Danielle tells her.

"Shhh." Paul quiets the girls.

"What is it?" Danielle asks.

"Did you hear that?" Paul says.

"Hear what?" asks Elida.

"The voice."

"What voice?"

"It sounded like the wind. It was a whisper. Someone whispered in my ear. It was a low voice."

Elida pulls her sleeping bag over her head. Through the bag we hear her ask, "What did the voice say?"

"It said," Paul pauses, lowering his voice to speak in a raspy whisper, "four . . . will . . . die . . . tonight."

Elida gasps. Danielle chuckles. Then there is silence.

"The voice could have been talking about anyone," I say. "It probably won't be us."

23 RANCH

PAUL MAKES A CALL TO BLACK BUTTE RANCH FROM the Bjurs's house and he secures a job for himself as a lifeguard. He also finds there is an opening in the housekeeping department and sets a time for me to interview. You will be a janitor, he says. You will be working with about twenty women. You will love it, he assures me.

Black Butte Ranch is a large, active cattle ranch in the mountains of central Oregon. It is a resort, but it's also a summer home for wealthy people from Portland and folks who come up from California. The ranch is just up from the high desert, set in the foothills of the Cascade Range. Paul says you can see the Three Sisters, Mount Washington, and Mount Jefferson from the meadow beneath Black Butte. Apparently, every summer, students come from all over the country to live in the woods and work on the ranch. Two cultures coexist, those who live in the woods and work the ranch, and the teenagers and college students who spend the summer here in their parents' summer homes, their parents, most of the time, not around. There are hundreds of miles of bike paths and thousands of miles of forest service roads that venture out from the ranch property. It's a great place to spend the summer, Paul tells me.

"When is my interview?" I ask.

"First thing tomorrow morning."

Danielle looks upset. We've been with the Bjurs for more than a week. We started out as moochers, but then the Bjurs

217

wouldn't let us go. Shirley kept us there, really. She'd say we should stay for another meal, then another, then we'd get to talking over coffee and sooner or later, we'd end up staying the night, sleeping on the lawn, telling stories, and pondering Mount St. Helens off in the distance, the snow lit by the moon. We'd go into Portland at night, buy a case of beer and sit outside a club getting toasted, then go in and dance a little, smoke a few cigarettes and walk the streets, window-shopping at four in the morning. I got drunk last weekend and Paul, Danielle, and Elida laughed at me as I threw up behind a Taco Bell. It was an idiot thing to do, and I felt terrible when Shirley found out about it. They really have become like family. That was the night I confessed my love for Elida, to which she responded by rolling her eyes. Luckily, we were able to laugh about it the next day.

Something did spark between Paul and Danielle, though. Whether it works out, and how it could, given the fact we will be living in the woods for the summer, remains to be seen. But they both seem levelheaded and patient. Randy and Shirley enjoyed the unfolding of their romance. They approve of Paul.

Danielle will be leaving for Sacramento soon, where she will live with her grandparents and attend summer school. She is on track to receive her bachelor's degree in a short three-year span. Two of those years are behind her.

We pack the van slowly, taking most of the afternoon. Paul is in no hurry to leave and neither am I. Paul and Danielle go for a walk down by the river and I take the van over to Elida's school where she told me to wait in the parking lot. I sit in the van, waiting for her to come out, when I notice a window in one of the classrooms opens and a backpack comes falling out, spilling a few books onto the lawn. After the backpack comes Elida, falling atop the pack and lying low, peeking back into the window to see if the teacher noticed. She gathers her books, reaches into the classroom and closes the window, then runs toward the van as though it were a prison break. Elida and I go over to Burgerville, where she works summers, and get a milk shake. She brings up the fact that I am in love with her several times and I tell her to knock it off. Am I embarrassing you? she says. *High school girl, Don. Can't seem to keep the older boys from taking interest, I guess.*

We get back to the house and find Randy dillydallying around, pretending he has things to do at home that prevent him from going to work on time. He looks at me and Elida and shakes his head. "You're skipping school?" he questions, giving her a stern look.

Elida covers her mouth and coughs. "I'm not feeling well, Daddy." "You a part of this?" he asks me, looking over Elida's shoulder.

Paul and Danielle come back from the river covered in dead grass. I whisper to Paul that the two of them look like they've been rolling around in a barn and he quickly swipes the dirt and grass off of his sleeve and belly. Danielle notices what he's doing and does the same, smiling and turning red. I grab the last of the bags and throw them in the back of the van. We said our good-byes to Nate earlier, before he was taken to school, and Shirley has been busy packing lunches for us. She brings them out and hands them to me and I set them in the passenger's seat, giving her a hug.

Randy gathers us around the van and says a prayer. He asks God to protect us and teach us whatever it is He wants us to know. Randy thanks God for introducing us to them, and making us a part of the family. There's nothing we can say after that, so Paul and I give everybody hugs and climb in the van, with Paul at the wheel and head down the driveway. I take a long look at Mount St. Helens as we round the neighbor's barn and find the main road. I imagine two thousand feet of the mountain blowing off the top, sending a cloud of ash more than a mile high. Paul has a dazed look on his face and it is obvious he is thinking about Danielle.

IF THERE IS A HIGH DESERT IN OREGON, THE VALLEY on the Pacific side of the mountain shows no hint of it. Highway 26 runs through Gresham, a town east of Portland, then climbs for about twenty miles into the town of Sandy. Beyond Sandy we get into thick forests of evergreen and pass through towns with names like Rhododendron, Welches, and Government Camp. The thick green climbs right up to the tree line of Mount Hood. The air is clean and thin up here. The terrain dips down into a canyon on our right and lifts to eleven thousand feet on our left. Mount Hood is all snow and ice coming up out of the earth like a sleeping thing, giving you the feel that at any moment it is going to roll over and crush you. Its full-white brightness in the midday sun seems to light up all the aspen and evergreen off its wings. Rock is exposed here and there, but most of it is snow and ice, brown ice pushed off the road to form thick, dirty walls of melting shoulder. The evergreens climb to the left till their lungs can't breathe, and frame for the mind the great steep of bubbled lava. In places Mount Hood appears as a perfect cone, but then another mile down the road and you see a jagged spot on top, then another mile and it is a perfect cone again. A photographer could take twenty photos from twenty locations and convince an amateur that he's shot twenty separate mountains.

Leaving Mount Hood in our rearview mirror, we begin our descent into central Oregon. Paul is right about the terrain changing abruptly. From the deciduous landscape of the valley, we climbed into dense forest with little undergrowth, and now we have settled into rocks, sand, and sagebrush. In only three hours, it feels like we went from Scotland to Utah. The clouds that roll in off the Pacific are too thick and heavy to pass over the Cascades, so central Oregon gets much less rain. Paul tells me the winter brings occasional snow, but the summers are perfect. Warm and sunny and dry.

Black Butte rests in the foreground of at least six visible snowcapped mountains. Paul names them as the North Sister, the Middle Sister, and the South Sister, Mount Jefferson, Mount Washington, and Three-Fingered Jack. He says he's climbed them all. The Pacific Crest Trail, he tells me, runs right between them, up from Mexico through the Sierra Nevada, over to Mount Hood and then across the Columbia River into Washington before finding Mount Rainier and then Canada. His lifelong dream is to hike the PCT from Mexico all the way north. It will take him more than six months, he says.

When we find the town of Sisters, it is just as Paul described. There are cone lickers and rows of shops. It's a western town with wooden walks in front of the shops. You can see the hills lift to the east. We are at the base of Black Butte now. It is a perfect cone of a hill, five thousand feet high, if not more. It should be called a mountain. It is big and dark with clouds around its head and thick forest all the way to the summit.

The entrance to Black Butte Ranch is only twenty miles beyond the town of Sisters. The road climbs all twenty of the miles. We have circled back into the Cascade Range, and the air is the cleanest I've breathed since we left Texas. You can feel the cleanness of the air against your skin, and it is as though you can see it, or see other things through it, as though somebody had cleaned your glasses. Sunlight filters through the pines and paints bright, moving abstracts against the roads and forest floor. Creeks slide out over rock beds and under bridges and you can smell the moisture and coolness in the air as we pass over.

Paul signals a left turn and we slow, downshift, and pull into the entrance of the ranch. There is a guardhouse and a gate, and Paul navigates to the window at the house (about the size of a tollbooth). The fellow asks what we are doing and Paul tells him he is a lifeguard showing up for the summer. The fellow lifts the gate and we enter. The ranch is all I expected and more. Before us is a meadow surrounded by forest and through the meadow (a square mile in size) runs a stream, and near the stream are horses and cattle. We park in the lot closest to the lodge and step out. Above the clouds, in the distance, stand the Three

Sisters, three towering peaks. Next to the Sisters are Three-Fingered Jack and Mount Jefferson. Behind us is Black Butte.

Paul points out the pool he will be guarding. It backs up to the pond and sits in front of the tennis courts. There are three pools, he says. We rotate, but I usually get assigned to this one. It's nice, he says, because he usually has friends who work in Honkers Café and they bring him food. Went all last summer without buying a meal, he says.

PAUL'S BEEN PRETTY QUIET FOR THE LAST HALF HOUR. We've been driving around the place and every few miles he will stop and look into some stretch of forest as if to recall some distant memory. We round what I think is the backside of the ranch and get a view of the Three Sisters, three matching peaks all folded into each other at their timberlines, each distinct and noble and yet humble, one not reaching to out-rise the others. We navigate back into the forest and I note the size of some of the houses, manors, more like, and some mansions. The golf course runs in and out of the forest, following streams that build to ponds and small lakes before the greens.

"Where are we going now?" I ask.

"To make camp. We need to do it before the sun goes down. We have about an hour."

We round back by the entrance gate but bypass it for a road that swings left. Not long onto it, we come upon another security gate. Paul looks at a little sheet of paper and punches the code, the gate swings open, and we drive through. Several enormous homes are tucked into the trees that surround this part of the meadow. There is a paved sidewalk that stitches one home to another, but they are each set on an acre or more of land. The road weaves back into the homes and crosses the golf course and pond and then back into more homes. Paul points out an empty lot that backs up to a fence and then dips down into a small ravine covered in aspen. He explains that we will make camp across the fence and down into the woods. It's illegal to camp back there, he warns. He says that the forest service would fine us if we were to get caught. It's a stealth operation, apparently.

"Here's what we'll do," he explains. "Let's drop our gear off in this ditch; we'll park the van and come back for the gear."

"Whatever," I tell him.

He stops the van, opens the side door, and removes his backpack. The ditch is twenty yards off the road, so he slides his backpack down into the ditch, comes back for his sleeping bag, and does the same with a few other items. I pull my gear out and imitate Paul. He has one tent. We've not used it the entire trip so I didn't know he had it, but he removes it from the van and slides it into the ditch. Then, in an instant, we are driving away. We round a turn or two and park the van in the parking lot of another community pool. Nobody will bother the van here, he tells me.

"Why don't we just live in the van?" I ask.

"Ranch security will make sure nobody is living in it. It's okay to park it here for a while, as long as we move it every couple of days, but we can't sleep in it. They will make us leave."

I have a hundred more questions but Paul does not seem to be in the mood to answer questions. He is home, I guess.

I realize it now. All this time I've known Paul, he has been the new guy. Now I am the new guy. It's an odd switch. This is clearly his comfort zone: the woods and all.

We are at a quick clip back to our gear, and Paul checks over his shoulder before pacing down the length of the ditch. Follow me, he says, and shoulders his pack and runs. I grab mine and run behind him. He tosses his pack over a fence and it rolls down a ledge of exposed rock. He heads back for the rest of the gear, being careful nobody sees him pick it up and run into the woods. We need two trips apiece to collect our things.

We jump the fence, boulder down the ledge, and gather our stuff at the bottom. Paul leads the way through the thick forest, through a hundred yards of baby aspen, all growing only a few feet apart, and into a clearing where there is a tent established. Henry, Paul says. Henry has already set up camp.

"Who is Henry?" I ask.

"An old friend," Paul answers. "You'll love Henry, Don. He's great." Paul walks over to the opening of the tent and drops his gear. "Hank!" he yells. Nobody answers. "He isn't here," Paul says, looking in the tent. "Well," he continues, "we should go ahead and set up the tent."

"Small tent," I say.

"We're not going to sleep in it," he tells me. "We'll just put our gear in there during the day. We should put it over here, under this tree. That way nobody will spot it." Paul begins unrolling the tent. I help him but I don't know what I'm doing, so finally I just stand back and watch, handing things to him when he needs me to.

"Maybe you can go back and get the rest of the gear at the ledge," Paul tells me.

"Sure. Just bring it all back here, right?"

Paul is busy with the tent. He talks to me without looking up. "Here would be the place."

I venture back through the aspen. On the way, I encounter two deer. They are nibbling at grass. I see their graceful brown bodies in splotches through the thick of trees. When they hear me, they become stiff, move in sudden jerks, find my eyes, stare me down, then leap off.

24 THE WOODS

BECAUSE BLACK BUTTE RANCH IS AT FOUR THOUSAND feet, and because there isn't a city for twenty miles, the stars at night feel as though they are falling into the meadow. At midnight it feels there is more light in the sky than darkness, as though God took a fistful of stardust and threw it upward where it shimmers at the apex of its ascent, as though what we know as creation exists only for this brief second before it all comes crashing down again. Brilliant blue clusters spread thick and dense and they sparkle and fade, sparkle and fade. It is silent music, the night sky. God does well to live atop them. And I wonder, as I lie in the meadow with a piece of grass between my teeth, if angels look down upon the sky to which we look up? And I wonder at all the other creation that must be out there, in some other dimension, in some other compartment of God's imagination. I wonder how much more of *it* there *is* out there, or anywhere, or nowhere. Scientists have always been baffled about all of this something having to have come from nothing, and I wonder what kinds of worlds the nothingness must inhabit. I wonder at what Paul said back in Portland, how God is good, how it doesn't do any good to run from Him because what He has is good and who He is, is good. Even if I want to run, it isn't really what I want—what I want is Him, even if I don't believe it. If He made all this existence, you would think He would know what He is doing, and you would think He could be trusted. Everything I want is just Him, to get lost in Him, to feel His love and more and more of this dazzling that He does. I wonder at His beautiful system and how it feels better than anything I could choose or invent for myself. I wonder as I gaze up at the night sky, this love letter from God to creation, this reminder that somewhere there is peace, somewhere there is order, and I think about how great His kingdom is, and is going to be, and I wonder, in this rare and beautiful moment, how I could ever want to walk away from it all. There are so many stars I will dream of them. I open my eyes and see stars, then close them and see stars. In the morning the sun will rise, the flowers will bloom in the spring, squirrels will perform acrobatic jumps from treetops to treetops, babies will gurgle, and I consider how delightful everything is. I remember as well what Paul had said in the canyon, about how what we used to want was cars and money and stuff and then all we wanted was a bowl of cereal, and I actually laugh out loud about it because right now we're here. I have absolutely nothing. I have no money and no home and nothing but a pair of shoes and a sleeping bag, and I am finally seeing how good life is, how beautiful it is.

I start realizing that this is the first time I have encountered beauty in nature. I've read poems that have made my heart race. I've read scenes in novels that have caused me to close the book, set my head in my hands, and wonder how a human could so brilliantly orchestrate words. But nature has never inspired me until now. *God is an artist*, I think to myself. I have known this for a long time, seeing His brushwork in the sunrise and sunset, and His sculpting in the mountains and the rivers. But the night sky is His greatest work. And I would have never known it if I had stayed in Houston. I would have bought a little condo and filled it with Ikea trinkets and dated some girl just because she was hot and would have read self-help books, end to end, one after another, trying to fix the gaping hole in the bottom of my soul, the hole that, right now, seems plugged with Orion, allowing my soul to collect that feeling of belonging and love you only get when you stop long enough to engage the obvious.

I FALL ASLEEP IN THE MEADOW AND WAKE UP COLD A few times, rolling over on myself to get some warmth. I finally get up about the time the sun makes it over the mountains. It is cold, though, and the ground is a bit damp. The sun has been up for an hour or so, and there is a bed of bent grass where my body lay. Having no idea what time it is, I walk back through the meadow toward camp. When I get there, I see Paul rummaging around in the tent. When he hears me he comes out and immediately scolds me for missing my interview.

"What interview?" I ask.

"You have an interview with housekeeping this morning, you idiot!"

"I forgot," I say. "I'll go tomorrow."

"No, Don. You have to go. We both have to get jobs," he tells me.

"If I'm late, I might as well go tomorrow."

"No!" he shouts. "You have to go. Apologize to them for being late."

"You should go," a strange voice says.

"Who is that?" I ask.

"Don, this is Henry. Henry, this is Don. He's a friend from Texas." Henry comes out of the tent, dragging a backpack behind him.

"The Lone Star State," Henry says with a smile. He must have slipped into camp last night. He is a wiry fellow with big blond hair sticking out in all directions. A handsome guy with big teeth and the sort of smile that probably gets him stuff for free.

"Nice to meet you, Henry."

"Good to meet you, Don. I understand you are going to be a janitor."

"Yes," I say. "And what is it you do?"

"I'm a lifeguard."

"Tough job," I say, rolling my eyes.

"Someone has to do it," he says.

I look over at Paul, who is wearing a worried expression and looking at the sun through the aspen.

"It's eight thirty, Don. You better hustle. Your interview was at eight."

"You can tell the time by looking at the sun?" I say, having already known that from our time in the canyon.

"Yes. It's late. You better go."

"I didn't know you could do that," I said, trying to bring back up the old conversation.

"Do what?" Paul questions.

"Tell time by looking at the sun. Native Americans do that, you know."

"Get out of here, man." Paul looks at the sun while he's talking. "Do you remember how to get there?"

"Just go up the road and take a left. Two miles, right?"

"Two miles," Paul clarifies.

"How do I look?" I ask.

"Terrible," he says. "Do something with your hair before you talk to them."

"You look fine," Henry says, broadening his grin. "I'd let you clean my toilet any day."

"Thanks, Henry," I say, motioning to Paul to take notice of his good manners.

"Meet me at the main pool when you are done," Paul tells me. "Do you remember where it is?"

"I'll find it," I say, stepping over a fallen tree and heading into the aspen.

"Cool guy," Henry says to Paul as I walk off.

"He's going to be late," Paul states.

Though it is late, the woods are growing out of a mist this morning. There are patches of cloud hanging thick in the aspen. It is cold. Must be forty degrees, if not colder. I find a good stride and stick to it, more to warm up than to make my interview. Not more than a hundred yards from camp I stumble upon the deer I saw yesterday. There are two, one with horns. They look up and freeze, staring at me for at least thirty seconds. I lean toward a step and they are off through the woods. With spurts of grace they fire through the mist like arrows, slowing at the top of their jumps and bounding off the ground, turning quick around trees.

The road to the housekeeping office rounds hills and is lined by trees and houses. There must be a thousand homes here at Black Butte Ranch. Earlier, when Paul suggested working on a cattle ranch, I pictured us roping cows and driving teams of wild horses. But this is a resort. It might have started as an active cattle ranch, but now it is a giant real estate project. I wonder what a house out here would cost, and how much money a family would have to have to use one of these as a *second* home.

"ARE YOU DONALD MILLER?" A DARK-HAIRED WOMAN asks as I enter the housekeeping department. She comes out of her office with a clipboard in her hand. She looks to be stressed: pale white face with lips traced in red lipstick. Her hands are weathered. One hand grips the clipboard and the other holds a walkie-talkie. She barks a command into the walkie-talkie and then tells me to wait in her office. I can hear her dividing up houses. Team one is to take houses 1–40 and team two is to take 41–80 and so on and so on, all the way through team ten. She makes small talk with one of the workers and then comes back into the office.

"You are late," she says.

"Yes, ma'am. I'm sorry about . . ."

"Do you make it a habit of being late to interviews?"

"No, ma'am. It's just that . . ."

"I don't need to hear your personal problems. If you want to work here, you need to be on time."

"I understand," I tell her.

"You understand," she says in sarcasm. "If you understood, you would have been on time. But you didn't understand. You understand now, but you didn't understand before or else you would have been on time. Do you understand?"

"Is this a trick question?" I say with a smile.

"Very funny. We've got a smart aleck, do we?"

"No, ma'am. I didn't mean it like that." I'm hesitant with my words. "I was just breaking the ice, I guess. I won't be late. I promise you that much."

"You don't have the job yet, Mr. Miller. You may not have the opportunity to show up on time."

The tension in the room is broken when an older, broad-shouldered, motherly woman steps into the office with a pile of folded towels in her hands. I gather that my interviewer's name is Lucy, because this woman calls her Lucy. And the motherly woman's name is Laurel.

Laurel tells Lucy she will need more towels if she is going to clean the condos and houses 1–40. Lucy tells her to take more, but to make sure and write it down so she knows where they are. Before leaving, Laurel looks down at me and says, "Fresh meat." She smiles as she says it, so I smile back and laugh. Laurel laughs.

"I'll take this one," Laurel says. "We could use some muscle on my team."

"He has a habit of being late," Lucy says to Laurel.

"I'll whip him into shape," Laurel says and looks at me with a grin. I grin back.

"You've got him," Lucy tells her. "If he gives you any trouble, tell me. I have already found out he has an attitude."

"What's his name?" Laurel asks. Nobody bothers to ask me.

"It doesn't matter," Lucy says and slaps Laurel on the back. "He won't last long."

Laurel exits and walks back into the laundry room to get more towels.

"All right, Donald Miller," Lucy begins, "what is your social security number?"

I give her the number.

"And your address?"

I give her my Texas address.

"Coming in all the way from Texas, are you? That's a long commute, don't you think?"

I tell her I don't have an address around here.

Lucy leans back in her chair. She sets her pen down and runs her hands through her long, unkempt hair. She looks out the window.

"Donald, you know that people aren't supposed to live in the woods around here, don't you?"

That's it, I guess. I messed up. "I've heard that, yes, ma'am."

Lucy takes a long look at me, shakes her head, picks up her pen, and begins to write an address on the form.

"There is a shower in the back," she says.

"Pardon me?"

Lucy points through her office door toward a door on the other side of the laundry room. "Through that door," she says, "there is a shower. If a person needed to take a shower in the morning, a person could do it through that door."

"I see."

"Be here at seven thirty tomorrow morning," she says. She doesn't look up; she just writes on my form.

I sit there and look at her. I cross my legs. I uncross my legs.

"You can go," she says.

"Thank you," I tell her.

"Be on time," she says.

"Yes."

"My name is Lucy. Call me Lucy, but I am not your friend. One mistake, and you are gone."

"I understand," I say.

"You did not understand this morning. You may understand now, but you did not understand this morning."

Laurel snickers when she sees me walk out of the office.

BIKE PATHS LINE EACH STREET ON THE RANCH. THE streets are dark asphalt, and the bike paths are half as wide as the street. I weave through the streets, not really knowing where I am going. I decide that if I continue walking north, I will find the main pool, where Paul is supposed to be working. So I wander, between and around big, expensive homes. Yuppie couples in Volvos pass me. None of them wave.

The bike path breaks away from the road, away from the houses, into a thicket of trees. It is here that I see the woman of my dreams. She is riding a bike, alone. A girl this pretty should not be riding alone. She passes me quickly and grins. She's wearing a Black Butte polo-style shirt. She must work on the ranch somewhere. I bet Paul knows her. I turn around to watch her pedal through the trees and disappear as the bike path weaves right, which is probably the direction I should be walking. She had long brown hair and looked polite and innocent. *What's a nice girl like you doing in a forest like this?* I think to myself.

The bike path opens up into the meadow where Mount Washington, Three-Fingered Jack, and Mount Jefferson are visible. This is where I slept last night, but the fog has lifted. The mountains are snowcapped, lit by the midmorning sun, and simply beautiful. All is silent, but in my mind I hear the cold wind blow furiously across the mountaintops. Clouds are high and scattered. Beyond the clouds is deep, endless blue. The meadow is a mile wide, it seems. The farther I walk into the open, the more spectacular the view becomes. Black Butte lifts to my right, and behind me are the Three Sisters and Broken Top. Six mountains, as well as Black Butte, are all visible from the center of the meadow. *Stunning,* I think to myself. *Colorado, eat your heart out.*

AS FAR AS I AM CONCERNED, THE PRIMARY OCCUPATION of a lifeguard is to swing a whistle around in your hand, working the rope through each finger, then swinging the other direction until the rope unwinds. Lifeguards who are good at their job can do it for half an hour without getting tangled.

I find Paul sitting up in his chair, twirling his whistle. Henry is preparing chemicals to put into the pool. Paul asks me if I got the job and I tell him I did. Good, he says. We both need to work. You call this working? I say to him, holding my hands out at the pool. Somebody has to do it, he says. *Saving lives is a man's job.*

"You hungry?" Paul says.

"I could eat," I answer.

"Henry, would you mind if I took lunch?"

"Bring me some," Henry says.

"Will do." Paul climbs down from his post.

"See you later, Henry," I tell him.

"Yeah, dude. I'll see you tonight. Are you going with us to the cave?"

"What cave?" I ask.

"I haven't told him yet," Paul says.

I nod at Henry and he turns to watch the pool. He takes his position atop the chair and starts twirling his whistle. He tells one of the kids (there are *two* kids to protect today, one for each lifeguard) not to run.

Paul and I cross the lawn and take seats on a deck outside Honkers Café, named after the ducks in the lake. I ask him how we can afford to eat, since we only have twenty dollars or so. He tells me the owner of the café always takes care of the guys who live in the woods. The kids who live in their parents' houses pay, but the folks who live in the woods eat for free.

"Do we order?" I ask.

"Nope. We just sit here, and sooner or later food finds its way to the table. He gives us only what he has too much of. You know, leftover pizza and that sort of thing."

"I get it."

"So, Don, how much are they going to pay you?"

"I didn't ask."

"You didn't ask?"

"Didn't think of it. She was kinda tough, you know. She was mad because I was late."

"Told you," he says.

"I didn't think they took housekeeping so seriously."

"Oh, yeah," he says. "They're like the army. They drive around in those big white vans and almost run people over, talking on their walkie-talkies and all. Those women could take over a small third world country. They're serious."

"I gathered that."

A young girl comes through the door and says hello to Paul. It's the girl from the meadow. The girl on the bike. Paul gets up and gives her a hug. He calls her Molly. "Molly, this is my friend, Don."

"Nice to meet you," she says. She doesn't remember me from the meadow.

"Nice to meet you," I tell her.

"I suppose you guys are hungry," she says to us.

"Starved," Paul tells her.

"How does a calzone sound? Sound good?"

"Sounds great," Paul says.

Molly walks back into the café.

"Where does she live? Is she from Oregon?" I start asking.

"I thought you were in love with Elida," Paul states.

"She's in high school, you sick creep. Where is Molly from? Is she in the woods somewhere?"

"I don't know where she's from. She goes to school some-where in Minnesota. But I don't think she is from Oregon. She stays here every summer with Jodie."

"Who's Jodie?" I ask.

"Jodie is who she stays with."

"You said that already."

"She's a friend. Jodie is a friend. Her family has a summer home on the ranch. Jodie is a lifeguard."

"And Molly is her friend."

"Yes," Paul clarifies. A moment later, "Speaking of infatua-tion . . ."

"I'm not infatuated," I tell him. "I just like the way she rides a bike."

"How do you know how she rides a bike?" Paul asks.

"Everybody rides a bike the same," I say.

"What are you talking about?" Paul asks.

"What are you talking about?" I say.

"Anyway," he begins, rolling his eyes. "Speaking of infatu-ation. Guess who called today?"

"Who?"

"Danielle."

"Danielle called you?"

"She called us. She called the lodge and they transferred the call to me at the pool."

"What did she have to say?"

"She's coming here. She's coming by on her way to Sacramento."

"How long is she going to stay?" I ask.

"Just for the day. She'll drive all night to get down to Sacramento. She's coming three weeks from now. Friday, possibly. Three weekends away, right?"

"What is today, Paul?"

"Today." Paul thinks to himself for a second. "I think it's Tuesday. But I'm not sure."

"Tuesday," I clarify.

Molly comes out with two huge calzones and sets mine down with a smile. She asks if I'm going to the cave tonight. I give her a confused look and then glance at Paul.

"I haven't told him yet," Paul says.

"Fine. Well, have fun," Molly says.

"Don here likes the way you ride a bike," Paul says, and I give him a death stare.

"I don't understand," Molly says, her blue eyes coming off her pale complexion like lake water.

"I was saying to Paul that it would be nice to go for a bike ride around here, saying that I thought I saw you in the meadow earlier."

"I don't remember this conversation," Paul says, shrugging his shoulders.

"That's because you're an idiot," I say. "Shut up or I am not going to teach you how to read."

"Yeah, it is a good place to ride a bike," Molly says, looking out toward the meadow. "Do you have a bike here?" she asks.

"He could ride on your handle bars," Paul says. "The two of you could get drunk later and Don could tell you how he feels." After he says this I kick him in the shin.

"Well, sounds fun. I better get back to work. Nice to meet you, Don," Molly says.

"Nice to meet you, Molly. Have a great day. I will see you around."

I will see you around, Paul mocks in a girly voice.

"I'm telling Danielle you're a recovering homosexual," I say to him. "Seriously, Paul, I am telling her you found Jesus and have barely wanted a man since, that she has nothing to worry about, that you will always like her and most of the time those conversions really stick."

25 THE CAVE

WE ARE NOT SLEEPING IN THE WOODS TONIGHT. PAUL tells me that everyone is headed to the cave. Apparently there are long lava tubes that tunnel under these mountains. There is a special one these guys camp in every year. It holds all sorts of memories.

We have been at the café most of the day. I talked with Paul for a while over lunch, then Henry came and joined us, leaving the lifeguarding to one of the locals. Some of the other guys showed up and Paul introduced me to them: Eddie, Pat, Brick, and Owen. All of these guys are out of NYU, I guess, and all of them literature majors, Bruce Springsteen fans. Owen is an epic poet and keeps notebooks with him always, writing down thoughts about girls and rocks and water and the metaphor of flight. Paul goes back to work and Eddie and I get to talking about girls, about how long it has been since he has had sex. Apparently it has been a whole month. I keep my mouth shut, just nod like it has been at least a month for me too. To be honest, he's not too calloused about sex like some guys are, but actually associates a kind of emotion to the act, as though he is good at falling in love for a night or two and then moving on. It really is about the connection, he says to me, admitting that with him the "connection" doesn't last very long.

The guys have moved their stuff out to aspen camp, and Brick starts telling me stories about years past when he and Paul stole a whole set of patio furniture off somebody's back deck. They had a regular living room set up out in the forest. They went back in the middle of the night to steal a barbeque grill but had to leave it in the middle of a field when security rounded the corner with their lights flashing. The security officers chased them along the road for a while but Brick and Paul dipped into some woods and disappeared like deer. I ask about the cave and Eddie says it's a tradition, once we all get here, to go sleep in the cave. It's up in the mountains a bit, Eddie says, looking over at Brick as if to ask whether he remembers where it is.

BRICK TAKES THE VAN UP STEEP, DARK ROADS LIT SOFTLY by moonlight through clouds. He is commenting to Paul on the handling. He says it's not bad for a van this old. Paul tells him about the mechanic in Nevada and about the junkyard, about how God showed up to answer our prayers. Brick isn't the spiritual type, so he shrugs it off. He pulls the van over into some trees. Pines scrape the side of the van and Owen has a tough time getting the door open. Nice parking, Eddie says. Brick thanks him. Outside the van, everyone acts like they know what they are doing. They grab sleeping bags and Brick throws one at me. Eddie asks about matches and Pat says he has a lighter, proving it by lighting a cigarette.

"We running?" Eddie asks.

"Sure we are," Paul tells him.

With that, Eddie bolts into the woods as Pat and Owen follow him, Pat holding his cigarette out before him like a torch. He runs smooth and fast around small trees and over logs. Owen, the biggest of the gang out of NYU, simply runs through the trees. He makes his way through the forest like some sort of poet beast, cracking branches with each stride. I am behind them, and Paul and Brick are behind me. Henry is running parallel. It's quite a sight, all of us running in and out of moon shadows. *If there were music to the scene, it would be bagpipes,* I think to myself. All of us are breathing heavily, and it's cold, so mist rises out of our mouths. Nobody screams or yells; they just run quickly. I don't know why we are running like this. Seems sensible to walk. But I don't want to get lost, so I run. And we run. And we run. About twenty minutes into the forest, we come to the top of a hill.

"This is it," Paul says, taking a breath.

"I don't see a cave," I tell him.

Paul points to a hole in the ground. It's not a large hole, about five feet by five feet. But he says it's the mouth of a cave. Brick takes a flashlight out of his pack and shines it down into the hole. "The ladder is down," he says.

"Happens every year," Eddie grumbles.

Brick takes some tubed webbing out of his pack and ties it around his waist. He has a headlamp that he straps around his head. The guys grab the rope and Brick lowers himself into the cave. His light throws shadows against the rock wall and I can tell the cave is pretty large.

Brick picks up a handmade ladder from the floor of the cave and pokes it through the opening. Eddie is the first to descend, then Paul, then me with Henry, Owen, and Pat right behind. Paul and Brick are the only ones with lights, which they shine deep into the cave.

I follow the light about a hundred yards down to where Paul and Brick reveal an old fire pit. There is wood scattered around the cave, old firewood, some of it unused, so we begin foraging for a fire. Pat lights the thing with his lighter, lighting another cigarette while he is at it. As it comes to life, the fire illumines the cave. The rock is deep and jagged, but the ground is smooth. The back of the cave extends at least two hundred yards, beyond which it is too dark to see.

"You ever been to the back of this thing?" I ask Paul.

"Nope. We've been back about a mile or so, but it's just more of the same, really. Doesn't get any smaller, doesn't get any bigger."

"Any animals in here?" I ask him.

"Never seen any. The opening is kinda tough on animals. I

would think if they fell in, they'd die from the fall. If that didn't get them, they'd die of thirst pretty quickly."

"I see," I say.

We make small talk for a few hours, mostly stories about drinking and stealing and girls on the ranch from years past. Eddie, Pat, and Owen spread out their sleeping bags and lie down. Owen is writing something and Pat is tinkering with his pocketknife. Eddie pulls out a pipe and fills the air with sweet-smelling smoke. I lean over to whisper to Paul.

"You know I have to be at work at seven thirty tomorrow. Earlier if I want to take a shower."

"Don't worry, I'll get you there. You'll be fine," he assures me.

Eddie overhears us. "Where you working, Don?"

"Housekeeping," I tell him.

"Militant types," Brick says.

"You can say that again," Henry chimes in.

One of the guys asks how long I intend to stay. I tell them it depends on whether I get a job in Colorado or not. I applied for a position at this camp out there, but I haven't called them to see if I got the job. If so, I hope to make enough money in housekeeping to get a plane ticket to Colorado Springs. Paul looks surprised at this. We never really talked about what I was going to do when the trip was over. But that's the plan.

"I didn't know you were thinking of Colorado," Paul says.

"It's not final or anything. I just sent an application in before we left. They start sessions in June, so I would be here for a month, no matter what."

"That's cool. I'd just hate for you to miss a summer in the woods."

"Summer in the woods is good, Don," Brick tells me. "Nothing to do but swim, flirt with rich girls, drink beer, swim, flirt with rich girls, go to parties at rich girls' houses, you know, just good vibes all around."

"Sounds good," I say, nodding my head.

"You a religious type, too, Don?" Eddie asks.

"I am. I mean, I always have been, been wondering about it, you know, but had a good night in the meadow last night. Just the stars, you know, really got me feeling like there was something more, something good."

"Aliens?" Owen asks.

"God," I say.

"Very good," Henry says, glowing out into a grin.

"You believe in God?" I ask Henry.

"Does God believe in me? That is the question." He says this through the same big grin. I laugh at him and Paul laughs. Eddie looks over at Owen.

"A poem!" Eddie says.

Owen pulls out his notebook, flips through the pages, and reads us a few lines. Eddie lays his head back on his sleeping bag and I follow suit. Owen's voice gets inside his craft, and you can hear the long deliberation that went into each line, each phrase. He reads for a few minutes and stops, everything getting quiet.

Everyone gathers themselves into their sleeping bags, and I lie there and watch the fire shadows slide up and down the rocks. The smoke drifts to the top of the cave and glides out through the opening. Before long I hear the gentle tap of rain and see the droplets of water reflect against the fire. Water pools on the ground beneath the opening of the cave. I wonder to myself whether Paul put my sleeping bag back into the tent before he left aspen camp this morning.

"I believe in God," Owen says to us, some of us already asleep.

"And God believes in you," Henry says, after a few seconds of silence.

• • •

PAUL LIFTS THE END OF MY BAG AND I SLIDE OUT ONTO the dirt floor of the cave. The fire has gone out, but morning light shines in through the opening.

241

"It's six, Don. Time for work."

"I don't have to be there till seven thirty," I tell him.

"We're an hour away. I have to drop you off and come back for these guys. Come on. It's a good hike back to the van. You can't be late again."

"I'm up," I say. "I'm up. Give me a second here." I find my boots and a rock to sit on. I pull my cold boots over my cold feet. I look at my warm sleeping bag and all I want to do is climb back into it. Henry uncovers his head and smiles through his big teeth with his blond straight hair going in all directions. "Clean a toilet for me," he says.

"I'll be thinking of you the entire time," I tell him. He has a good laugh at that.

"Off to fight the war," Eddie says.

Paul rolls his bag and stuffs it into his backpack. He does the same with mine and before I can lace my boots, he is on the ladder, climbing out through the roof. I follow him up into the sky. Everything on the ground is wet. Rain drips from the trees. Patches of snow have settled on the ground. *It's spring,* I think to myself. *It's spring and there is snow on the ground.*

I follow Paul through the forest. There is no trail to speak of, so we head downhill, letting gravity do all the work. I'm getting dirty sliding over fallen logs, covered in moss and dirt. My hands are brown and muddy. I wonder out loud how I am going to look for Laurel and Lucy.

26 RANCH LIFE

BLACK BUTTE RANCH BEGAN IN THE EARLY 1900S when a development company decided that the twenty-nine thousand families in the state of Oregon who made more than $40,000 might very well be interested in a second home in the mountains. Their aim was to settle 5 percent of these wealthy families into vacation homes that would sit empty during the winter months. It was a bold move. Today, one might call it absurd. But back then it worked. Homes were sold and a summer village began. Today homes sell for $700,000 or more. There are more than seven hundred properties on the ranch. Some structures are simply two-bedroom cottages and some are nine-bedroom manors. Paul and I have been here three weeks now and settled in well. We live for free. We don't even have to pay taxes.

I've found that I fit well among a group of militant cleaning women. Even Lucy likes me, these days. I show up for work early and take a shower, folding towels till the ladies show up. Laurel has become like a mother to most of us, all the young girls and me. A couple girls from Washington, DC, studying at American University, have become pretty good friends. Every condo we go into, we check the fridge to see if the vacationing families left any ice cream, and if they did, we take a break, sitting on the beds, and tell stories of how terrible boys are, how they just don't know how to treat women these days. I nod my head in agreement and suck off another spoonful of Häagen-Dazs. "It's tough to be a woman these days, that's for sure," I say. "You can say that again," one of the girls comments. And while the work is hard, the girls do make it fun. But the real life, the life where I am finding faith and friendship and peace, is out in the woods.

On several occasions, someone from the ranch will offer me a place to stay. But I always refuse. Only last night we were up late at a party where we drank coffee, played Scrabble, and listened to John Prine records when the fellow who owned the house offered to let me stay the night in a spare bedroom. It was well below freezing last night, but I turned him down all the same.

I suppose it takes about a week to get used to sleeping outside. But once accustomed to it, a person can't easily go back to having a roof over his head.

If a man's senses are either sharpened or dulled by the way he rubs against time, mine have become increasingly sharp over these last three weeks. I am hungry, so I appreciate food and thank God for it whenever I find ice cream or other perishables in a condo I am cleaning. I appreciate friendship and don't need a television to keep me company. I appreciate birds chirping, as there is no radio to seduce my ears. I appreciate God, because I live in the house He has made, as opposed to a house I purchased by my own means.

I've learned, too, that I don't really know very much about anything. I mean, I used to have all these theories about life. I thought I had everybody figured out, even God, but I don't. I think the woods, being away from all the clingy soot of commercialism, have taught me life is enormous, and I am very tiny in the middle of it. I feel, at times, like a droplet of water in a raging river. I know for a fact that as a grain of sand compares in size to the earth itself, I compare in size to the cosmos. I am that insignificant. And yet the chemicals in my brain that make me feel beauty when I look up at the stars, when I watch the sunset, indicate I must be here for a reason. I think I would sum it up this way: life is not a story about me, but it is being told to me, and I can be glad of that. I think that is the *why* of life and, in fact, the *why* of this ancient faith I am caught up in: to enjoy God. The stars were created to dazzle us, like a love letter; light itself is just a metaphor, something that exists outside of time, made up of what seems like nothing, infinite in its power, something that can be experienced but not understood, like God. Relationships between men and women indicate something of the nature of God—that He is relational, that He feels love and loss. It's all metaphor, and the story is about us; it's about all of us who God made, and God Himself, just enjoying each other. It strikes me how far the commercials are from this reality, how deadly they are, perhaps. Months ago I would have told you life was about doing, about jumping through religious hoops, about impressing other people, and my actions would have told you this is done by buying possessions or keeping a good image or going to church. I don't believe that anymore. I think we are supposed to stand in deserts and marvel at how the sun rises. I think we are supposed to sleep in meadows and watch stars dart across space and time. I think we are supposed to love our friends and introduce people to the story, to the peaceful, calming *why* of life. I think life *is* spirituality.

If I could, if it would be responsible, I would live in these woods forever: I would let my beard grow, hunt my own food, chart the stars, and write poems about mountains. But I know these days are passing. This morning I made a call to Colorado and the camp out there offered me a job. I will be leaving Oregon in a week, leaving behind Paul, Henry, and the boys. Leaving behind the meadow. I start wondering if, when I leave this place, when I leave all these guys who don't share my faith, when I leave these militant women always complaining about men, when I leave the starlight above the mountains, if I will go back to my old faith habits, jumping through hoops, trying to please God or, worse, subscribing to self-help formulas and calling it faith. I hope not. I hope I never lose this perspective. Walking through the meadow on the way over to see

Paul, I promise myself if I ever get frustrated with life again, if I ever get into river-deep debt, I will sell it all and move out into the woods, find some people who aren't like me and learn to love them, and do something even harder, let them love me, receive the love of somebody who doesn't share my faith system, who doesn't agree with me about everything, and I will sleep beneath the stars and whisper *thank you* to the Creator of the universe, as a way of reacquainting myself to an old friend, a friend who says you don't have to be smart or good-looking or religious or anything; you just have to cling to Him, love Him, need Him, listen to His story.

PAUL WORKED THE EARLY SHIFT THIS MORNING SO HE could be free when Danielle arrives. We're expecting her sometime before lunch. She's only staying the day, then driving south to Sacramento so she can live with her grandparents and attend summer school.

I'm sitting on the deck outside Honkers. The pool is unusually full of children. It's a Saturday and all the rich folks are here using their summer homes, so Paul has his hands full. He waves from atop his chair and I wave back. From the deck all the mountains are visible above the meadow, where a creek divides the landscape in two. A cowgirl is driving horses into a pen, where she will saddle them and give people trail rides for a fee.

Out in the distance, I see Molly. She is just on the other side of the pond and heading to the café for work. Nothing ever happened between Molly and me. She got word through Henry that I thought something about her but she didn't respond. Henry says she's hooked on Eddie even though Eddie is hooked on some New York ballerina that we've all heard a dozen stories about. Still, there is something beautiful about the girl that won't have you. Molly is turned sideways now, trying to straighten a bow on the back of her dress. You have to love a girl who wears a dress to work.

Paul comes down from his chair and Henry takes his place. Henry offers a wave from the high post. Paul jumps the railing and sits down next to me.

"Any sign of Danielle?" he asks.

"Yeah. She was with some football player earlier. They were making out."

"Very funny."

"No," I say. "I haven't heard from her. When is she supposed to get here?"

"Anytime now. She should have been here by eleven, but she is probably running late."

Paul waves at Molly, who is peering through the glass doors. She mouths and asks us whether we are hungry and Paul nods his head yes.

"So,"—Paul rests easy in his chair—"where you been all morning?"

"I worked a short shift with the girls."

"Just one of the girls," Paul says, raising his eyebrows.

"Just one of the girls," I confirm.

"You had a good time here?" he asks.

"Can't thank you enough," I say to him. Paul and I had purchased a box of wine a few nights ago and sat here on the deck and drank and talked about what a great trip we had, how God showed up when we needed Him to show up, and how good it was to know each other. It occurred to me then, and I said it to Paul, that there is something God made that is better than starlight. *What is it?* he asked me. *It's you, man,* I said. *Me?* he asked. *You,* I said, *you know, friends, people, it's beautiful, really, that we don't have to be alone. I appreciate you,* I told him. Paul went on about how much he appreciated me, too, and I even shed a few tears about it. He said he thought I was a good guy, that I was funny but also deep, and wasn't judgmental like some people have become these days, impossible to be around without making you feel like crap about yourself. *We're going to be best friends, you realize that,* Paul said. I hadn't realized it, to be honest. Paul is a better guy than I, better looking, more athletic, smarter. I didn't know whether he thought of me that way, you know, but apparently he did. It's great when somebody who is better than you in all those ways that don't matter but always matter lets you be an equal. Molly comes out with some sandwiches and pats me on the back, saying it is good to see me. I tell her it is good to see her, too, and smile. Paul bites into his sandwich and looks out over the meadow.

"You think we've been on a pilgrimage?" Paul asks, talking with his mouth full.

I look out over the meadow, at the mountains in the distance. "I think we've been on a pilgrimage," I say.

27 SUNRISE

I DON'T THINK WE CAN REALLY UNDERSTAND HOW TIME passes. We can't study it like a river or tame it with a clock. Our devices only mark its coming and going. I dropped an anchor three months back but time didn't slow. Some things have to end, you know. You feel like life is always leading up to something, but it isn't. I mean life is just life. It's all happening right now, and we aren't going to be any more complete a month from now than we are now. I only say this because I am trying to appreciate everything tonight. I will be leaving soon, and I want to feel this, really understand that it is happening because God breathed some spark into some mud that became us, and He did it for a reason, and I want to feel that reason, not some false explanation.

Everything plays like an art film tonight. Owen is listening to Bruce Springsteen on the jukebox. He says Bruce is as good as Bob Dylan. Danielle is sitting across from me at the table and she's flipping pages in a book of poems Eddie bought in Sisters a few days ago. Molly is making everybody yogurt. She closed the café several hours ago but let us in to hang out because Paul told her I was leaving and everyone decided to throw a "going away" celebration. We've been sitting around for hours. It's late, and Danielle has a look of frustration because she knows every minute she waits will make for a longer, more weary drive to Sacramento. Henry and Jodie are arm wrestling and laughing because Henry keeps letting her win.

"When are you leaving?" Eddie asks me, trying to remember.

"The end of the week," I tell him.

Molly comes over with yogurt. Paul told Danielle about my crush so Danielle offers a gentle smile when Molly hands me my cup. Molly rounds the table and gives everyone as they'd asked: chocolate or vanilla or both swirled together.

"I think you should stay," Henry says.

"Stay, Don," Jodie offers.

"He's already made up his mind," Paul tells them.

"Where are you going again?" Molly asks.

"Colorado," I tell her.

"Last I checked, we had mountains here," Owen says, dropping another quarter into the jukebox.

"Well, Don," Danielle begins, "I'm jealous. I'd love to be going back to Colorado. I think you're making the right decision."

Paul looks over at Danielle like she's crazy. Danielle just shrugs her shoulders and grins.

Molly swipes the table with a wet cloth. She laughs at us but then tells us she needs to get going. She has to work in the morning and it's already four o'clock. She's not going to get much sleep.

"It's four in the morning!" Danielle exclaims.

"It is," Paul confirms.

"Oh, heavens. I've got to get going."

"Danielle!" Paul gives her a confused look. "You can't drive. You haven't slept."

"I've had about seven cups of coffee. I have to get to Sacramento. I'll be fine."

"Stay here," Paul tells her. "Stay here and camp for the night. You can get started tomorrow."

"I have to go," she says into Paul's lovesick eyes.

"Sleep out under the stars with me," Paul says.

"Not a good idea," Danielle says, smiling and shaking her head.

"You can sleep at my place," Jodie tells her.

"You can sleep out under the stars with me," I say.

"No. I need to go. I'm good about driving at night. I'll pull over and sleep if I need to. Besides, the sun will be up in an hour or so. Don't worry. I'll be fine."

I tell the guys thanks for the send-off, and that I will see them soon.

"We're going to the Sisters rodeo tonight," Owen says. "You in?"

"I'm in," I tell him. Molly shoos us out and gives me a hug good-bye. I tell her I will see her again before I leave and she says I better.

"It's been great having you here, Don," Eddie says. "It's been real good. If you're ever in New York, you have a place to stay, friend."

"Thanks," I tell him. "You going to the rodeo tonight?" I ask.

Eddie puts his heels together and bends his knees up and down like he's riding a horse. "Wouldn't miss it," he says.

Paul and I walk Danielle to her car and they exchange a close hug. Danielle gives me a hug, too, but it's one of those "old friend" types of hugs, not like the "I can't wait to see you again and I am going to cry all the way to Sacramento" hug she gave Paul. Danielle gets into her car and closes the door. Paul doesn't blink or shift his eyes while she fastens her seat belt.

"Pull over as soon as you get tired," he tells her. "Someplace safe. Not a rest area. A police station or something."

"I will," she says with a laugh. Then she tells us she loves us. Paul grins when she says it.

"She said she loves *us*, not just you," I tell him under my breath.

Danielle's brake lights glow on the asphalt as her car sputters around the parking lot, down the road, and out toward the main gate. Paul watches her all the way out, never taking his eye from the little head above the driver's seat.

"You think she'll be all right, Don?" he asks.

"I think so. She's a smart girl."

"You know, Don. I think she's the one."

"What are you talking about? You haven't known her a month."

"One month is a long time," he says.

"One month is one month."

"That's a long time," he says. "Besides, it's been longer than that. It's been a month and a few days."

"The few days make a difference."

"Sure it does," Paul says, shifting his weight around. We walk across the parking lot toward the road without saying a word. Black Butte is visible in the fading moonlight. The sun will be coming up in an hour or so and the earth is beginning to ready itself. Distant birds chirp and clouds are perching themselves on the backs of the mountains.

"You want to catch sunrise?" Paul asks.

"Sounds good. It's not like we're going to get any sleep tonight."

"Where?" he asks.

"How about the meadow? We can see the entire horizon from the meadow."

"Sounds good."

I trail Paul to the center of the meadow. I'm walking with my hands in my pockets, watching closely at his feet, being careful not to step off the dark trail. "See those clouds, Paul? Those will light up," I say.

"It should be good," he says. "Forest fires are blazing south. It should be good." Our voices sink deep into the meadow silence, landing soft against the wet grass and marshes.

THE EARTH AROUND THE MEADOW IS HEAVY IN ANTICIpation. The mountains are silhouetted like sleeping dragons. There is a deep, blue coolness at the western edge of the landscape, where a few stars linger, their last flickered flames shimmering.

Paul wraps his arms around his chest, unfolds them, blows warm air into his cupped hands, then slides them into his pockets. He's shifting his stiff weight from foot to foot and squinting his eyes, breathing thick mist into the air around him.

"Thanks, Don."

"Thanks for what?"

"Just thanks. I'm going to miss you around here."

"You should come to Colorado, Paul. You'd love it."

"I'll think about it," he says.

And if these mountains had eyes, they would wake to find two strangers in their fences, standing in admiration as a breathing red pours its tinge upon earth's shore. These mountains, which have seen untold sunrises, long to thunder praise but stand reverent, silent so that man's weak praise should be given God's attention.

It is a wonder that those exposed to such beauty forfeit the great questions in the face of this miraculous evidence. I think again about this small period of grace, and thank God for it, that if only for a season, I could feel the *why* of life, see it in the metaphor of light, in the endlessness of the cosmos, in the miracle of friendship. And had these mountains the ability to reason, perhaps they would contemplate the beauty of humanity, and praise God for the miracle that each of us is, pondering the majesty of God and the wonder of man in one bewildering context.

Their brows are rumpled even now, and their arms are stretched toward heaven.

ABOUT THE AUTHOR

Donald Miller is the director of The Burnside Writers Collective, coeditor of *The Ankeny Briefcase,* and the author of *Blue Like Jazz, Searching for God Knows What* and *To Own a Dragon.* He lives in Portland, Oregon.

www.Bluelikejazz.com

To order copies of Don's books or his lectures on CD, please visit **www.burnsidewriterscollective.com**.

And for even more great literature, Don recommends: **www.ankenybriefcase.com**.

P.S. Paul and Danielle did get married.

ACKNOWLEDGMENTS

I OWE HEARTFELT THANKS TO PAUL HARRIS FOR GIVING me the sort of friendship a guy could write a book about.

And to Terry Glaspey, who originally acquired this book years ago, as well as the original group of readers who read it. I hope you don't mind the changes. Thanks to Kathryn Helmers, who read over the rewrite and gave me the encouragement to wrap it up and obey the gut. Thanks to everybody at Thomas Nelson who works so very hard to get these books out there. I can't think any more fondly of a group of people.

This true story would not have been written without the real-life characters who make my life more interesting than television. Kind thanks to Randy and Shirley Bjur, Danielle, Elida, and Nate, Wes and Maja, Grampa and Grandma Bjur, and the whole Ridgefield/Sacramento clan. Also, Ben Bonham, Betty and Bob from the truck stop, and Mrs. Tucker and Mike from California.

While writing, I listened to Derek Webb, The Daylights, Jars, Ryan Adams, James Taylor, U2, Lyle Lovett, Dwight Yoakam, John Gorka, Over the Rhine, David Barnes, Rosie Thomas, Steve Earle, and Mindy Smith.

A number of people read the early stages of the manuscript and gave criticism that helped the book like medicine. Kim Moore proofread the project and made me look smart by correcting my rotten grammar and spelling. John and Terri MacMurray read and praised every chapter, and I would not have sent it to a publisher save for their kindness and encouragement. Also Mary Miller, Evelyn Hall, Nathan and Sara Pylate,

Shelly Burke, Andy Whipps, Amy Martin, Missy Tygert, Adam Rehman, Jamie Bushek, Sara Mathews, Matt Jacobson, Don Jacobson, Jeff Baldwin, Ross Tunnell, Michaela Frick, Kim Kemper, Dave Beitler, Lonnie Hull-Dupont, Gregg Harris, Matt and Julie Canlis, Randy and Jan Demlow, Angie Rabatin, Scott Armstrong, and David Gentiles. Special thanks to Curt Heidschmidt and Rick Crosser for their friendship and encouragement. Much gratitude to Jeff Olson for countless conversations and for giving me the opportunity to read portions of the manuscript to Mosaic. Thanks to Jim Small for all he does to get the word out. I owe a debt of gratitude to Fred "One Page a Day" Willis for giving me Robert Pirsig's book with a little note on the inside cover. And thank you to Anne, for your incredible kindness, and for all those beautiful words. Thank you for giving so many of us permission to feel God, and to be ourselves. You are a dear saint.

Thanks to Amy Bowers, Tony Kriz, Penny Gruener, Tara Brown, Jim Chaffee, Leslie McKellar, Laura Long, Kurt and Donna Nelson, Heirborne, Rick McKinley, Drew Goodmanson, Eric Brown, Jeff Marsh, Christina Reagan, Jordan Green, Grant and Blake Gaskill, Wes and Stacy Gorton, Mike Tucker, Eric and Josiah, Jon Foreman, Jamie Tworkowski, Kaj and Lib, the boys in Jars, Laura Gibson, Chris Seay, the folks at Imago and Ecclesia, and all the other good friends who are as important to this process as ink itself.

And as always, thanks for reading this book. I love doing this and couldn't do it without you picking up a copy here and there. I wanted to take a break from the deep theological stuff and just take you on an old journey I took once and introduce you to some wonderful people. I am so glad you were able to come. Much love and gratitude to you, and all God's blessings.

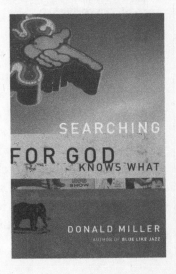

"I spent several months backtracking this trip, trying to remember all that happened to Paul and me on the road. I brought along a few hundred CDs, knowing music would be critical to get "the feel" right. About half way through my trip, I heard a band called the *Robbie Seay Band*, picked up their CD, and for the rest of my trip (about six weeks) I didn't take these guys out of my stereo. All this to say, Robbie's CD *Better Days* is to me the soundtrack for the revised edition of this book. I am pleased to introduce it to you."

— Donald Miller